WOMEN ENTREPRENEURSHIP IN THE INDIAN MIDDLE CLASS

WOMEN ENTREPRENEURSHIP IN THE INDIAN MIDDLE CLASS

Interdisciplinary Perspectives

JEEMOL UNNI
VANITA YADAV
RAVIKIRAN NAIK
SWATI DUTTA

Orient BlackSwan

WOMEN ENTREPRENEURSHIP IN THE INDIAN MIDDLE CLASS: INTERDISCIPLINARY PERSPECTIVES

ORIENT BLACKSWAN PRIVATE LIMITED

Registered Office
3-6-752 Himayatnagar, Hyderabad 500 029, Telangana, India
e-mail: centraloffice@orientblackswan.com

Other Offices
Bengaluru, Chennai, Guwahati, Hyderabad, Kolkata,
Mumbai, New Delhi, Noida, Patna

First published by Orient Blackswan Private Limited 2021

ISBN 978-93-5442-145-7

Typeset in
Constantia 10.5/13
by Le Studio Graphique, Gurgaon 122 007

Printed in India at
Thomson Press, New Delhi 110 020

Published by
Orient Blackswan Private Limited
3-6-752 Himayatnagar, Hyderabad 500 029, Telangana, India
e-mail: info@orientblackswan.com

Dedicated to the loving memory of
Preet Rustagi

Contents

Abbreviations

3Ms	Markets, Money and Management
AIIMS	All India Institute of Medical Sciences
APS	Adult Population Survey
ASCI	Administrative Staff College of India
ASI	Annual Survey of Industries
CES	Consumption Expenditure Survey
CGTMSE	Credit Guarantee Fund Trust for Micro and Small Enterprises
CTO	Chief Technology Officer
DIC	District Industry Corporation
E3V	Environment, Energy and Enterprise Ventures
EPF	Employees' Provident Fund
EUS	Employment and Unemployment Survey
GEM	*Global Entrepreneurship Monitor*
GST	Goods and Services Tax
IEA	Individual Entrepreneurial Aptitude
INR	Indian Rupee
IRMA	Institute of Rural Management, Anand
KMVS	Kutch Mahila Vikas Sangathan
KOV	Kurmanchal Organic Ventures
KSRTC	Karnataka State Road Transport Corporation
MOSPI	Ministry of Statistics and Programme Implementation
MPCE	Monthly Per Capita Consumption Expenditure
MSME	Micro, Small and Medium Enterprises
NCAER	National Council of Applied Economic Research
NCR	National Capital Region

NGO	Non-Governmental Organisation
NSIC	National Small Industry Corporation of India
NSSO	National Sample Survey Office
OAE	Own Account Enterprise
OAW	Own Account Worker
OBC	Other Backward Classes
OECD	Organisation for Economic Co-operation and Development
PBC	Perceived Behavioural Control
PF	Provident Fund
PPP	Purchasing Power Parity
SC	Scheduled Castes
SMEs	Small and Medium Enterprises
SSI	Small Scale Industry
ST	Scheduled Tribes
STPI	Software Technology Park of India
TAI	Travel Another India
TEA	Total Early-Stage Entrepreneurial Activity
TPB	Theory of Planned Behaviour
UFW	Unpaid Family Worker
UNDP	United Nations Development Programme
VAT	Value Added Tax
WBES	World Bank Enterprise Surveys

Tables and Figures

Tables

Figures

Acknowledgements

This book draws extensively on material from a research project on women entrepreneurship, but is an entirely new manuscript written over a period of two years. The idea of writing a book on women entrepreneurs came during one of our research project meetings. The project, lasting over three years (2015–17), provided rich, in-depth insights on women entrepreneurs in India. Our research used mixed methods, quantitative and qualitative material, secondary and survey data to gain macro as well as micro perspectives on the subject.

We would like to thank the unknown reviewer, assigned by Orient BlackSwan, for very detailed comments on the first manuscript submitted to the publisher. It helped us rewrite the entire manuscript into a more readable form for a larger audience, and improved the flow of the arguments discussed.

We would like to express our sincere thanks to the Indian Council of Social Sciences Research (ICSSR) for funding our research project on women entrepreneurship. Our special thanks to Revathy Vishwanath, Assistant Director, Research Project Division, ICSSR, for support.

We are grateful to Rakesh Basant and Amirullah Khan for feedback, valuable inputs and continuous support during our research work on women entrepreneurship in India. We are particularly grateful to Rakesh Basant, Indian Institute of Management (IIM), Ahmedabad, for reading and reviewing our book drafts. His insightful inputs helped us greatly in our study and book-writing process.

We owe our thanks to the academic and administrative support we received from the Institute of Rural Management (IRMA), Anand, where Jeemol Unni, Vanita Yadav and Ravikiran

Naik were based during major part of the ICSSR project in 2015–17. We acknowledge the support of the Directors and Director-in-Charge, and all administrative staff and members of the faculty at IRMA for providing a congenial atmosphere to undertake this study.

The major part of this book was written while Jeemol Unni was at Ahmedabad University, where she continues as Professor of Economics at the Amrut Mody School of Management (AMSOM). She is grateful to Abrar Ali Saiyed, faculty at AMSOM, for the fruitful discussions and suggestions based on his insights on entrepreneurship. We gratefully acknowledge the academic and administrative support provided by Devanath Tirupati, Dean, AMSOM. We acknowledge the support of the administrative staff at Ahmedabad University.

Vanita Yadav moved to Central Queensland University, Australia, after completing the ICCSR project work in India. She completed the chapter drafts and book-writing, including updating the chapters and completing the review process, at the Central Queensland University's Sydney campus. We gratefully acknowledge the resources and research support provided by the School of Business and Law, Central Queensland University, Australia.

We would like to especially thank all the women entrepreneurs who participated in the research study and shared their entrepreneurial journey with us. We are also thankful to Sunetra Deshpande from Vox Populi for her support towards the case study research on women entrepreneurs in India.

Swati Dutta was based at the Institute of Human Development (IHD), Delhi. We are thankful to Alakh N. Sharma, Director, IHD, and the research and administrative staff of IHD for their constant support.

Writing this book would not have been possible without the support of our dear family and friends. We thank all of them for their support during the writing of this book.

We gratefully acknowledge our research collaborator, Preet Rustagi, who left us during the course of the ICSSR project, for her work on attitudes and perceptions towards entrepreneurship among India's youth. Her work will be beneficial for readers, researchers and policy-makers for years to come. We are left with fond memories of her very amiable and supportive nature and her active academic contributions. Thank you, Preet for being with us during a large part of the ICSSR research study.

We dedicate this book to the loving memory of Preet Rustagi.

Introduction

Economic growth in India has given rise to a new middle class. The Indian middle class grew from nearly half of India's 1.2 billion population to two-thirds between 2004–05 and 2011–12. The middle class accelerates growth by its savings and investments, values human capital accumulation and incubates the next generation of entrepreneurs who create employment opportunities (Boushey and Hersh 2012). The middle class also provides stable demand for goods and services. Access to labour markets and quality of employment is closely linked with economic background/class, especially for the middle class (Lahiri 2014). Though we cannot assert that the middle class is the only critical factor for economic growth, evidence suggests that its significance is increasing in economic, social and political spheres across countries. A strong middle class can also have an important effect on reducing poverty (Ravallion 2009) and inequality. A growing middle class can reduce the gender gap in economic participation by enabling women to pursue career options.

India currently faces a massive challenge of high levels of youth unemployment, especially among the educated urban population. The formal labour market in India is saturated, unable to absorb the ever-increasing labour force. Therefore, the role of small and medium enterprises (SMEs) in creating employment opportunities is vital for economic prosperity and social stability in a developing country like India.

Further, half of the world's population and one-third of the global manufacturing workforce are women (de Groot 2001). Women have made significant contributions to economic growth over the past century (Ghani et al. 2012). At the same time, remunerative opportunities in industrial development have improved women's quality of life, literacy, life expectancy and ability to fight poverty (de Groot 2001). Thus, empowering half the potential workforce has yielded significant economic benefits, which go beyond promoting gender equality (Banerjee and Duflo 2005; World Bank 2012). Numerous studies advocate the significance of entrepreneurship, and particularly women entrepreneurship, for continuous economic development (Allen et al. 2008). 'An entrepreneur is an entrepreneur' it is said; yet the differences in the experience of male and female entrepreneurs provide compelling reasons to inquire into the struggles, challenges, and aspirations of middle-class women entrepreneurs. This is the broad motivation of this book.

THE FIELD OF ENTREPRENEURSHIP

The 1980s saw renewed interest in entrepreneurship with the growth of SMEs in Europe and America. Entrepreneurship and leadership programmes became very popular in the business schools of Anglo-Saxon universities. Entrepreneurship as a discipline was captured by management literature and became a part of strategic management learning. It addressed two core questions: who starts a new business, and what are the non-financial pre-conditions of successful business growth (Chepurenko 2015). A consensus emerged that entrepreneurship is a study of the 'emergence of new activity'. Scott Shane and S. Venkataraman suggested that the fundamental starting point of entrepreneurship research is the question 'How, why and when do entrepreneurial firms discover and exploit opportunities?' (Shane and Venkataraman 2000).

Views of entrepreneurship differing from this Anglo-Saxon view of the commercial, profit-driven innovator and creator of new business activity have emerged. In 'poor countries with resource-driven economies' (Chepurenko 2015), exploration and exploitation of new opportunities may be the only source of obtaining reasonable well-being. Cross-country studies using

Global Entrepreneurship Monitor (GEM) data have shown that levels of entrepreneurship were higher in poor countries rather than in the established market economies. This may be seen as being driven by necessity, rather than by opportunity, in poor and developing countries. Entrepreneurship is often based on the existence of networks and social capital, and limited economic and human capital. In such a context extended family labour, and remittances as capital and female entrepreneurship play an important role. Antoinette Schoar distinguished between two kinds of entrepreneurship: *subsistence* and *transformational* entrepreneurship (Schoar 2010). Subsistence entrepreneurs, who run tiny businesses that do not grow into large firms but merely provide an alternative source of employment to the entrepreneur and his family, form the majority. Transformational entrepreneurs, who build large businesses, create jobs and are true engines of growth for the economy, are rare. According to Schoar, subsistence entrepreneurs form the majority in India and China.

Mainstream management literature on entrepreneurship since the 1930s assumed a gender-neutral stance. A sub-theme of women entrepreneurship emerged in the 1970s (Jennings and Brush 2013; Yadav and Unni 2016). The contribution of women entrepreneurship research was in emphasising the distinction between necessity-driven versus opportunity-based entrepreneurship (Shapero and Sokol 1982). Early entrepreneurship theory focused on *pull* factors (for e.g. a supportive entrepreneurial ecosystem in the region), but Albert Shapero and Lisa Sokol argued that *push* factors (for e.g. a lack of jobs in the formal sector) may also apply to the entrepreneurial activities undertaken by minority groups (ibid.). This extends the existing belief that push factors are mainly associated with highly innovative and technology-driven innovations. Further, the motivation of women entrepreneurs may be very different from that of men, and for those among the lower middle class it may be very different from that of the upper middle and upper classes. We explore some of these issues in this book.

Our focus is on enterprises that are more than three or five years old, depending on the data sets used, and not on start-ups or recent entrants. In Chapters 2 to 6, we include case studies of successful middle-class women entrepreneurs who have an established business that is running for at least five years. Hence, ours is not a story of 'creation of new enterprise'. We are interested in understanding what makes an entrepreneur grow within the constraints of the informal sector and innovate in response to the institutional environment in the formal sector. And further, how women entrepreneurs fare in India's socio-economic milieu.

BUILDING THE THEORY OF ENTREPRENEURSHIP

The theory of entrepreneurship has borrowed from the disciplines of economics, sociology and psychology. However, the field of entrepreneurship is currently strongly embedded in the discipline of management, in the sub-field of strategy. Entrepreneurship literature rarely gives a sense of the substance, magnitude or dynamics of the research context. There is a great need to describe the research site, country or region, and 'contextualise' the research, linking it to theory, research objectives and the site of study (Zahra 2007). In this book, we take a pluralist approach to the study of entrepreneurship and draw heavily from the fields of management and economics, and partly from sociology, psychology and gender studies, for a more holistic understanding of entrepreneurship.

We also define entrepreneurship more broadly to include not just 'new economic activity' but operation of all economic enterprises, to understand what motivates a large proportion of the labour force in India to operate micro and small enterprises that do not seem to grow to scale and have relatively low returns. The Indian economy continues to be *dualistic*, with tiny and small enterprises operating in the informal sector, and large, technologically advanced enterprises in the formal sector. The formal sector can be broadly defined to include firms that are registered with a statutory body and are mandated to follow all financial and labour laws. Enterprises in the informal sector are relatively small, are not formally registered and operate with or without hired labour. They may not be included in the financial and tax net of the country and are not compelled to follow labour laws, such as the provision of social protection benefits to workers.

In an interesting study on contextualising theory-building in entrepreneurship research, Shaker A. Zahra discusses linking theory to the context or the research phenomenon by considering its stage of development (Zahra 2007). Through these two axes, Zahra suggests that theorising can be slotted into four quadrants: established theory and established phenomenon; established theory and new phenomenon; new theory and established phenomenon; and new theory and new phenomenon (ibid.).

An example of the first quadrant, established theory and established phenomenon, is using agency theory to explain motivations for corporate venturing. Most of these studies focus on corporates but do not articulate the assumptions or question them. In economic theory, the Porter framework benefited from relaxing assumptions of perfect competition (Porter 1979), and is widely used in entrepreneurship literature.[1]

The second quadrant is of studies using established theory to understand new phenomenon, implying unpacking the content of entrepreneurial decisions or the process followed in arriving at these. Variables that identify processes are difficult and messy to capture and may require the use of multiple theories. An example is the use of social networks to explain the internationalisation of new ventures, drawing on network theory and industrial organisation.

The third quadrant consists of studies that use new theory to explain an established phenomenon. This could imply importing old theory from other disciplines to study an established phenomenon. For example, economics and game theory can be used to map out strategies of new entrepreneurial ventures.

Finally, applying new theory to new phenomena, the fourth quadrant, tend to be fishing exercises with vague descriptions of the phenomenon under study. Theorising implies 'framing a debate, seeing things afresh, offering fresh insight into things we know or should know...Theory should be able to enrich and add to the body of knowledge and not simply rewrite what we know' (Zahra 2007).

While we do not make any claims to building theory in this book, we can say that our study falls into the second quadrant, as we use established theory from management and economics to study women entrepreneurship contextualised to include the micro and small enterprise sector in India. This book contends that by attempting to apply old theories from diverse disciplines to the study of entrepreneurship in a developing country like India, we are 'framing the debate' afresh, from which a new multidisciplinary theory can be developed.

ECONOMIC CLASS, EDUCATION AND LABOUR MARKET PARTICIPATION

Participation in the labour market and quality of employment is closely linked with an individual's economic background. Participation in economic activities and access to good quality employment depends on the socio-economic status of households, which is determined by class, caste and gender. The middle class significantly differs from the poor in terms of access to and attainment of education, economic opportunities and labour market outcomes. The continued growth of the middle class is associated with the accelerated growth of middle-class employment. Phu Huynh and Steven Kaspos found that economic participation rates were higher among the poor compared to the middle class in developing countries, which substantiates the fact that economic participation declines the higher the income class, and the poor are more likely to participate in any available economic opportunity (Huynh and Kaspos 2013). This is more so for poor women, on whom the final burden of feeding the family falls. Along with income class, cultural and social factors such as caste and religion also restrict participation in the labour market or determine the type of economic activities that can be carried out.

In India, as well, economic participation of poor women is higher, falls with the middle class and falls further with the upper-income class (Huynh and Kaspos 2013). Educational attainment and economic participation are linked through economic class. Further, educational attainment and better-quality employment outcomes were also found to be associated with class (ibid.). The middle class is equipped with higher levels of education and has better access to decent and productive employment. Middle-class workers are more likely to have high-skilled occupations compared to poor workers.

India is a country of rich cultural, social and economic diversity. At the same time, Indian society is entangled in class and caste hierarchies, which is also reflected in economic occupations. Besides class, social background (caste and religion) also affects socio-economic outcomes (Unni 2006). The recent emergence of the Indian middle class has complex implications for the economy, for Indian politics and class dynamics.

India is a young country, with nearly one half of its population aged below 30 years. Even with its *demographic transition*,[2] the youth bulge is large, and this will continue for a few decades to come. Youth in the age groups 15–29 years comprise 27 per cent of India's population. The rural–urban differences in India's human capital attributes are stark, with urban female literacy being higher than that among rural males (Central Statistics Office 2016). Work participation rates of urban females, however, are very low compared to rural females and all males, rural or urban.

Is the scenario different for those women among the youth who are educated? High youth unemployment rates, especially among women who are educated beyond the higher secondary level, indicate their willingness to work on the supply side and poor avenues of their absorption on the demand side. Basic education appears increasingly inadequate for access to employment opportunities, leaving many educated youth unemployed globally. The pursuit of labour market participation finds them entering into informal, irregular, part-time contracts.

Some who are relatively better educated or skilled utilise their resources to initiate entrepreneurial activity, even as they await success in their job search efforts. These comprise the interim entrepreneurs who are not in it to continue but will quit as soon as they find alternative employment. With increased competition due to higher education levels among the unemployed, people at the bottom of the pyramid are being left out of the labour market. What prospects do they have for entrepreneurial avenues?

Economic growth in India has accompanied jobless growth in the past and there is little guarantee that this will change with time. Given the large share of the young population and ever-growing new entrants to the labour force, the supply of labour is increasing while there is a shortage of demand for labour. There are structural and economic factors which can serve as constraints to increasing demand for labour, hinting at continuation of already high unemployment among educated youth. Self-employment with low returns is a recourse that the unemployed opt for during times of economic crises, leaving them in the category of working poor. In addition, human capital attributes, such as technical and managerial skills, can limit absorption of the available labour supply for entrepreneurial ventures.

Given this scenario of lack of jobs, what factors support or aid the process of entrepreneurship development and sustenance? Most research has focused on access to credit, assets, infrastructure, knowledge and networks for promotion of entrepreneurship. An equally important dimension on the supply side that has not been adequately examined relates to the attitudes and intentions towards entrepreneurship held by agents, their households and society at large. The agent concerned and her/his attitude to elements characterising entrepreneurship such as autonomy, risk, work effort, income and net perquisites, influence the choice towards undertaking it. The likelihood of opting for entrepreneurship is higher among individuals who want more independence, income and other benefits. In this book, we examine these individual, social and human capital attributes to gain further insights into the occupational choice of entrepreneurship.

ENTREPRENEURSHIP: WHY IS IT IMPORTANT?

Entrepreneurship is a crucial mode of utilising youth power and generating employment that will in turn contribute to the economy's growth and development, especially for those who aspire to be owners and employers rather than employees. Understanding the intentions and constraints to being motivated for entrepreneurial endeavours is critical for designing and formulating appropriate policy initiatives. Encouragement of the 'enterprise spirit' or 'animal spirit' among young people is a precondition for success in employment, growth, competitiveness and innovation. For India, which is suffering from high levels of unemployment and an increasing number of discouraged jobseekers among urban youth, this precondition can be linked to an urgent need for the promotion of enterprising activity as a potential solution to youth unemployment.

According to the GEM Report 2012 (Xavier et al. 2012), India is ranked far lower than many developing countries involved in GEM. India ranked low in terms of priority towards encouraging entrepreneurship among the educated in particular, for research and training in entrepreneurship, and effective transfer of these skills to new entrepreneurs. However, in terms of internal market openness and physical infrastructure, India is ranked significantly high. This clearly suggests that there is huge potential in India to provide a base for entrepreneurship among the youth if suitable policy is framed.

If we consider the Total Early-Stage Entrepreneurial Activity (TEA)[3], a key measure used by GEM to compare entrepreneurship levels, India stands at a lowly 9.9 per cent—one of the lowest-ranked countries in the world in 2013 (GEM 2013 Global Report). India also ranked among the bottom three countries in the world in terms of the ratio of opportunity entrepreneurship to necessity entrepreneurship. Compared to its development-level peers, the report also found that India ranked below average on job growth expectations, innovation and internationalisation. In fact, India ranked far below Sub-Saharan Africa in terms of innovative orientation.[4]

It is now widely accepted that a matriculation certificate does not guarantee employment for those wishing to enter the labour market after school. Gideon Horn, for instance, offered several reasons for this phenomenon, such as: ill-prepared learners; an inferior schooling system; teachers with insufficient motivation and knowledge to transfer the skills required for the modern world of work; an economy that is not conducive to job creation; affirmative action; and other reasons such as increased mechanisation in the industrial sector (Horn 2006). Further, scholars also argue that the 'traditional classroom delivery' method of basic education in a majority of developing countries like India (Co and Mitchell 2006) may not be conducive to the development of an enterprising spirit among young learners. Allan A. Gibb proposed that enterprising approaches to small business education and training may be important for programmes aimed at promoting business initiation (Gibb 1993). Further, the transfer of enterprising knowledge and skills should be ingrained in the goals of basic education if young learners completing school are expected to participate meaningfully in economic activity. Many developed and developing countries have confirmed the importance of entrepreneurship as the driver of sustainable job and wealth creation (Döckel and Ligthelm 2005). In this book, we study the entrepreneurial attributes of students in colleges in the National Capital Region (NCR) of India to understand how a pipeline for entrepreneurship can be built among the youth.

THE BOOK

This introductory chapter presents our motivation for the study of women entrepreneurship in the middle class in the context of India. Chapter 1 reviews the phenomenon of women entrepreneurship from a management perspective and documents the evolution of the discipline chronologically. It surveys existing literature reviews in established management journals on the subject. It also uncovers the various management theories used in prior literature to study the phenomenon of women entrepreneurship. In Chapter 2 we expand the scope of the review of literature on entrepreneurship to include economic and sociological aspects, including those from a gender perspective. We discuss the wider literature on debates related to the middle class, occupations and mobility, informal employment, women's work participation and self-employment. This literature will be referred to and empirically analysed in the subsequent chapters.

Chapter 3 provides evidence of the growth and character of entrepreneurship in India using various national sources of data. We discuss various definitions of the middle class and provide estimates of its size and growth. The middle class is not homogenous. Hence, we describe the nature of occupations and entrepreneurship within segments of the middle classes. This chapter helps to provide the context in which we discuss women entrepreneurship in India.

Entrepreneurship may be driven by individual motivations or may be influenced by the external eco-system. In economics these are considered under the streams of behavioural and institutional economics. In Chapter 4, we explore behavioural traits such as preference for risk, overconfidence or optimism with regard to individual abilities, and the influence of non-pecuniary benefits such as being one's own boss in the decision to take up entrepreneurship. In this chapter, we use the concepts of 'opportunity-based' and 'necessity-driven' entrepreneurship from management literature, and behavioural traits from economics literature to study the drivers of entrepreneurship.

The Indian economy continues to be dualistic after nearly three decades of economic reforms. In Chapter 5, we explore the impact of external and institutional eco-systems on entrepreneurship in the informal and formal sectors of the economy. This contrast will help present a more nuanced understanding of the behaviour of formal and informal businesses in the eco-entrepreneurial systems in which they operate. In this chapter, we draw on the idea of institutional voids from management literature and external institutions from economics literature to study their impact on entrepreneurship in the context of the dualistic structure of industry in India. This multidisciplinary framework draws on Zahra's conceptualisation of theory building (Zahra 2007).

In India, we know little about the youth's attitudes, aspirations, willingness and key obstacles to becoming an entrepreneur. Who wants to be an entrepreneur? What determines the entrepreneurial aptitude of the person? Chapter 6 explores the attitudes, motivations and constraints towards entrepreneurship among educated youth across technical and non-technical colleges in the NCR. We estimate the aptitude and entrepreneurial spirit among youth, both boys and girls, in these colleges.

The theme of gender pervades the entire book. To enrich the discussion further, we use qualitative insights from 10 real-life case studies of established women entrepreneurs from eight different industry sectors in India, spread across Chapters 2 to 6. Data from personal interviews with these women entrepreneurs was used to create these brief case studies. Each case study presents interesting insights on the background of the woman entrepreneur, her motivation and choice of industry sector. Importantly, the cases reveal the challenges of setting up an enterprise in India and offer practical recommendations to women aspiring to become entrepreneurs.

In Chapter 7, we summarise the debate on women entrepreneurship using a multidisciplinary framework. We highlight the way forward in future women entrepreneurship research. Finally, we present possible pathways for encouraging entrepreneurship among women. This includes expanding the scale and scope and enabling innovation among women-owned or operated enterprises within the current policy framework. We hope that the multidisciplinary view presented in this book will help frame the debate on entrepreneurship afresh and lead to the development of theory in this area.

NOTES

[1]Porter's framework enumerates five forces that help organisations understand the business environment and thereby increase profitability, namely: competitive rivalry; supplier power; buyer power; threat of substitution; and threat of a new entry (see Porter 1979a, and 2008).

[2]*Demographic transition* is a declining fertility rate leading to an increase in the proportion of youth in the population. This is considered an advantage as it increases the proportion of workers in the population and reduces the *dependency ratio* or proportion of people dependent on the working population.

[3]TEA includes individuals in the process of starting a venture and those running a new business that is less than three and a half years old (GEM 2013).

[4]Schumpeter's view of innovative entrepreneurship was of new product-market combinations destroying older, obsolete products and services, and pushing the production frontier forwards (Schumpeter 1942). GEM Reports define innovative orientation using two measures: i) Percentage of TEA that declare they have a product or service that is new for all or some of their consumers; and ii) Percentage of TEA that declare they are new in the market, with few or no other businesses that offer the same product or service (GEM 2013 Global Report).

I

Management View of Women Entrepreneurship[1]

Till the 1990s, mainstream academic journals and leading newspapers in the United States perceived women-owned firms as only small lifestyle businesses or sole proprietorship firms (Baker et al. 1997). The male-centred business model was considered the natural model of doing business. However, research on women entrepreneurs reveals that entrepreneurship is a gendered phenomenon and entrepreneurial activities can be rooted in families (Jennings and Brush 2013).

Emerging literature suggests that women can play a significant role in the larger entrepreneurship phenomenon and economic development (Sarfaraz et al. 2014). Thus, there is an urgent need to investigate various dimensions of women entrepreneurship. Existing theoretical concepts need to be expanded to better explain the uniqueness of women entrepreneurship as a subject of research inquiry.

Addressing this need to build a better understanding, this chapter attempts to present an overview of the field and highlight future research directions. First, we discuss the growth and chronological history of the field of women entrepreneurship. Then, we discuss the research review approach followed in each paper and present the findings from our search of e-databases. Next, we present a summary and analysis of the literature review papers published from the 1980s till 2016. Finally, we discuss directions for future research.

WOMEN ENTREPRENEURSHIP: A CHRONOLOGICAL HISTORY OF THE FIELD

Literature on mainstream entrepreneurship primarily focusing on the male entrepreneur emerged in the 1930s. The late 1970s witnessed the emergence of an explicit sub-domain of women entrepreneurship (Jennings and Brush 2013). This section outlines the chronological history of the development of the literature on women/female entrepreneurship. Table 1.1 presents a summary of the key historical milestones in this sub-domain.

In 1976, Eleanor B. Schwartz published the first academic paper on female entrepreneurship in the *Journal of Contemporary Business*. The first policy report in this area, titled 'The Bottom Line: Unequal Enterprise in America', was released by the President's Inter-agency Task Force on Women Business Owners in 1979 in Washington DC. R. D. Hisrich and M. O'Brien made the first academic conference presentation on women entrepreneurs at the Babson College Conference on Entrepreneurship in 1981. The first academic book on female entrepreneurs, *Women in Charge: The Experience of Female Entrepreneurs* by Robert Goffee and Richard Scase, was published in 1985.

Initial research on entrepreneurship assumed that male and female entrepreneurs were generally the same and there was no specific need for a separate investigation (Bruni et al. 2004). Hence, the sub-domain of women entrepreneurship did not develop as a significant area of research until the late 1990s to early 2000s (Jennings and Brush 2013) with the launch of two dedicated conferences: the policy-oriented Organisation for Economic Co-operation and Development (OECD) Conference on Women Entrepreneurs in Small and Medium Enterprises, first held in 1998; and the academic Diana International Conference, first held in 2003.

TABLE 1.1: Chronological summary of the first studies on women entrepreneurship

Year	Type of study	Reference
1976	First journal article	Schwartz 1976
1979	First policy report	President's Inter-agency Task Force on Women Business Owners 1978
1983	First conference paper presentation	Hisrich and Brush 1983
1985	First academic book	Goffee and Scase 1985
1998	First policy-oriented conference on women entrepreneurship	OECD Conference on Women Entrepreneurs in SMEs: A Major Force in Innovation and Job Creation (http://www.oecd.org/cfe/smes/womenentrepreneurskeymessages.htm)
2003	First academic conference on women entrepreneurship	Diana International Conference on Women's Entrepreneurship Research, Babson College
2006	*Global Entrepreneurship Monitor's* special report on women and entrepreneurship	GEM Report on Women and Entrepreneurship
2009	First dedicated journal	*International Journal of Gender and Entrepreneurship*

Source: Authors

It was not until 2009 that a niche journal titled the *International Journal of Gender and Entrepreneurship* was launched. Eventually, leading mainstream entrepreneurship journals recognised the growing need for research on women entrepreneurship. The journal *Entrepreneurship Theory and Practice* published a special issue on women entrepreneurship in 2006–07 (de Bruin et al. 2006), and then again in 2012 (Hughes et al. 2012).

The *Global Entrepreneurship Monitor* (GEM) also published a special report on women and entrepreneurship in 2006, followed by subsequent reports in 2010, 2012 and 2015. In 2015, the Global Entrepreneurship Development Institute published the Female Entrepreneurship Index report that analysed conditions for fostering women entrepreneurship in 77 countries. According to the report, the top 10 countries for female entrepreneurs in

2015 were the United States, Australia, the United Kingdom, Denmark, the Netherlands, France, Iceland, Sweden, Finland and Norway (Terjesen and Lloyd 2015).

REVIEW METHOD

We considered online discovery services like EBSCO, ProQuest and Google Scholar as the main source for articles. Our first objective was to identify and analyse the leading research journals in the broader area of entrepreneurship with a focus on women entrepreneurship papers. This analysis would help us reflect on the progress of the field and act as a potential source of published research reviews on women entrepreneurship.

McDonald et al. reviewed the research methods used in entrepreneurship from the year 1985 to 2013 and identified six top entrepreneurship journals (McDonald et al. 2015). These include three top American journals (*Journal of Business Venturing*, *Entrepreneurship Theory and Practice* and *Journal of Small Business Management*), and two top European journals (*International Small Business Journal* and *Entrepreneurship and Regional Development*), having impact factors ranging from 1.33 to 2.97. We extended this list and added six more entrepreneurship journals from the Harzing journal quality list (Harzing 2016), which is a compilation of journal rankings from various sources like the Australian Business Deans Council Journal Ranking List, WU Wien Journal Rating, HEC Paris Ranking List, and others.

Altogether, we considered 12 established entrepreneurship journals having journal quality rankings ranging from A*, A, B and C (Harzing 2016). Next, an advanced search for articles on women entrepreneurship was conducted, with a combination of the keywords 'women' or 'gender' in the paper title, using the EBSCO Academic Search Ultimate e-database of academic peer reviewed research journals, magazines, periodicals, reports and books. We carried out 12 separate searches individually for each of the shortlisted entrepreneurship journals. The scope of the search included journal papers that were available online in EBSCO till May 2016.

Table 1.2 and Figure 1.1 summarise our search results. Table 1.2 lists all the selected entrepreneurship journals along with all their papers published on women entrepreneurs from the 1900s till 2016—a total of 185 papers were found. Among the mainstream entrepreneurship journals, we found that the *Journal of Small Business Management* published the first paper in 1973, followed by the *Journal of Business Venturing* in 1988. The *Journal of Small Business Management* had the maximum number of papers. Interestingly, two mainstream entrepreneurship journals, *Economics of Innovation and New Technology* and the *International Journal of Entrepreneurial Behaviour and Research* had no papers on women entrepreneurship till as late as 2016.

TABLE 1.2: List of entrepreneurship journals and papers published on women entrepreneurs, 1900–2016

	Journal name	Year of publication of first article	Total papers (1900–2016)
1.	*Economics of Innovation and New Technology*	–	0
2.	*Entrepreneurship & Regional Development*	1998	11
3.	*Entrepreneurship Theory & Practice**	1991	34
4.	*Industry and Innovation*	2010	1
5.	*International Journal of Entrepreneurial Behaviour and Research*	–	0
6.	*International Journal of Entrepreneurship and Innovation*	2007	5
7.	*International Review of Entrepreneurship*	2015	1
8.	*International Small Business Journal*	1998	18
9.	*Journal of Business Venturing**	1988	26
10.	*Journal of Small Business and Enterprise Development*	2003	16
11.	*Journal of Small Business Management*	1973	46
12.	*Small Business Economics*	1996	27
	Total number of papers		**185**

Note: *Journal is a leader in the entrepreneurship field (Harzing 2016)
Source: Authors

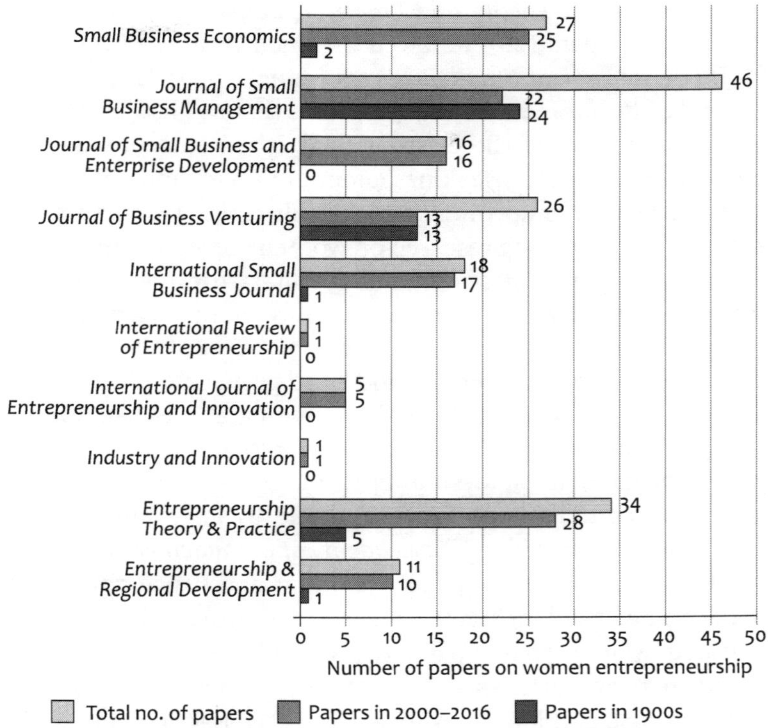

FIGURE 1.1: Papers on women entrepreneurs in established entrepreneurship journals

Source: Authors

Figure 1.1 graphically illustrates the number of papers on women entrepreneurs published in the 1900s and 2000–2016 in the 10 journals. The two journals *Economics of Innovation and New Technology* and the *International Journal of Entrepreneurial Behaviour and Research* that had no papers on women entrepreneurship were dropped from this graph. We found a total 138 papers published from 2000 to 2016. This clearly illustrates a substantial increase from the total 46 papers published during the 1900s. Except for two journals, the *Journal of Business Venturing* and the *Journal of Small Business Management*, there is a visible trend of increased publication of papers.

Entrepreneurship Theory and Practice published the maximum number of papers (28), followed by *Small Business Economics* (25), the *Journal of Small Business Management* (22) and the *Journal of Business Venturing* (13). Note that the list in Table 1.2 is only indicative of the existing established entrepreneurship journals, and scholars seeking potential publication outlets can also consider other upcoming and interdisciplinary journals that are open to publishing research on women entrepreneurship.

Our next level of search was for literature review articles published on women entrepreneurship in management and social science journals. We used a combination of the keywords 'female' or 'women' or 'gender' and 'entrepreneur' and 'review' or 'literature' in the paper title field, using e-databases like EBSCO, ProQuest and Google Scholar. Only relevant review articles were shortlisted for analysis after reading the abstracts. We also selected a comprehensive review article by J. E. Jennings and C. G. Brush published in *The Academy of Management Annals* as our foundational review paper (Jennings and Brush 2013). This paper helped us identify a few more review articles that were not revealed by our search of paper titles. In all, we found 19 relevant literature review articles on women entrepreneurship published between 1986 and May 2016. These are discussed in detail in the reviews section that follows.

REVIEWS OF PAPERS ON WOMEN ENTREPRENEURSHIP

An increase in the number of papers on women entrepreneurs resulted in publications of literature reviews to comprehend the state of the field of research in this area. Table 1.3 presents a summary of the literature reviews published in research journals from 1986 to May 2016. The two review papers published in the 1980s, five in the 1990s and 12 in the 2000s up to 2016 are covered in detail in the following sub-sections.

Reviews in the 1980s

D. D. Bowen and R. D. Hisrich published the first review paper on women entrepreneurs in 1986. They found only piecemeal studies on male and female entrepreneurs till the 1980s (Bowen and Hisrich 1986), which did not examine the causal factors likely to encourage a person to choose an entrepreneurial career. Further, they reported that very little was known about female as compared to male entrepreneurs. Using the lens of career theory, Bowen and Hisrich proposed a career model[2] including determinants of women's entrepreneurial behaviour. This first research review attempted to develop insights in this area and encourage women entrepreneurs in non-traditional industries.

The second review published by Sue Birley in 1989 studied whether female entrepreneurs were different from male entrepreneurs and found that the major difference was in their market-entry choices. Birley reported that nearly all the studies examined were descriptions of basic backgrounds and characteristics, and that there was a need to examine subtle factors like cultural conditioning and experiences. She proposed that the differences between men and women entrepreneurs should be observed in a situational and cultural context. Till the 1980s, the role of women in most Western economies was seen as that of a wife and a mother. Women drew heavily upon the home front for ideas and lacked basic commercial networks. As a result, the market entry choices of women differed from those of men. The review paper proposed that the advent of women-founded businesses was one reflection of a changing society. In future, the profile of women entrepreneurs would likely match changing situations and become closer to that of male entrepreneurs.

Reviews in the 1990s

The third review published by D. P. Moore in 1990 suggested that focused studies on female entrepreneurship were a relatively new phenomenon in the late 1980s (Moore 1990). The field was in an initial stage of paradigm development. Moore reviewed 21 studies on female entrepreneurship and reported that these were fragmented and unrelated, and provided descriptions of only a small section of female entrepreneurs. Further, these studies borrowed theoretical concepts from other areas that were not valid for the women entrepreneurship domain. Moore suggested that a statistical research base be established and typologies, models and theories be developed in this area.

The next review by C. G. Brush in 1992 suggested that not only had the number of women business owners grown considerably over the past decade, but there had also been an increase in the number of research studies on women business owners (Brush 1992). She reported that research over the past decade had shown some similarities and some differences between male and female business owners. Similarities had been reported in demographic features, some psychological traits and business skillsets. Differences had been reported in educational background, occupation, motivation to start a business and approach to business creation and growth. Brush further suggested that the differences had not been fully explained in the literature, and proposed an integrated perspective rooted in psychological and sociological theories to explain gender-based differences. This perspective suggested that women perceived their businesses as a cooperative network of relationships comprising family, society and personal relationships. It differed from the economic perspective of firm creation and was likely to offer explanations for differences between male and female entrepreneurs.

The fifth review by E. M. Fischer, A. R. Reuber and L. S. Dyke in 1993 also suggested the need to build theoretical foundations in women entrepreneurship research. They reported that even though such research had grown considerably, there was still largely atheoretical speculation on the differences between male and female entrepreneurs. They used the perspectives of liberal feminism and social feminism to interpret past research on women entrepreneurship. Additionally, the article also presented findings from a survey of 136 manufacturing firm owners (including 11 women), 156 retail firm owners (including

29 women), and 216 service firm owners (including 20 women). The article reported no strong evidence for women-owned firms being impeded by the owners' lack of education or experience (Fischer et al. 1993). From a policy perspective, this study suggested that access to apprenticeship in the industry for women entrepreneurs could be beneficial as it was the best way to prepare for launching a business in a particular industry. Further, women entrepreneurs could also benefit by being exposed to business start-ups. They proposed that the theories of liberal feminism and social feminism could be used to further understand undefined male and female socialisation differences, which could possibly explain why men and women ran their businesses in different yet equally effective ways.

The sixth review by T. Baker, H. E. Aldrich and N. Liou in 1997 reported a paradox: even though women business ownership had grown substantially in the United States, the number of articles on women business owners/entrepreneurs in newspapers (like *The New York Times* and *The Wall Street Journal*) and leading academic journals had declined (Baker et al. 1997). They reported two dissenting voices: scholars researching on sex and gender issues reasoned in favour of systematic empirical differences in male and female work behaviours; and women's advocacy groups stated that not only were women different but women business owners also possessed unique advantages over men. Mainstream academic journals and media journalists perceived women-owned firms as small lifestyle businesses or sole proprietorship firms. Baker et al. (1997) suggested that rising dissenting voices had been ignored by journalist and academic groups due to androcentrism, which assumes that the male-centred business model is the natural model or way of doing business. Their review found small but significant gender differences in social behaviour and leadership-related studies that could offer interesting insights for understanding the subtle characteristics of women business ownership behaviour.

K. Mirchandani's 1999 review of female entrepreneurship literature used the lens of feminist theory on gendered work (Mirchandani 1999). This review also tried to identify and provide explanations for similarities and differences between female and male entrepreneurs. The paper proposed that the field of women entrepreneurship could be advanced via deliberations on two topics. Firstly, scholars needed to focus on the very construction of the female entrepreneur category, which lays greater emphasis on gender over other types of stratification. Secondly, there was a need to understand relationships between gender, occupation and organisational structure and their impact on female versus male entrepreneurs.

Reviews from 2000 to 2015

A research review by L. K. Gundry, M. Ben-Yoseph and M. Posig in 2002 suggested that the number of women-owned enterprises and research studies on women entrepreneurship had grown steadily in the preceding two decades (Gundry et al. 2002). The review summarised key topics and findings and offered directions for future research. Gundry et al. underscored the need to study comparisons between different sectors of industry and understand the impact of factors like industry, family, culture and goal-orientation in women-founded enterprises. They also highlighted the need for research on women entrepreneurs in developing countries (ibid.).

Helene J. Ahl's 2006 review article presented a critique using discourse analysis of 81 women entrepreneurship research articles published between 1982 and 2000 (Ahl 2006). The review focused mainly on articles from four leading entrepreneurship research journals: *Entrepreneurship Theory and Practice*, *Journal of Business Venturing*, *Journal of Small Business Management* and *Entrepreneurship and Regional Development*. Ahl suggested that there was a need to expand the research object and move from an individualist focus of examining the female entrepreneur to include more factors and contingency studies or comparative studies that include researchers from different countries. Contingency studies could examine external factors like legislation, social norms, family policy, economic policy, labour market structure, degree of women entrepreneurs' participation, and others. Ahl also highlighted the need to make a shift in epistemological position from how gender is done (how women entrepreneurs construct their lives and businesses) to how social orders are gendered (examples include business legislations, policy, support systems, cultural norms, labour divisions). This paper suggested new research directions that were not reproductions of women's subordination but offered a richer perspective on women entrepreneurship grounded in feminist theories.

The next article by Anne de Bruin, C. G. Brush and F. Welter in 2006 is an introduction to a special issue of the journal *Entrepreneurship Theory and Practice* on women entrepreneurship (de Bruin et al. 2006). It presented an overview of the sub-field and a review of the research articles submitted in response to the special issue's call for papers. The journal received a total 52 submissions from 132 authors in 21 countries. Of these, 11 articles were published as special issues in two volumes of the journal, in 2006 and 2007. De Bruin et al. suggested that research on women entrepreneurship was still at an early childhood stage. They proposed that there was a need to pursue more research that is connected to theory, which could capture the heterogeneity in women entrepreneurship research. Further, they suggested that the field of entrepreneurship could advance by encouraging the growth of several scholarly communities that focus in depth on closely defined subject areas. The area of women entrepreneurship could be one such scholarly community. De Bruin et al. also mention the Diana Project that was initiated in 1999 to study women entrepreneurship in the United States. The project now has participants from 20 countries and can be considered a good example of developing focused professional communities in this area.

The next article, again by de Bruin, Brush and Welter, was an introduction to the second volume of the *Entrepreneurship Theory and Practice* special issue on women entrepreneurship, published in 2007. They presented an analysis of the existing and future research themes in women entrepreneurship. The themes included financing of the venture; networks or social capital; firm performance covering growth, growth strategies and success; and individual characteristics like entrepreneurial orientation, self-efficacy, intentions, motivations and decision models. They highlighted that very few authors had explicitly studied the entrepreneurial processes of women entrepreneurs. Further, there was paucity of research on the environment for women entrepreneurship that covered studies from different countries, regions (such as rural or urban) and different business sectors. They also outlined methodological issues and argued whether there was a need for a separate theory on women entrepreneurship. They suggested that research on multiple levels involving multiple units of analysis was required to advance the field, and that existing theoretical concepts needed to be expanded to better explain the uniqueness of women entrepreneurship (de Bruin et al. 2007).

Brush, de Bruin and Welter in 2009 used an organisational framework to review academic literature on women entrepreneurship. They proposed a gender-aware framework for a holistic understanding of the phenomenon of women entrepreneurship. Founded on institutional theory, they built a framework around the 3Ms (markets, money and management), and added two more constructs (motherhood and meso/macro environment) to build a 5M framework to study women entrepreneurship. In this framework, the motherhood construct was a metaphor representing the female entrepreneur's household and family context, which could potentially have a much larger impact in the case of female as compared to male entrepreneurs. Going beyond the domain of markets, the meso/macro environment construct tried to capture influences of society, culture (macro), and intermediate structures and institutions (meso) on ventures run by women (Brush et al. 2009).

The next review by H. Ahl and T. Nelson in 2010 presented an analysis of research trends on gender and entrepreneurship and offered recommendations for new directions. They suggested there was a need to contrast empirical findings using male/female entrepreneurs as independent variables. More research was required on differences between male and female entrepreneur's behaviour in the context of social forces that impact them. They highlighted the need to re-frame the perspective on gender (differing from biological sex) in entrepreneurship research to include aspects of men, women, femininity or masculinity. They asserted that a better dialogue could be achieved by using the word gender as a socially constructed phenomenon. In other words, scholars needed to focus on understanding the distinguishing process of 'doing entrepreneurship' in terms of 'what women do' and 'what men do' (Ahl and Nelson 2010).

D. M. Sullivan and W. R. Meek in 2012 reviewed literature on women entrepreneurship from 1993 to 2010. They organised the literature review under the process model of entrepreneurship including pre-launch, launch and post-launch phases, which was initially proposed by R. A. Baron and R. A. Henry (Baron and Henry 2011). Sullivan and Meek extended this model and called it the process model of gender and entrepreneurship. They reported that research on women entrepreneurship had increased in the previous two decades but there was still a greater need for more studies in this area. They suggested that women were likely to face barriers to entry due to unequal access to assets or resources or education, and were likely to face differing societal attributions and expectations. To mitigate some of these concerns, women could be encouraged to pursue education in fields associated with high-growth industries (Sullivan and Meek 2012).

H. Ahl and A. Marlow in 2012 argued that an occluded gender bias existed within the entrepreneurship discourse. This was contrary to neo-liberal views on entrepreneurship that proposed only personal efforts as determinants of reward and status. They highlighted that even though there had been calls to use feminist theories as analytical frames, there was scant evidence of such applications. They argued that gendered assumptions limited the epistemological scope of research in this area and positioned women entrepreneurs as either failed or reluctant subjects. They proposed the building of a reflexive critical perspective, which could help evaluate the prevalent theoretical approaches on women entrepreneurship within the broader ambit of entrepreneurship research (Ahl and Marlow 2012).

The next article by K. D. Hughes et al. in 2012 characterised women entrepreneurship research as being on the brink of adolescence that year. This characterisation was based on visible growth indicators in the field, like increasing number of conferences, special issues in existing journals, calls for papers and the launch of niche journals on the subject, such as the *International Journal of Gender and Entrepreneurship*. Further, there were examples of other publications like GEM reports, chapters and books on women entrepreneurship. This paper was an introduction to the second special issue of the *Entrepreneurship Theory and Practice* journal on women entrepreneurship in 2012, and presented a critical review of the state of research and of the articles submitted for the special issue (Hughes et al. 2012). The issue received a total 40 submissions from 90 authors in 14 countries, including the United States, United Kingdom, Belgium, France, Canada, Germany, China, Netherlands, Finland, Spain, Sweden, Saudi Arabia and Taiwan. This was fewer than the papers received for the first, two-volume special issue in 2006 and 2007, which could have been due to the presence of niche journals on women entrepreneurship by 2012.

Hughes et al. (2012) reported that there were advances in the type of questions being asked and the explanations being offered. They suggested the need for inclusion of diverse voices and the application of a constructionist approach to answer traditional and non-traditional questions. They also indicated that most of the research collaborations in the area of women entrepreneurship were still restricted within national boundaries and that future research needed the building of networks across transnational borders (ibid.).

The next review paper by Jennings and Brush in 2013 is a comprehensive review that documented in detail the development of research on women entrepreneurship over 30 years. It presented an assessment of research contributions with reference to the larger context of the entrepreneurship domain. It also discussed the challenges and opportunities for scholars studying the niche area of women entrepreneurship. Jennings and Brush used the lens of informed pluralism, which seeks to explore women entrepreneurship using extensions to and by general research on entrepreneurship. They further discussed entrepreneurship as a gendered phenomenon, and that entrepreneurial activities could be rooted in families (Jennings and Brush 2013).

The next article by P. Goyal and V. Yadav in 2014 is a review of challenges faced by women entrepreneurs in developing countries like India. They reported that female entrepreneurs faced challenges of higher magnitude compared to their male counterparts. These challenges were unique and more complex for women living in developing countries. Women in developing countries struggled to gain access to finance, faced socio-cultural biases and experienced low self-esteem, they found. They reported that developing countries had institutional voids and low levels of entrepreneurial education, and highlighted the need to address these complex challenges comprehensively, which could assist research and policy work on women entrepreneurs in developing countries (Goyal and Yadav 2014).

C. Henry, L. Foss and H. Ahl in 2016 reviewed the literature published on gender and entrepreneurship in 18 journals over a period of 30 years. They identified methodological trends in this area and discussed methodological innovations needed for future research. They found there were large-scale empirical studies that primarily focused on comparisons between male and female entrepreneurs. There was often less information given on the industry sector or the sampling methods employed. They suggested there was a paucity of feminist critique and that future scholars needed to engage with post-structural feminist approaches. They highlighted the need to adopt innovative methods like in-depth qualitative approaches to study life histories, case studies or discourse analysis (Henry et al. 2016).

TABLE 1.3: Summary of literature review articles published on women entrepreneurship

Sl. No.	Author Year	Journal	Key findings	Theory
1.	Bowen and Hisrich 1986	*Academy of Management Review*	First literature review paper on female entrepreneurs. Examined literature from an entrepreneurial career perspective and posited a career model containing determinants of women entrepreneurial behaviour.	Career theory
2.	Birley 1989	*Journal of Small Business Management*	The major difference between female and male entrepreneurs was in their market-entry choices. There was a need to examine subtle factors like cultural conditioning and experiences.	Proposed a new theory: the supply of entrepreneurs is situationally and culturally bound
3.	Moore 1990	*Journal of Business Ethics*	Current studies were limited, fragmented and unrelated. Statistical research base, typologies and models need to be developed. The field was in an initial stage of paradigm development and there was a need to build theories.	
4.	Brush 1992	*Entrepreneurship Theory and Practice*	Research over the decade had shown some similarities and differences between male and female business owners. Similarities had been reported in demographic features, psychological traits and business skillsets. Differences had been reported in educational background, occupation, motivation to start a business and approach to business creation and growth.	Proposed an integrated perspective, rooted in psychological and sociological theories, to explain gender-based differences
5.	Fischer, Reuber and Dyke 1993	*Journal of Business Venturing*	There were theoretical speculations on the differences between male and female entrepreneurs. No strong evidence for women-owned firms being impeded by the female owners' lack of education or experience was found. Further, access to apprenticeship in target industry for women entrepreneurs could be beneficial.	Liberal feminist theory and social feminist theory can help explain why men and women run their businesses in different yet equally effective ways

(Contd)

Table 1.3 (Contd)

Sl. No.	Author Year	Journal	Key findings	Theory
6.	Baker, Aldrich and Liou 1997	*Entrepreneurship and Regional Development*	Reported a paradox: even though women business ownership had grown substantially in the US, the leading press and academic journals had remained silent. Small but significant gender differences in social behaviour and leadership studies could offer interesting insights on gendered differences in business ownership.	Social behaviour theory
7.	Mir-chandani 1999	*Gender, Work and Organization*	Research on women entrepreneurship could be advanced via reflections on: (i) construction of the 'female entrepreneur' category that lays greater emphasis on gender over other types of stratification; (ii) examination of relationships between gender, occupation and organisational structure, and their impact on female versus male entrepreneurs.	Feminist theory
8.	Gundry, Ben-Yoseph and Posig 2002	*Journal of Enterprising Culture*	Suggested the need to study comparisons among sectors, examine impact of factors like industry, family, culture and goal orientation in women-founded enterprises, and study women entrepreneurship in the context of developing countries.	
9.	Ahl 2006	*Entrepreneurship Theory and Practice*	Highlighted the need to expand the research object and move from an individualist focus of examining the female entrepreneur to include more factors and studies, like contingency studies or comparative studies. Also highlighted the need to make a shift in epistemological position from how gender is done to how social orders are gendered.	Feminist theories: liberal feminist, social feminist, psychoanalytical feminist, radical feminist, social constructionist and post-structural feminist theory

(Contd)

Table 1.3 (Contd)

Sl. No.	Author Year	Journal	Key findings	Theory
10.	de Bruin, Brush and Welter 2006	*Entrepreneurship Theory and Practice*	Research on women entrepreneurship was still at an early childhood stage; there was a need to pursue research that is connected to theory. Nurturing professional academic communities in this area, like the Diana Project, was needed to advance the field.	
11.	de Bruin, Brush and Welter 2007	*Entrepreneurship Theory and Practice*	Existing theoretical concepts needed to be expanded to better explain the uniqueness of women entrepreneurship. Research on multiple levels involving multiple units of analysis was required to advance the field.	Proposed use of feminist theories to expand entrepreneurial theories on process, opportunity recognition, opportunity exploitation, value creation, entrepreneurial environment and institutional theory
12.	Brush, de Bruin, and Welter 2009	*International Journal of Gender and Entrepreneurship*	Proposed a gender-aware framework for a holistic understanding of women entrepreneurship. Founded on institutional theory, they built a framework around 3Ms (markets, money and management) and added two more variables (motherhood and meso/macro environment) to construct a 5M framework.	Institutional theory, propose gender as a social construct theory
13.	Ahl and Nelson 2010	*International Journal of Gender and Entrepreneurship*	Re-framed the perspective on gender (differing from biological sex) in entrepreneurship research. Used the word 'gender' as a socially constructed phenomenon. Focused on understanding the distinguishing process of 'doing entrepreneurship' in terms of 'what women do' and 'what men do'.	Use institutional theory to examine gender and entrepreneurship

(Contd)

Table 1.3 (Contd)

Sl. No.	Author Year	Journal	Key findings	Theory
14.	Sullivan and Meek 2012	*Journal of Managerial Psychology*	Extended the research examining relationships between I/O psychology and entrepreneurship studies. Presented the review as a process model of gender and entrepreneurship.	Expectancy theory, regulatory focus theory, social cognitive theory to study process model concepts (entrepreneurial opportunity recognition, motivation, resource acquisition, success/performance)
15.	Ahl and Marlow 2012	*Organization*	An occluded gender bias existed within entrepreneurial discourse, which was contrary to the neo-liberal views on entrepreneurship. Gendered assumptions limited the epistemological scope of research and positioned women entrepreneurs as either failed or reluctant subjects. There was a need to build a reflexive critical perspective.	Feminist theories
16.	Hughes, Jennings, Brush, Carter and Welter 2012	*Entrepreneurship Theory and Practice*	Research on women entrepreneurship was still at an adolescent stage. Inclusion of diverse voices and application of constructionist approaches to answer traditional and non-traditional questions was needed. Research collaborations in the area were still restricted within national boundaries; future research needed the building of networks across transnational borders.	

(Contd)

Table 1.3 (Contd)

Sl. No.	Author Year	Journal	Key findings	Theory
17.	Jennings and Brush 2013	*The Academy of Management Annals*	A comprehensive review of the sub-field documenting in detail the evolution of research work on women entrepreneurship over a period of 30 years. Used the lens of informed pluralism and reported that entrepreneurship is a gendered phenomenon, entrepreneurial activity is embedded in families, entrepreneurship can result from necessity as well as opportunity and entrepreneurs pursue goals beyond economic gains.	Feminist theory, process theory, motivation and goals
18.	Goyal and Yadav 2014	*Psychosociological Issues in Human Resource Management*	Reviewed challenges faced by women entrepreneurs in developing countries, which had institutional voids and low levels of entrepreneurial education. Women struggled to gain access to finance, faced socio-cultural biases and experienced low self-esteem. There was a need to address these complex challenges comprehensively to assist research and policy on women entrepreneurs in developing nations.	
19.	Henry, Foss and Ahl 2016	*International Small Business Journal*	Reviewed literature published on gender and entrepreneurship in 18 journals over a period of 30 years. There were large-scale empirical studies that primarily focused on comparisons between male and female entrepreneurs, and often less information was given on the industry sector or the sampling methods. There was a paucity of feminist critique and future scholars needed to engage with post-structural feminist approaches. There was a need to adopt innovative methods like in-depth qualitative approaches.	Post-structural feminist theory

Source: Authors

DIRECTIONS FOR FUTURE RESEARCH

Till the 1980s, there were only piecemeal studies and little was explicitly known about female entrepreneurs (Bowen and Hisrich 1986). Initial studies were fragmented and unrelated, providing descriptions of only a small section of the larger population of female entrepreneurs (Moore 1990). The role of women in most Western economies was seen as that of a wife and a mother till the 1980s. As a result, women lacked basic commercial networks and their market entry choices differed (Birley 1989). The advent of women-founded businesses was considered one of the reflections of a changing society.

Build Theoretical Explanations for Gender-based Comparisons of Business Owners

In the 1990s, as the number of women business owners grew, the number of research studies on women entrepreneurs also grew (Brush 1992). Initial research was primarily focused on listing similarities and dissimilarities between male and female business owners. Differences were reported on educational background, occupation, motivation and method of business creation and growth. Researchers like Fischer, Reuber and Dyke suggested that the differences reported in literature between male and female entrepreneurs were speculations and largely atheoretical in nature (Fischer et al. 1993). There was a need to build more theoretical explanations and move beyond recording differences.

For example, Brush (1992) proposed an integrated perspective explaining gender-related differences using psychological and sociological theories. This is different from the economic perspective of firm creation and assumes that women entrepreneurs perceive their businesses as cooperative networks of relationships involving family, society and personal relationships. Fischer et al. (1993) suggested using theories of liberal feminism and social feminism to understand undefined male and female socialisation differences, which could help explain why men and women ran their businesses in different yet equally effective ways.

Extend Existing Theories of Entrepreneurship Using a Feminist Perspective

There is debate in the literature reviewed about whether a new theory on women entrepreneurship is required. Many researchers have suggested that existing concepts of entrepreneurship can be used in conjunction with feminist theories to extend the theoretical foundations of the larger entrepreneurship field. In the past, many theoretical lenses have been used to examine the phenomenon of women entrepreneurship. For example, Bowen and Hisrich (1986) used career theory to propose a career model of women's entrepreneurial behaviour; Brush (1992) used psychological and sociological theories to explain gender-based differences; Brush et al. (2009) used institutional theory to propose gender as a social construct; and Sullivan and Meek (2012) used expectancy theory, regulatory focus theory and social cognitive theory to study entrepreneurial process model concepts. Ahl (2006) reported the use of feminist theories like the liberal feminist theory, social feminist theory, psychoanalytical feminist theory, radical feminist theory, social constructionist and post-structural feminist theory. To advance our understanding of this field, there is also a need for a shift in epistemological position from how gender is done to how social orders are gendered (Ahl 2006; Ahl and Nelson 2010). Research efforts in this direction are likely to offer a richer perspective on women entrepreneurship. Scholars can use the existing concepts of entrepreneurship and ground them in feminist theories.

Study Entrepreneurial Processes of Women-founded Business Models

Women entrepreneurs comprise about half the human resources in developing economies (World Bank 2009). Despite an influx of women into the field of entrepreneurship in developing countries (Gichuki et al. 2014), very few authors have explicitly examined the entrepreneurial processes of women-founded businesses (de Bruin et al. 2007). In reality, women in developing countries are more likely to face complex barriers to entry and unequal access to resources and networks (Goyal and Yadav 2014). Thus, there is a need to build an in-depth understanding of the business models of women-founded firms from pre-launch to launch and post-launch phases (Sullivan and Meek 2012). Scholars can use the lens of process theories to understand the influence of gender in business models.

Expand the Scope of Research on Women Entrepreneurs: Context and Content

Our review findings suggest that there is a need to expand the scope of research on women entrepreneurs involving the context as well as the content of research. Bruin et al. (2007) report that the *Entrepreneurship Theory and Practice* journal's special issue had generated interest on the topic in the researcher community and the special issue's countries of submission included countries like United States, United Kingdom, Canada, Bulgaria, Denmark, Germany, Switzerland, Finland, Italy, Norway, Sweden, New Zealand, Spain, Australia, China, France, India, Malaysia, Iran, Pakistan and Ghana. Despite the interest, we find that most of the literature on women entrepreneurship reported empirical studies primarily from the West. There are very few studies that explore this phenomenon in a developing economy context, and there is a need for research on women entrepreneurs in developing countries (Gundry et al. 2002; Goyal and Yadav 2014).

Further, the context can also be expanded in terms of the women entrepreneurship environment to study comparisons among classes (upper, middle and lower), sectors (manufacturing, services and others), regions (urban and rural) and nations. Scholars can design studies to examine the impact of factors like industry, family, culture and goal orientation in women-founded enterprises (Gundry et al. 2002). It would be interesting to observe socio-cultural and economic class differences across nations with different cultural backgrounds.

Content-wise, there is a need to move beyond the individualist focus of the female entrepreneur and include more factors like contingency studies and comparative studies (Ahl 2006). For instance, contingency studies can explore external factors like legislation, social norms, family policy, economic policy, labour market structures, and the degree of female business owner's involvement. From a macro perspective, scholars can explore links between income class, educational attainment and women entrepreneurship. To foster entrepreneurship among young women, it would be useful to explore entrepreneurial intentions of young women from varied socio-economic and class backgrounds in different cultural contexts.

Embrace Innovative Research Methods to Study Women Entrepreneurs

Our review of literature reveals that most of the papers on women entrepreneurship fall under the positivist research paradigm.[3] Many are empirical studies focusing on male and female entrepreneur comparisons, which provide less information on industry sectors or the sampling methods used (Henry et al. 2016). There is a need to adopt inductive methods of qualitative analysis that can help increase our understanding of entrepreneurship as a gendered phenomenon (Mirchandani 1999) and advance theory in this area. For example, research methods like in-depth qualitative approaches can be used to investigate life histories, ethnographies and case studies or discourse analysis. Further, scholars can research the phenomenon of women entrepreneurship on multiple levels using multiple units of analysis (de Bruin et al. 2007).

CONCLUSION

The field of women entrepreneurship has come a long way since its emergence in the late 1970s. Our review of literature published between 1986 and 2016 found that the initial studies on entrepreneurship primarily assumed male and female entrepreneurs to be the same and found no explicit need for a separate investigation. As a result, research on women entrepreneurship did not develop as a distinct domain until the late 1990s to early 2000s. This development witnessed the emergence of professional communities like the Diana Project, dedicated conferences and niche journals in this area. Mainstream entrepreneurship journals also acknowledged the need for research in this area and came out with special issues to advance the body of knowledge on women entrepreneurship.

Many studies in the past borrowed theoretical concepts from areas that were not valid for the women entrepreneurship domain. There is a need to be inclusive of diverse voices and consider constructionist approaches to explore traditional as well as non-traditional questions. Particularly, there is a need to use the lens of feminist theories to capture heterogeneity in women entrepreneurship research and extend existing entrepreneurial theories. There is also a need to study entrepreneurial processes of women-founded business models and adopt innovativeness in research method choices.

Our review results can also be beneficial for start-up managers and women entrepreneurs. In practice, aspiring women entrepreneurs can benefit by gaining access to apprenticeship in target industries. This experience can help them prepare better prior to launching their own business in that particular industry. Specifically, gaining exposure to a business start-up can be beneficial. Further, most of the collaborations in the women entrepreneurship area are still restricted within national boundaries and there is a need to build research as well as practice networks across transnational borders.

NOTES

[1]This chapter is an adapted version of a paper previously published in 2016 as an Open Access article, titled 'Women Entrepreneurship: Research Review and Future Directions', in the *Journal of Global Entrepreneurship Research* under the Creative Commons Attribution License 4.0 International License (https://creativecommons.org/licenses/by/4.0/); the authors retain the copyright (Yadav and Unni 2016).

[2]Bowen and Hisrich (1986) proposed a career model or framework explaining factors that encourage a woman to enter the entrepreneurial career. They suggest that the factors that determine entrepreneurial behaviour are spread over life spaces (i.e., work, personal and family space) for an individual (man or woman), and tend to evolve over time from childhood to adulthood.

[3]A positivist research paradigm involves studies that are quantitative in nature like surveys or experiments. These studies aim to explain and predict relationships between variables using hypotheses testing and statistical analysis methods.

II

Multidisciplinary View of Women Entrepreneurship

Mainstream management literature has been challenged by emerging pluralist economics literature, giving rise to a cross-disciplinary approach towards the study of entrepreneurship. Insights from behavioural economics suggest that perceptions (including individual traits and motivations) matter in entrepreneurial decisions. Institutional economics has highlighted the role of institutional factors (the entrepreneurial ecosystem, such as procedures and costs to start a business) in entrepreneurial activities. Feminist literature critiques the treatment of women informal workers as a 'gendered entrepreneurial subject' (Boeri 2018). Even though research on entrepreneurship challenging mainstream understanding is increasing, the literature on women entrepreneurship from a pluralist perspective, especially from transitional economies and developing countries, is still under-developed.

In Chapter 1, we reviewed the literature on entrepreneurship and women's entrepreneurship, in particular from a management perspective. A key takeaway from the review using the lens of informed pluralism was that besides being a gendered phenomenon embedded in families, 'entrepreneurship can result from necessity as well as opportunity and entrepreneurs pursue goals beyond economic gains' (Jennings and Brush 2013). A woman's decision to become an entrepreneur can be precipitated by both push or pull factors.

In this chapter, we critically discuss the extant empirical literature on women entrepreneurship from a pluralist, mainly economic perspective. We also examine the broader issue of women's work participation in India and whether self-employment constitutes entrepreneurship. Another dimension of the debate considered is the role of the middle class in fostering entrepreneurship. We also present two case studies of women entrepreneurs as real-life examples of women exploring diverse business sectors in India.

ECONOMICS

Economists attribute the terms 'entrepreneur' and 'entrepreneurial spirit' to Joseph A. Schumpeter. In Schumpeter's theory of economic development, the key role of innovation by entrepreneurs is acknowledged as the driver of the dynamic and consistent process of economic change (Schumpeter 1934a). In his theory, economic development progresses through business cycles (ibid.). The term 'creative destruction' attributed to him implies that old technologies give way to the new through innovation, and this process drives economic growth. Thus, innovative entrepreneurs are key drivers of the process of economic growth. In an uncertain economic situation, the entrepreneur is a risk-taker and is motivated by the joy of creation, the will to conquer and the desire to be commercially successful. More generally, economists define an entrepreneur by the functions he or she performs: risk-taking, coordination of productive resources, innovation and provision of capital.

Schumpeter defines an entrepreneur as a person who is willing and able to convert a new idea or invention into a successful innovation. According to him, the essence of entrepreneurship is the discovery of new economic opportunities. An entrepreneur achieves success by introducing a completely new product or service, thereby starting the creative destruction of an existing market equilibrium. Broadly, entrepreneurs are classified into *innovation* entrepreneurs, *arbitrage* entrepreneurs and *need-based* entrepreneurs. According to Schumpeter, only innovation entrepreneurs are real entrepreneurs as they create a disequilibrium force. However, according to Israel M. Kirzner, an individual who can identify opportunities and make profit from the existing scenario can also be termed an entrepreneur (Kirzner 1997). Such a person makes profit through arbitrage opportunities that exist either within the market or among different markets. The third type of entrepreneurship arises due to economic constraints existing in society. This need-based entrepreneurship is most prevalent in developing countries. The profile of the need-based entrepreneur is very different compared to the other two kinds of entrepreneurs, mainly because of his/her reasons for choosing entrepreneurship. Two strands in economics literature—behavioural economics and institutional economics—have taken the concept of entrepreneurship forward.

Behavioural Economics

Behavioural economics draws from psychology to study an individual's process of economic decision-making by examining behavioural, emotional and social factors. Contrary to traditional economics, behavioural economics contends that people may not always behave as expected or as reported, and may act irrationally. Suggestive persuasion designed by observing human traits and motivation can be used to 'nudge' people into desired forms of behaviour. 'Nudge' is a non-parametric tool developed by the discipline, a non-regulatory approach that tries to influence people by altering their options or choices. Adam Oliver argued that behavioural economics can also be used to inform regulation or policy that can direct people towards desired behaviour (Oliver 2015). We follow this line of argument in Chapter 4.

Traditional economic models predict that people choose entrepreneurship when returns are higher than wage or salaried employment. However, this traditional model came into question when studies in the United States found that entrepreneurship tends to be an activity with low median returns and high variance (Astebro et al. 2014). Only a few entrepreneurs succeed and many fail or receive meagre returns. Further, despite low odds of success, entrepreneurs persist in running businesses for long periods with low returns (Hamilton 2000). This puzzle contradicted the entrepreneurship theory of pursuit of business opportunity and profit-orientation and the expected utilities framework. In a review of the development of the field of behavioural economics, M. Kremer, G. Rao and F. Schilbach (2019: 415–417) note that firms in developing countries may deviate from the neoclassical framework of profit maximisation.

Behavioural economics seeks to explain this puzzle of the entry into entrepreneurship through three main factors. First is a preference for risk, 'because they get utility out of risk itself' (Arrington 2010). Entrepreneurs are less risk-averse and attracted to the possibility of large gains from risky ventures. However, some empirical studies using various methods, including experimental, did not find evidence that entrepreneurs were more risk-taking than non-entrepreneurs (Astebro et al. 2014). The second explanation for continued entrepreneurial activity in the face of low returns is overconfidence (Moore and Healy 2008; Weinstein 1980). The entrepreneur's confidence in his or her abilities and optimism with regard to the business environment makes the entrepreneur ignore the fact that ventures can fail, or start small and remain small. A third explanation is that the non-pecuniary benefits of entrepreneurship, such as the advantages of being one's own boss, can motivate individuals (Hurst and Pugley 2011; Yurdagul 2017).

Thomas Astebro et al. (2014) suggested various directions in which the behavioural roots of entrepreneurship were proceeding. First, there were attempts to disentangle the multiple explanations and interpretations for entrepreneurship; second, attempts were made to understand the social context of the behaviour of entrepreneurs, such as intergenerational correlation with self-employment; and third, it was seen that excessive entry into entrepreneurship may be a positive feature in creative destruction, leading to positive externalities like a breakthrough innovation beneficial to society.

Institutional Economics

There is a significant stream of research in management literature on the impact of institutional voids, such as government legal and regulatory mechanisms, on entrepreneurship (Puffer, McCarthy and Boisot 2010). Informal institutions, essentially society's norms and beliefs, define codes of socially acceptable behaviour (North 1990). Both formal and informal institutional voids can impact entrepreneurship. Informal institutions such as accepted gender norms have a significant impact on women entrepreneurship.

William Baumol's idea of productive and unproductive entrepreneurship as shaped by institutions is a significant contribution to economics of entrepreneurship literature (Baumol 1996). He extends Schumpeter's view of innovations to innovations in rent-seeking behaviour and criminal activities, which he terms 'unproductive entrepreneurship', as opposed to productive and growth-oriented entrepreneurship. Baumol proposed a fascinating insight, that the nature of entrepreneurship was influenced by the 'rules of the game that govern the payoffs to entrepreneurship' (ibid.).

> When institutions provide secure property rights, a fair and balanced judicial system, contract enforcement, and effective constitutional limits on government's ability to transfer wealth through taxation and regulation, it reduces the profitability of unproductive political and legal entrepreneurship. Under this incentive structure, creative individuals are more likely to engage in the creation of new wealth through productive market entrepreneurship. (Sobel 2008)

The role of institutions takes a new meaning in this narrative of entrepreneurship.

Extending Baumol's framework, Justin W. Webb, Theodore A. Khoury and Michael A. Hitt developed a model to analyse how formal and informal institutions affect the nature of entrepreneurship in a continuum, from formal productive to informal productive to destructive economic activities (Webb, Khoury and Hitt 2019). They also distinguished between productive activities by the individual's objectives: driven by growth, lifestyle- or subsistence-based. We broadly follow this literature to distinguish the influence of formal institutional voids on the growth of informal enterprises and innovation among formal enterprises in Chapter 5.

Zoltan Acs and José Ernesto Amorós argued that the institutional environment facing the country has an impact on entrepreneurship (Acs and Amorós 2008). This can help explain why the volume and nature of entrepreneurship varies across and within countries. Candida G. Brush, Anne de Bruin and Friederike Welter used an organisational framework to review the academic literature on women entrepreneurship (Brush, de Bruin and Welter 2009). They proposed a gender-aware framework for a holistic understanding of the phenomenon of women entrepreneurship. As mentioned in Chapter 1, they built a framework around the 3Ms, and added motherhood and meso/macro environment to construct a 5-M framework of study that would also try to capture influences of society, culture (macro), intermediate structures and institutions (meso) (Yadav and Unni 2016).

Gender studies expand the context of institutional factors to include social and traditional institutions as well. Ahl (2006) suggested a need to expand the research object and move from an individualist focus of examining the role and behaviour of the female entrepreneur to include external institutional factors. This should include legislation, social norms, family policy, economic policy, labour market structure, degree of women entrepreneur's participation, among other factors. The study suggested a need to shift from an epistemological position of how gender is done (how women entrepreneurs construct their lives and businesses) to how social orders or institutions are gendered (examples include business legislations, policy, support systems, cultural norms, labour divisions). It offers new research directions that are not reproductions of women's subordination but provide a richer perspective on women entrepreneurship grounded in feminist theories.

Erica Field, Seema Jayachandran and Rohini Pande (2010) addressed the question of what constrains entrepreneurship choices among poor women in India. Do institutions place constraints on the behaviour of women? They hypothesised that traditional institutions of caste and religion may pose unique barriers to business growth and profitability for family-run enterprises. In an experimental research study, they discussed the impact of attending training on economic outcomes and found that training encourages upper-caste women to start or expand business.

WOMEN'S WORK PARTICIPATION AND SELF-EMPLOYMENT

There has been an active debate on women's participation in the workforce in India. Despite relatively high economic growth, women's labour force participation has been declining continuously in the last two decades. The decline has been attributed to an income effect: with rising household incomes women prefer to withdraw from the workforce (Sundaram and Tendulkar 2006). The phenomenon of withdrawal of women from the workforce has also been attributed to a discouraged worker effect rather than an income effect. It is argued that if there is demand for their labour, women would seize the opportunity based on the nature of work available and its quality (Unni and Raveendran 2006). A large proportion of women are self-employed in India, particularly in the agricultural sector. Hence, changes in demand based on a good or bad agricultural year affects demand for women's labour in agriculture. A poor agricultural year also affects the non-agriculture sector as a large part of the demand for goods in rural India comes from the surplus generated in the agricultural sector. This can lead to a decline in women's work participation due to the discouraged worker effect.

Self-employment

Standard economic theory of wage determination in labour markets assumes that self-employment and wage employment are substitutes of each other. While self-employment with low returns may be like wage work, the two are not perfect substitutes due to various differences in initial endowments. The decision to participate in self-employment may be dependent on small investments in capital/land, and not based on the market wage (as in the case of the wage worker). Or it may depend on the availability of complementary inputs (like raw material, e.g. bamboo), or technology (like machinery or equipment, e.g. sewing machine), and/or on the endowment of specialised skills for particular economic activities. Standard economic theory also assumes perfect ease of entry into the wage labour market while in reality employment may be constrained by class, caste, religion, gender and, in the case of self-employment, by the interlocking of price and non-price factors across markets, e.g. land and credit. Hence, while some segment of self-employment may be a substitute to wage employment, a large part may have its own independent reason for the choice of this form of employment.

James Heintz (2008) argued for adopting a broader definition of the labour market to include both wage and self-employment. One of the implications of doing so would be that

> the conceptual framework based on the dichotomy of 'labour demand' and 'labour supply' may no longer be universally operational. For example, in the typical demand/supply framework, the self-employed must be considered both buyers and sellers of their own labour. This could be interpreted to imply that the self-employed are economic schizophrenics, at war with themselves as to where their self-interest lies. ...it suggests that the traditional apparatus for theorizing labour markets—with its intersecting supply-and-demand curves—will need to be reformed to adequately capture the employment relationships that dominate the labour markets of developing countries. (Heintz 2008: 14)

Traditional theorising of labour markets assumes an unadulterated notion of profit maximisation, which may not always be appropriate. Poor households may be trying to sustain household incomes by working longer hours than is considered 'optimal' by traditional theory. In contrast with the logic of labour markets, non-monetary factors may also be important for the self-employed. 'Models of imperfect labour markets abound in the economics literature, and not just among heterodox practitioners or the radical fringe of the discipline. Despite a well-developed critique, even among many in the mainstream, rarely do these theoretical insights alter the dominant policy prescriptions in a meaningful way' (Heintz 2008: 14).

Self-employment involves investment in human (skill) and physical (fixed) capital assets, as well as social capital (contacts) and undertaking risk, unlike wage employment. Wage employment involves sale of human capital (labour) to an employer. In some cases, self-employment also involves recruitment of labour.

Stephen Marglin wrote a classical paper titled 'What Do Bosses Do?' in which he argued that wage employment is about discipline and control (Marglin 1974). Perhaps a similar argument could be advanced for the new forms of self-employment, e.g. industrial outwork and disguised wage employment.

Traditional self-employment, whether in single persons or family units, is often embedded in social relationships: workers (both paid and unpaid) are often recruited from networks of family, kinship and community; intra- and inter-firm relationships are often non-contractual; household and enterprise accounts are often not separated; entry into self-employment often involves inheriting a parental business or carrying on the kinship group's line of work. These features reflect what some observers call 'family-embeddedness' and 'intergenerational inheritance' of self-employment (Arum and Müller 2004). Richard Arum and Walter Müller argue that self-employment could mean having more flexibility in working hours and the freedom to choose the nature of work (ibid.). For others, it may mean entrapment in low-paying jobs.

According to Janet Hotch, 'In the light of these ambiguities, self-employment can carry connotations of independence, agency, and self-fulfilment, despite the hardships it may entail; or it can mean drudgery and uncertainty' (Hotch 2000: 143). The self-employed are exposed to market risks but cannot afford to insure themselves, nor enjoy employment-linked social protection (ibid.).

The role of the state is generally to balance the choice of equity versus efficiency. In general, economic policy chooses efficiency, as indicated by standard economic theory. Self-employment with very low productivity and income per worker is treated as an inefficient unit in the economy. Hence, if a self-employed small enterprise dies or closes down, such closure is considered efficient in theory, and consequently in policy. Economic policy is not concerned with the consequences of such closure of small enterprises on the economics of the household unless it becomes an economy-wide phenomenon, as the farmers' suicides have in recent years (seen as the closure of small and micro farms). If economic policy were more concerned with equity rather than efficiency, the survival of small, self-employed enterprises would be of greater concern. An important policy issue for a self-employment enterprise would be how to scale up its economic activity, which requires policy support.

The Self-employed and Entrepreneurship

Poor and developing countries, particularly in Asia and Africa, have a significant proportion of self-employed workers and enterprises. The self-employed consist of employers, own account workers (OAWs, or enterprises based on family labour alone with no hired workers), and unpaid family workers (UFWs). As in the discussion in the previous section, the self-employed could be independent enterprises with small scale operations or engaged in subcontracted work for large enterprises. In this context, important questions to pose are: is the self-employed person an entrepreneur? Are all self-employed workers entrepreneurs engaged in profit maximisation? It has been argued that a self-employed person or enterprise hiring at least one worker, i.e. an employer, is more likely to be an entrepreneur and more likely to be an opportunity-based one (Daymard 2015).

In a study in Sri Lanka, Suresh de Mel, David McKenzie and Christopher Woodruff asked the question, 'who are the own account workers?' (de Mel, McKenzie and Woodruff 2008). They found that roughly two-thirds of own account workers should be classified as wage workers rather than entrepreneurs. Ability, motivation and a competitive attitude are critical in the differentiation of small and micro enterprise owners from those of larger business enterprises. The implication of this theory is that among the self-employed, an own account worker is likely to offer herself for wage employment if she finds a remunerative job. Such self-employed workers can also be classified as necessity-driven entrepreneurs.

'The concept of entrepreneurship is multifaceted and is surely not synonymous with self-employment. However, it is common in the entrepreneurship literature to call individuals having a preference for being self-employed "latent entrepreneurs"' (Blanchflower et al. 2001; Gohmann 2012), and to call individuals who are taking steps to start a new business 'nascent entrepreneurs' (Davidsson 2006). Women who were competitive were more inclined to be self-employed or 'latent entrepreneurs' (Bönte and Piegeler 2013).

The gender dimension of entrepreneurship literature is also derived from the fact that a significant proportion of self-employed women in developing countries are own account workers, who can be classified as necessity-driven entrepreneurs. The economist's definition of an entrepreneur as risk-taking innovators looking for an opportunity, or that of the psychologist as high achievers, may not suit these women entrepreneurs. Karen Hughes reported that people who were forced into self-employment had lower income and displayed a lower level of satisfaction than their counterparts who started a business deliberately (Hughes 2003).

The Self-employed as Informal Workers

Self-employed and own account workers can be characterised as informal workers, broadly defined as those who do not receive social protection support from an employer. Feminist literature strongly critiques the construction of women informal workers as an 'abstract gendered entrepreneurial subject' (Boeri 2018). It raises strong objection to the neoliberal development agenda of micro enterprise expansion relying on informal work in the face of loss of formal work (Karides 2010). Jan Breman objects to the idea of labelling informal work as an opportunity, overlooking the cycle of pauperisation (Breman 2013), while Barbara Harriss-White labels such work as occurring due to limited choices for women given the social structures and production relations (Harriss-White 2003).

One of the contentions of this line of argument is that the woman in most developing economies must fulfil the social reproduction function which inhibits her capacity to engage fully in entrepreneurship. She is pushed into self-employed work largely due to poverty or the need to enhance household income. She is engaged in subcontracted work with little autonomy and mainly works from home in the informal economy. This literature objects to such self-employed women workers being regarded as entrepreneurs, while reducing social security budgets (Boeri 2018). Mainstream entrepreneurship literature often ignores the social reproduction function performed by women that inhibits their capacity to expand their enterprise. Women informal workers working from home do not defy social norms (Kabeer 2010) and they fulfil their social reproduction function (Boeri 2018).

In the prevailing conception of entrepreneurship in management literature, the emergence of the strand of women entrepreneurship where women engage in work out of necessity rather than opportunity challenges the primacy of goals related to economic gain. The economics literature on self-employment and labour markets suggests various reasons for women's engagement in entrepreneurship other than profit maximisation. The pluralist approach, including management, behavioural economics and institutional economics, questions the construction of an entrepreneur as driven only by the desire to seize opportunity and chase profit. This line of argument will be explored in this book.

THE MIDDLE CLASS

Approaches to Defining Class

Social class is an established concept in sociology, originally propounded by Karl Marx (cited in Bottomore, Rubel and Fromm 1964) and Max Weber (1978[1909]). Marx emphasised the possession of assets and private ownership of capital in a capitalist society as a determinant of class. The struggle between capital and labour led to class conflict. Weber emphasised social stratification, including class, as returns to different forms of assets, status or prestige, and power.

In a series of articles, David B. Grusky, Kim A. Weeden and Jesper B. Sørensen defined classes based on occupational categories and called them 'micro-classes' as opposed to 'big classes' as defined by Marx and Weber (Grusky, Weeden and Sørensen 2001; Grusky and Sørensen 1998). Their reason for aligning class with occupation was because the exclusive focus on 'big class' had become disconnected with the institutional realities of the labour market. Weeden and Grusky identified three clusters of mechanisms or processes that are closely tied to these disaggregated occupations: a) allocation into the occupation, both through selection by employers and self-selection by job-seekers; b) social conditioning, including education and training, social interactions and occupational environment generating occupation-specific lifestyles and social attitudes; and c) institutionalisation through formal licensing, employer protocols in defining jobs, and practices of occupational associations (Weeden and Grusky 2005).

Michael Mann distinguishes three fractions of the middle class: 'The petite bourgeoisie: proprietors of small, familial business; Careerists: wage or salaried employees moving up corporate and bureaucratic hierarchies; and Professionals: "learned," collectively organized occupations licensed by the state' (Mann 2012). He identified three processes that link these three occupational categories into a class: diffused capitalist participation in economic hierarchy, a distinctive consumption pattern and converting surplus incomes into capital investment.

In a detailed analysis of the horizontal fractionalisation and vertical layering of the middle class, Erik Olin Wright considered the 'new middle class' of professionals and white-collar workers different from the 'old middle class,' or petty bourgeoisie of small, independent producers and shopkeepers. He, however, did not consider the middle class a true class but a 'contradictory location within class relations' (Wright 1985).

Closer home, Satish Deshpande argued that in India the middle classes were not homogeneous. The elite fraction of the middle class specialised in the production of ideologies, while the mass fraction 'engages in the exemplary consumption of ideologies, thus investing them with social legitimacy' (Deshpande 2003: 141). Pranab Bardhan defined the professionals among the middle class, including white-collar workers, based on their possession of human capital (Bardhan 1994). In his framework, state power is captured by three dominant groups: industrial capitalists, rich farmers and professionals.

Michael Kalecki, writing on the role played by social classes in mixed economies like India, argued that a group of middle classes together with the middle peasantry form a distinct class force that 'naturally' rises to power when political independence is not accompanied by an armed struggle (Kalecki 1972). The middle classes operate with state capitalism to expand the productive potential of the country. This allows for the development of the small firms or the self-employed and creates executive and technical openings for young men from the ruling classes.

The idea of the middle classes was developed by K. N. Raj to argue that these social classes were important since they stood between the proletariat and the bourgeoisie, formed the bulk of the population, and prospects for their growth had improved.

He attempted to define these middle classes as 'all those who had income from property, earned along with input of own labour', and called them the 'intermediate classes' (Raj 1973). Unlike Marxist literature, which only included tangible assets in property, Raj treated possession of certain types of education and skill (administrative, managerial, scientific or technical), which earned quasi rent, as a form of property (Unni 2006).

Emergence of the Global Middle Class

In an early exposition of the emergence of the middle class in America, Helen Hughes and Berhanu Woldekidan argued that the middle class is not synonymous with the middle income group (Hughes and Woldekidan 1994). They argued that the middle class has higher incomes and recognisable social, cultural, political and economic characteristics. It has distinctive behavioural characteristics and plays a key role in articulating the country's national cultural traits. The middle classes value freedom of choice and demand it with respect to where they live, work, educate their children and travel. As the middle classes grow, there is increase in demand and they influence production and consumption patterns in the country. They influence social and economic policies indirectly through pressure groups and directly through parliamentary processes. In short, the authors claim that the middle class is a narrowly self-interested group.

Hughes and Woldekidan argue that the concept of the 'economic man' is derived from the behaviour of the middle class with regard to consumption, savings, investment and production. The middle class is found to maximise personal utility and profits in production, these being the traits of the 'rational economic man' (Hughes and Woldekidan 1994). While other classes may do the same, the middle class articulates this approach more than others. This is what is seen as 'modernisation'.

Abhijit V. Banerjee and Esther Duflo argue that in developing countries there is not much difference between the consumption patterns and businesses of the middle class and the poor

(Banerjee and Duflo 2008). They note that small business owners work very long hours with very modest gains. About 15 per cent of businesses lost money, and if rent was included in the costs, the profits were mildly negative. However, women preferred self-employment as this form of work gave them more flexibility to take care of their children. According to the authors, these businesses were a means of sustenance, not an engine of growth, a way of 'buying a job'. Women's business was seen as complementary to the men's economic activity. These small businesses were under-capitalised, and in that sense the business of the middle class was not very different from that of the poor. In management literature, this form of self-employed business would be considered necessity-driven entrepreneurship.

The question posed by Banerjee and Duflo (2008) is: why do the middle classes not save more and grow their business? This is a puzzle as the middle class is seen to buy homes, invest in health and education and buy consumer durables such as televisions, while the business stays resolutely small. Their answer is that the middle classes do not grow their business because it is not their priority. Investing in human capital such as education of their children and health appears to be their priority. They subscribe to the view that only the richer segments of family business are really dynamic.

So, how are the middle classes different from the poor? They prefer a steady salaried job, while the poor have more casual jobs. If the middle classes run a petty business, they are likely to shut it down if they get a good job (Banerjee and Duflo 2008). This view of self-employment is the economic logic discussed earlier, implying that self-employment and wage employment are substitutes.

Alejandro Guarín and Peter Knorringa defined the 'New Global Middle Classes' as those that have been upwardly mobile due to the unprecedented economic growth in countries like China and India in the preceding decade. The reference to 'classes' and not 'class' was due to the diversity in their culture and behaviour, both from each other and from the Western middle class. These rising middle classes were global in the sense that 'the number of people with discretionary spending power is so large that the phenomenon has become global in scale' (Guarín and Knorringa 2014).

The rising middle classes were of two kinds, the old and the new. The old middle classes were more stable while the new were more likely to fall back into poverty in case of an economic crisis (Guarín and Knorringa 2014). Guarín and Knorringa agree with Banerjee and Duflo that the difference between the middle classes and the poor was not their income level, but that the former were more likely to have stable, salaried employment (Banerjee and Duflo 2008). These scholars from the Global North seem to follow the economic logic that for the new middle classes, self-employment and wage employment were substitutes.

The emerging global middle class in less developed countries was seen as a new consumer class already larger than the Western consumer class. Consumer research and multinational companies were now focused on this global middle class with discretionary purchasing power and the ability to pursue a consumption-focused lifestyle (Üstüner and Holt 2009). The question posed was: are the consumer preferences of this rising middle class similar to those of the Western middle class? This literature does not address how middle-class economic activity status is influenced by the consumer choices of this rising global middle class.

Social and Economic Mobility

Sociological approaches to class focus on the labour market and occupations. Robert Erikson, John H. Goldthorpe and Lucienne Portocarero (1979) classified occupations into:

> classes based on employment status (employer, employee, self-employed); sector of the economy (non-manual, manual, agricultural); skills (skilled, semi-skilled, unskilled); and authority in the workplace (supervises, does not supervise). The version of the class schema most commonly used in comparative-mobility analysis included seven classes, namely

> high-level professionals and managers (Class I); low-level professionals and managers (II); clerical workers (III); self-employed with and without employees (IVab); farmers (IVc); skilled manual workers (V þVI); unskilled manual workers (VIIa); and farm employees (VIIb). (Torche and Lopez-Calva 2013)

Erikson, Goldthorpe and Portocarero (1979) studied inter-generational class mobility in three Western countries, France, England and Sweden. They found that Sweden had the highest mobility based on origin and destination of classes across generations in the 1970s. It is possible that Sweden was undergoing rapid structural transformation during this period. 'In Sweden the sons of manual wage-workers, including agricultural workers, and also of lower-level white-collar employees have achieved what could be regarded as relatively long-range upward mobility into service-class positions' in this period (Erikson et al. 1979).

More recent literature addressed the issue of mobility and stability of the middle class in the era of economic liberalisation. While there were benefits of the growth of the middle class, the capacity to be the next high source of consumption depended on the stability of this class. A stable and secure middle class was more likely to invest in assets, both for consumption and production, and thereby stimulate growth. Is the middle class in countries able to withstand the impact of macroeconomic shocks or family restructuring (Torche and Lopez-Calva 2013)?

While economic literature tends to define the middle class based on income, sociological literature prefers indicators of status. Florencia Torche and Luis F. Lopez-Calva tried to take both views into consideration and define a latent socio-economic index including household income, housing quality and access to services (Torche and Lopez-Calva 2013). They presented a three-class model, defining the middle class as households that were above poverty or near-poverty but lacked the economic assets to ensure complete protection against poverty. They studied the impact of economic liberalisation on the middle class in Chile and Mexico in the early 2000s. They found substantial upward and downward mobility in the two countries during this period. They concluded that the middle class was not stable and a substantial proportion was subject to vulnerability, which threatened potential political and economic benefits of a strong middle class. They found that socio-economic mobility was largely mediated through labour market resources and human capital, while demographic characteristics like age, sex and marital status of the household head had a weak association with economic well-being. The middle class in Mexico was more vulnerable to falling into poverty than Chile, mainly because Chile protected its middle class with better social protection programmes than Mexico during the period of study. The importance of social protection in middle-class stability during the process of economic liberalisation was brought out in this study.

In India, the middle classes historically consisted of upper-caste groups, but in the past two decades, the composition of the middle classes has been changing to include some Other Backward Classes, religious minorities and some Scheduled Caste groups (Sridharan 2004; Unni 2006). E. Sridharan argued that economic reforms in India have been adopted gradually and that this is due to the changing composition of the middle classes (Sridharan 2004). The upper segment of the middle class was likely to support liberalisation as it opened the market to a wider range of consumer goods, and it perceived regulation pre-liberalisation as leading to corruption. However, the lower segments of the middle classes were likely to prefer regulation as it provides some support to small enterprises and greater chances of employment in the public sector.

CASE STUDIES OF WOMEN ENTREPRENEURS

In this section, we discuss two case studies of women entrepreneurs as qualitative -evidence of women-founded firms from three different industry sectors: transportation services, not-for-profits and agribusinesses. The cases are short narratives of their entrepreneurial journey and offer interesting real-life insights. The first case presents a woman entrepreneur who launched two firms together: the private limited Sakha Cabs company and a not-for-profit firm, the Azad Foundation. This is an example of a business model that creates synergy between two different firms with different forms of organisation. It is a case of a woman entrepreneur setting up an enterprise with dual goals: profit maximisation, and consciously thinking of empowering women from the poor social class.

The second case is of an agribusiness firm called The Altitude Store, which sells organic products in New Delhi. It serves as an example of a woman entrepreneur who successfully connected farmers growing organic produce with consumers in urban markets seeking organic food products. Here is another case of a woman entrepreneur setting up a business not just for profit, but also to provide better avenues and more profitable business for poor farmers. Both cases bring out the unique nature of women entrepreneurs who pursue dual goals and work to empower the lower segments of society. The studies present the entrepreneurship challenges faced and offer practical recommendations to women aspiring to pursue such unique models of entrepreneurship.

CASE STUDY 1: **Empowering Women through Innovative Business Models**

Entrepreneur: Meenu Vadera
Company: Sakha Cabs and Azad Foundation
Industries: Social Enterprise, Travel Services and Not-for-Profit

Meenu Vadera was born in New Delhi, and spent her entire childhood there. Meenu's late father was a freedom fighter who fought in the Indian National Army and, after independence, worked as a trade union leader. Her mother retired as a teacher. Meenu's educational background includes specialisation in management, public policy and development studies. She holds a postgraduate Diploma in Rural Management from the Institute of Rural Management, Anand (IRMA), and a Master's in Social Development and Public Policy from the London School of Economics, United Kingdom. Meenu has been working on women's issues for more than 20 years, and has been involved in grassroots-level initiatives in India and Uganda. She worked as country director of Action Aid, Uganda, from 1998 to 2003.

Meenu is a mission-driven individual and is committed towards working for empowerment of women. Her extensive work experience in the non-governmental (NGO) sector and her reflections on the social environment in Delhi inspired her to launch Sakha Cabs. During her international travels, Meenu had seen women-based cab services and she wondered why there were no cab services for women in Delhi, especially given the growing number of crimes against women in the city. A few five-star hotels in Delhi had also started allocating entire floors for women travellers to ensure their safety.

Meenu felt that a cab service 'for women and by women' was a great idea which would enable her to meet two objectives with just one intervention. Firstly, her firm would be able to provide livelihoods to poor women who could become cab drivers. Secondly, it would offer a safe means of transportation to women travellers. The entire public transport system, including taxis, was male-dominated in India, she said. Creating a 'mobility'-based work environment could potentially empower women travellers as well as women drivers.

Thus, Meenu decided to launch Sakha Cabs as a for-profit social enterprise providing livelihood opportunities to poor and disenfranchised women. She also launched a partner firm Azad Foundation to assist in training, development and women empowerment interventions. The role of Sakha Cabs was to provide livelihoods to the women who underwent counselling and skill-training at Azad Foundation. Once trained, the women would be employed in Sakha Cabs as cab drivers. Meenu co-founded Sakha Consulting Wings and Azad Foundation with two friends. She registered Sakha as a private limited company and Azad Foundation as a not-for-profit firm/NGO in 2008. Meenu's batchmates from IRMA and a few Ashoka Fellows[1] acted as mentors during the initial phases of the launch and helped shape her business idea.

Meenu launched Sakha with her own funds. Initially, she operated over the phone from home. Sakha Cabs shares most of its resources with Azad Foundation. Azad Foundation donors have also gifted cars to be used as taxis for Sakha Cabs. Meenu hired a chartered accountant (CA) to facilitate the legal process of incorporating the firms. She, however, recommends that 'as an entrepreneur one must not leave the entire process to the CA believing that they will manage everything'. Her first CA even forgot dates of scheduled meetings for company registration in government offices. As a result, she hired another CA and kept a track of her file progress along with the scheduled dates.

Meenu recalled that selecting a name for her firm was a challenge. She wanted to name her firm 'Women on Wings'. But while filing, she was told that the first word in the company name must be a proper noun and the next word has to explain what the business is about. Names like 'Pratima Cotton Spinning Mill' were cited as examples, which she found unimaginative and boring. She was also advised to add the word 'consulting' in the name as it defines anything and everything! As Meenu discovered, naming a firm was far from easy or straightforward. Finally, she submitted five options, including 'Women on Wings', 'Sakha Women on Wings', and 'Sakha Consulting Wings' among others. Sakha Consulting Wings was approved. Meenu was initially unhappy with the approved name as the words 'consulting wings' did not represent a for-women, by-women cab service. 'If you want to do some simple work, why should the government make it so complex for you?' she said.

Recommendations for women entrepreneurs

Overcoming gender bias and dealing with government departments: 'We've helped around 250 women get licenses, and I can say that 95 per cent couldn't have got them on their own. Is this not an example of a clear gender bias?' Meenu asks. She revealed that even though India's transport departments have the same policies for men and women drivers, in reality, it does not work that way. There is a great gender bias against women drivers. Another hurdle in getting a driving license for Sakha's women drivers was procuring documentation for applications. Most women who approached Azad Foundation and Sakha came from poor families, had never driven a car or even stepped out of their home without male supervision. As a result, getting address and identity proof for such women became a challenge. Even after getting the relevant documents, many women were sent away or forced to make several visits to the transport office to get their license processed.

Passionately believe in your idea and never give up: Meenu shared that it has been a very difficult and long journey for her as an entrepreneur. She passionately followed her vision of 'empowering women through mobility', and it was her self-belief that kept her going. 'When I first told people about my idea, the [typical] response was, first teach them [women drivers] how to park a car. People were sarcastic,' she recalled. Teaching women how to drive a car in a city like Delhi and building self-confidence in women who had faced great personal hardships was an even greater challenge for Meenu and her team. 'A large part of me is in development and as a feminist, women's rights are very, very core to me, so that is definitely my identity,' she said.

CASE STUDY 2: **Bringing Organic Products from Rural to Urban Spaces**

Entrepreneur: Ayesha Grewal
Company: The Altitude Store
Industries: Agribusiness and Retail

Ayesha Grewal's formative and schooling years were spent between Delhi and Mumbai. Her grandfather was in the Indian Administrative Service and her father worked in the corporate sector, with Citibank and the Tata Group. Her mother was an art historian and writer. Her parents believed in holistic child development, and encouraged Ayesha and her elder sister to participate in sports and extracurricular activities. Her father was also a sportsperson and had represented India in the Davis Cup Junior in tennis. Ayesha actively participated in extracurricular and sports activities in school, becoming house captain, school prefect, basketball captain, table tennis captain, among others. She holds a graduate degree in Liberal Arts and a Master's in Global Finance from the US.

After graduation, Ayesha worked in New York for about a year and then returned to India in 2000. Prior to launching The Altitude Store, Ayesha founded her own consulting firm, Environment, Energy and Enterprise Ventures (E3V) in 2002. She also founded an organic food processing company, Kurmanchal Organic Ventures (KOV), that sourced organically grown fruits from the Kumaon hills in Uttarakhand to make processed foods that were later sold in the National Capital Region.

The idea for starting a totally organic agribusiness store originated when Ayesha was running KOV. Ayesha had received many queries for organic products from both the supply and demand sides. She had partnered with farmers who were supplying jams and chutneys made from farm-grown apples, peaches, apricots and plums for KOV. They often asked Ayesha whether they could sell her their other produce like *rajma* (kidney beans), turmeric, etc. KOV's first sale of organic processed foods was to the Modern Bazaar supermarket. Gradually, people started calling Ayesha directly for more organic food options. On one hand, there were farmers who had all this organic produce, for which they weren't getting proper rates in the local markets. On the other hand, there were consumers in Delhi's urban markets who were desperate for organic products and willing to pay a higher price for them. That's how the idea for The Altitude Store was born.

Ayesha's parents acted as her informal mentors in her entrepreneurial journey. Her former colleague and business partner John, who passed away in 2012, was her formal mentor who had a major role in shaping Ayesha's business perspective. Ayesha used her own finances to launch The Altitude Store. A couple of years later, she felt the need to expand her business, buy more shelf space and procure more products.

Ayesha incorporated The Altitude Store as a private limited company. The legal name of her firm is Altitude Organic and Natural Products Pvt. Ltd. Ayesha took the help of a law firm and an accountant for incorporation. The law firm helped get the name for her firm approved and the accountant helped her get the tax licenses. Ayesha applied for a bank account for her company after getting a TIN number and PAN card, after which shareholders were able to put money into her firm. The accounting firm was very helpful and had also reduced its audit fees when business was slow in the initial years, she shared.

Recommendations for women entrepreneurs

Focus on the venture full-time: Ayesha was initially managing two tasks together: being an agribusiness entrepreneur, while working full-time as a business consultant. She struggled with managing finances for her start-up in the initial years. At that time, her store used to get around five to six orders a week. She had employed two people to run the store as she continued to work in her full-time consulting job. She had to pay salaries to staff, pay suppliers and meet the day-to-day store operating costs. She would meet these expenses from the money she earned from her consulting job. 'A lot of people told me this was not the way to do it. They said that if you are going to set up Altitude as a proper company, then you would have to give up your consulting work,' she said. Gradually, she accepted this and focused on The Altitude Store full-time.

Manage product storage: Ayesha needed to store all the products being procured for the store but did not have money for storage. 'In Delhi the rents are so high...so it was all in my basement. Even today my house is full of packaging materials, pickles, etc.', she said. Later, she was able to rent a place for storage and even procure cold-storage equipment for storing perishable products.

Legal advice: Ayesha suggested that hiring an accountant during the start-up stage is more beneficial than hiring a lawyer. 'Hiring a lawyer doesn't help, and it is better to go to an accountant. Lawyers will charge ten times what the accountant does. If one tries to do it all by oneself, it will take forever. Get a trustworthy accountant to help, someone who can guide you,' she advised.

CONCLUSION

In this chapter, we reviewed the literature on entrepreneurship and the middle classes from a pluralist perspective. This expands horizons on how to view entrepreneurship compared to the solely management view presented in the previous chapter. In this book, we take elements from management literature as well as economic and sociological perspectives on entrepreneurship and the middle classes for a more holistic understanding of the phenomenon of entrepreneurship in an emerging economy like India.

The main takeaway from the review of extant literature in all these fields is that entrepreneurs were heterogeneous in nature and in their motivation for undertaking business. The case studies presented in this chapter, and in subsequent chapters, illustrate the heterogeneity in the nature and motivation of women entrepreneurs for undertaking business. From management literature, we take the concept of motivation of opportunity versus necessity entrepreneurship. Using behavioural economics, the puzzle of entrepreneurship in a situation of low returns could be explained by behavioural traits like preference for risk-taking, overconfidence and non-pecuniary benefits of being one's own boss. Institutional economics tells us that the external macro policy environment and entrepreneurship eco-system motivates or inhibits entrepreneurship. In countries where a large proportion of the workforce is self-employed, it is important to ask if the self-employment was an entrepreneurial activity. Here again the self-employed can be seen as heterogeneous and motivated by opportunity or necessity. The upper segment of the self-employed should be seen as entrepreneurs, while for the lower segment self-employment and wage employment may be substitutes for wage labour, as suggested by traditional neo-classical theory.

We briefly review the economic and sociological understanding of class. What and who constitutes the middle class? The economic view of class was generally based on income groups and occupational categories, while the sociologist view was based on social status, prestige and power. Western literature saw the emergence of a global middle class defined as one with discretionary incomes and likely to influence consumption patterns. The literature from the Global South and developing countries was of the view that the middle classes were heterogeneous. The upper end of the middle classes tended to be in steady salaried employment and their priority was education and health. The lower segments of the middle classes in self-employment with under-capitalised enterprises, as in the neoclassical theory, were more likely to shut operation and take up wage employment if the returns were better. The caste composition of the Indian middle classes was also changing from mainly upper caste to inclusion of Other Backward Classes, religious minorities and Scheduled Caste groups.

The two case studies of women entrepreneurs highlight the dual goals pursued by them and their concern for empowerment of the lower classes. They truly depict the heterogeneous nature of entrepreneurship, particularly among women in India.

This review of literature from a multidisciplinary perspective and the review of management literature in the previous chapter tell us that the motivation for undertaking entrepreneurship could be different for different segments of the population. Our review of the concept of class showed that the middle class is also not a homogeneous group. In the subsequent chapters, we explore the heterogeneous nature of entrepreneurship within the middle classes.

NOTE

[1]See https://www.ashoka.org/en-in/program/ashoka-fellowship

III

Entrepreneurship and the Middle Class in India

Emerging Evidence

India has seen rapid economic growth in the past two decades, giving rise to entrepreneurship and a burgeoning middle class. Measuring the size of both the middle class and levels of entrepreneurship is fraught with controversy, as we have seen in previous chapters. However, before discussing the nature and drivers of entrepreneurship, it is imperative to get a sense of the dimension of both enterprises and the ubiquitous middle class in India.

We have discussed that entrepreneurship could grow due to opportunity or necessity. It is generally assumed that the segment that grows due to necessity is smaller in scale and more likely to be self-employed enterprises in the informal sector. In this chapter, we use various data sources to estimate the size, scale and growth of enterprises in both the formal and informal sectors. Entrepreneurial activity in the middle class is the other important segment we address in this book. We discuss various methods of estimating the middle class and provide alternative estimates. We also present two case studies of women entrepreneurs from the middle class in India. Finally, we discuss the nature of entrepreneurship in the middle class.

GROWTH OF ENTERPRISES: WHAT DOES THE DATA TELL US?

India has several data sets that can be used to study entrepreneurship. The Ministry of Statistics and Programme

Implementation's (MOSPI) Economic Census counts all enterprises in India. The Non-Agricultural Unorganised Sector Enterprises Surveys by the National Sample Survey Office (NSSO), MOSPI, provide an estimate of enterprises in the informal sector. We provide estimates using both these sources in this chapter. In later chapters, we use *Global Entrepreneurship Monitor* (GEM) and World Bank Enterprise Surveys (WBES) data to understand various dimensions of entrepreneurship in India. These international data sources provide information on the characteristics of enterprises such as behavioural traits of entrepreneurs (GEM), and the external institutional factors that influence innovation in enterprises (WBES), which are not available in the two Indian data sources noted above.

Economic Census[1]

The Economic Census of India periodically lists all non-agricultural enterprises, whether in the organised or unorganised sectors, and agricultural enterprises except those involved in crop cultivation. It lists enterprises operating from household premises and establishments in separate premises. The large proportion of unorganised enterprises in the country makes such estimation difficult and the census is thus not necessarily accurate. However, it still gives a picture of the number and proportion of organised and unorganised enterprises in the country. The last three Economic Censuses were conducted in 1998, 2005 and 2013.

According to Economic Census 2013, there were a total of 58.5 million enterprises operating in India, of which 45.4 million, or about 77.6 per cent, were engaged in non-agricultural activities.[2] Of the 58.5 million enterprises, 34.8 million, or nearly 60 per cent, were located in rural areas. The other 23.7 million enterprises constituting 40 per cent, were in urban areas.

Of the 45.4 million non-agricultural enterprises, nearly 30 million, or about 66 per cent, were own account enterprises (OAEs) or those employing only family labour. These were likely to be micro and small enterprises in the informal or unorganised sector. Approximately 5.2 million, or 11.2 per cent, were operated by women.

The number of all enterprises in urban areas registered a growth of above 5 per cent in the period 2005 to 2013, more or less similar to growth during the previous census period, 1998 to 2005 (Table 3.1). However, there was slower growth of non-agricultural enterprises (rural and urban) on average, dropping to approximately 3.4 per cent from 2005 to 2013. The slowdown in the overall growth of enterprises and non-agricultural enterprises in urban areas in particular in the latter period was perhaps due to the global financial crisis that began in 2008.

It is interesting that during 2005–13, the number of urban OAEs rose by 7 per cent overall, and by nearly 5 per cent for all non-agricultural enterprises. It has been noted that the informal sector grows during a recession or economic crisis as the poor have to find a means of livelihood to survive (Mehrotra 2009). The growth of OAEs is a manifestation of this phenomenon. The overall growth of OAEs in the period 2005 to 2013 was greater than that of all enterprises and enterprises in the non-agricultural sector (Table 3.1). The relatively higher growth of OAEs in comparison to all, as well as in both periods, was observed in overall industry and services. This phenomenon was also observed in manufacturing and construction in the industry sector, and in hotels, restaurants, transport and storage in the services sector. That is, the higher growth of small OAEs was true for most industry groups with a large unorganised sector.

We highlight another feature of informal OAEs using Economic Census 2013. Nearly one quarter of all enterprises in urban areas do not have a separate designated place of work and operate from within household premises (Table 3.2). About 30 per cent of OAEs and only 12 per cent of establishments operated from household premises. More than 50 per cent of OAEs in manufacturing, trade and real estate activities (e.g. brokers) and education (e.g. crèche, nursery and tuition activities) operated from home. These small OAEs were likely to be operated by middle-class and lower middle-class households

TABLE 3.1: Annual growth rate of all urban and OAEs, Economic Census, 1998, 2005 and 2013

	1998–2005		2005–2013	
	All	**OAE**	**All**	**OAE**
Total enterprises (agriculture + non-agriculture)	5.4	3.7	5.1	7.0
Non-agricultural enterprises	**4.7**	**2.8**	**3.4**	**4.8**
Industry	**7.0**	**4.5**	**4.0**	**6.3**
Mining and quarrying	19.3	–	0.1	–
Manufacturing	7.2	4.7	3.0	5.2
Electricity, gas and water supply	10.1	–	33.1	–
Construction	1.7	−0.7	25.5	27.9
Services	**4.1**	**2.3**	**3.1**	**4.3**
Trade, hotels, transport, storage and communication	6.6	4.6	2.2	3.0
Trade, hotels and restaurants	6.1	4.0	1.7	2.3
Trade	**6.4**	**4.2**	**1.1**	**1.8**
Accommodation and food service activities	3.6	1.7	8.0	9.5
Transport, storage and communication	11.5	11.7	6.4	8.3
Transport and storage	7.8	7.3	12.3	14.6
Information and communication	25.8	38.7	−6.3	−7.6
Financing, insurance, real estate and business services	12.8	12.4	4.5	8.6
Community, social and personal services	−2.3	−5.7	−3.3	−4.8

Note: OAEs are own account enterprises operating without hired labour
Source: MOSPI 1998, 2005 and 2013

with a minimum investment of own capital and funds borrowed from friends and relatives.

Operating from within household premises implies a small scale of operation, thus possibilities for growth are limited. OAEs operating from home may have to take recourse to illicit electricity connections, have poorer systems for waste disposal and poorer access to and quality of water and sanitation facilities. Lack of safe storage facilities in homes doubling up as workplaces may reduce opportunities for securing large job contracts as contractors may fear for the safety of materials and final products. All these could lead to low productivity and hence low incomes for these informal enterprises.

TABLE 3.2: OAEs and establishments operating within the household, Economic Census 2013, Urban

	Operate within household premises		
	OAE	**Establishments**	**Total**
Total enterprises	**30.8**	**12.5**	**23.6**
Manufacturing	57.6	21.6	42.4
Electricity, gas, steam and air-conditioning	16.1	4.1	7.4
Water supply, sewerage, waste management	15.7	8.3	12.5
Construction	8.3	9.5	8.7
Wholesale and retail trade total	62.2	10.0	28.8
Transportation and storage	6.3	4.8	6.0
Accommodation and food service activities	20.1	9.9	15.2
Information and communication	19.3	7.4	13.0
Financial and insurance activities	27.2	3.7	14.3
Real estate activities	54.8	14.3	46.2
Professional, scientific and technical	21.9	7.5	14.5
Administrative and support services	25.2	9.8	17.1
Education	59.9	8.3	27.8
Human health and social work activities	22.1	10.1	14.6
Arts entertainment, sports and amusement	16.7	6.7	11.9
Other service activities not classified or listed	20.3	9.1	16.1

Note: Establishments are informal enterprises employing at least one hired worker

Source: MOSPI 2013

Unorganised Non-Agricultural Enterprises Surveys

The NSSO provides a comprehensive database on informal enterprises by owner-entrepreneur/s' gender through its Unorganised Non-Agricultural Enterprises Surveys as part of the National Sample Survey (NSS). These, however, only provide data on unregistered enterprises. MOSPI's Annual Survey of Industries provides comprehensive data on enterprises in the organised sector but does not probe the gender of the owner-entrepreneur.

Earlier, the NSSO surveyed unorganised enterprises in the manufacturing, trade and services sectors separately every five years, but has now gradually switched to consolidated surveys of these industry groups. Three rounds of this consolidated Unorganised Non-Agricultural Enterprises Survey have been conducted by the NSSO in 1999–2000 (NSS 55th Round), 2010–11 (67th Round) and 2015–16 (73rd Round). All three rounds included all manufacturing and service sectors but excluded mining and quarrying, electricity, gas and water, and the 67th and 73rd Rounds excluded construction as well. We use data from the 67th and 73rd NSS Rounds in this book. The advantage of NSS data is that it computes value addition in enterprises and collects information on the characteristics of the owner and enterprise.

As expected, the large majority of informal/unorganised sector enterprises were OAEs, more so among women-owned enterprises (Table 3.3). A positive feature was that among all enterprises, the growth of establishments, i.e. informal enterprises employing hired labour, was higher (by nearly 14 per cent) compared to OAEs (nearly 10 per cent) during the period 2010–11 to 2015–16. Establishments are operated with at least one hired labourer, and are therefore larger in scale than OAEs. We assume that such establishments had higher productivity and consequently higher revenue.

What do we learn about women-operated enterprises? While there was no major difference in the growth of male- as opposed to female-owned establishments (larger enterprises), the number of female-owned OAEs (smaller enterprises) grew faster than male-owned OAEs during the period 2010–11 to 2015–16. Women-owned OAEs were more likely to be operating from household premises and also grew the fastest during the period 2010–11 to 2015–16. Both these features of women-owned enterprises—exceptionally large growth of OAEs and home-based nature

TABLE 3.3: Characteristics of urban unorganised non-agricultural enterprises by gender of ownership, 2010–11 and 2015–16

	2010–11			2015–16			Growth (percentage)		
	Male	**Female**	**Total**	**Male**	**Female**	**Total**	**Male**	**Female**	**Total**
Type of enterprise									
OAE	82.5	95.8	84.9	81.4	96.1	84.4	5.8	24.2	9.6
Establishment	17.5	4.2	15.1	18.6	3.9	15.6	13.6	14.1	13.7
Total	100	100	100	100	100	100	7.2	23.8	10.2
Location of enterprise									
Within household premises (%)	34.8	80.5	43.1	33.4	84.7	43.8	2.7	30.3	12.0
Age of enterprises									
<5 years	29.6	40.3	31.5	39.5	45.5	40.7	43.0	39.7	42.2
6–10 years	28.9	27.3	28.6	25.7	26.5	25.9	−4.6	20.3	−0.3
11–20 years	27.2	22.1	26.3	25.2	22.1	24.6	−0.8	23.7	2.9
>20 years	14.3	10.3	13.6	9.6	5.9	8.9	−27.7	−29.2	−27.9
Total	100	100	100	100	100	100	7.2	23.8	10.2
Social group									
SC-ST	17.2	18.2	17.4	16.0	19.2	16.6	−0.8	30.9	5.2
OBC	44.6	45.9	44.8	50.0	49.3	49.8	20.1	33.0	22.5
General	37.5	35.2	37.1	33.3	30.7	32.8	−4.8	8.0	−2.6
Total	99.4	99.3	99.3	99.2	99.2	99.2	7.1	23.7	10.1

(Contd)

Table 3.3 (Contd)

	2010–11			2015–16			Growth (percentage)		
	Male	**Female**	**Total**	**Male**	**Female**	**Total**	**Male**	**Female**	**Total**
Growth status of enterprise									
Expanding	32.6	26.9	31.6	30.8	24.9	29.6	−3.1	7.4	−1.5
Stagnant	43.7	42.0	43.4	45.1	48.5	45.8	5.8	34.2	10.8
Contracting	8.7	7.7	8.5	11.9	11.5	11.8	40.0	72.6	45.4
<3 years old	15.0	23.4	16.5	12.2	15.2	12.8	−16.3	−24.6	−18.4
Total	100	100	100	100	100	100	2.6	16.2	5.1

Note: Establishments are informal enterprises employing at least one hired worker

Source: NSSO 2013, 2018

of operations—implies that they were smaller in scale. Hence, these enterprises were more likely to have low-value assets, which in turn implied low productivity and revenue generation as compared to male-owned enterprises.

About 31 per cent of all enterprises were running for less than five years (start-up enterprises) in 2010–11. This rose to 40 per cent in 2015–16. Male-owned enterprises were more evenly distributed by duration of operation, while a larger percentage of women-owned enterprises were start-up enterprises. Start-ups grew by about 40 per cent during this period. By social group, the Other Backward Classes (OBCs) dominated, owning nearly 50 per cent of all enterprises. They also dominated in growth of enterprises, perhaps indicating dynamism in this caste group. However, an increase in caste groups designated as OBC in recent years may partly account for the large increase during this period.

With such a large increase in unorganised enterprises, particularly OAEs, women-owned enterprises and start-ups, the question of how they are faring arises. Both NSS rounds asked owners of unorganised enterprises running for more than three years whether the enterprise was expanding, stagnating or contracting. In both rounds, nearly one-third of enterprises reported that they were expanding operations. This was true irrespective of gender of ownership. Over the period 2010–11 to 2015–16, the number of enterprises that reported expansion unfortunately declined, though women-owned enterprises reported that expansion grew by 7 per cent. Nearly 45 per cent of enterprises reported that they were stagnating and about 50 per cent reported that they were contracting, with nearly 70 per cent of women-owned enterprises reporting this.

It is disheartening to learn that more than half of unorganised enterprises were contracting over the five-year period to 2015–16 and a large proportion were stagnating. However, we focus on the positive. Nearly 30 per cent of enterprises reported that they were expanding in 2015–16. Further, there was a growth of 7 per cent in expanding women-owned enterprises. In Chapter 5, we attempt to identify what factors enabled these enterprises to expand.

WHAT CONSTITUTES THE MIDDLE CLASS IN INDIA?

Though many people feel that they belong to the 'middle class', there seems to be no consensus on just who constitutes the middle class. Subjective definition always takes the form of self-ascription, while there are too many objective definitions. A recent study suggested that there are as many as 156 definitions of the middle class (Förster 2014). There is no agreement among economists on the appropriate income/consumption thresholds to identify the middle class—not even on whether it is relative or absolute income that matters, or on whether the identification should be based on a country, a region or a global standard. A common practice is identifying some middle portion of classes categorised by income distribution within a country as the middle class. Some use global distribution of income/consumption to identify middle classes in a country.

There is a significant amount of literature on defining and measuring the middle class, mostly in the context of developed countries. Early literature (Hughes and Woldekidan 1994) suggested possible measurement of the middle class by income, education, occupation and consumption. Helen Hughes and Berhanu Woldekidan's income approach was not found useful, as a median income group actually measures middle income and not the middle class, the latter having certain social and cultural traits. It was also not useful due to differences in purchasing power parity (PPP). Their education approach was also rejected as composition changes rapidly over time in any group, moving from the prominence of secondary to tertiary and higher education. Hughes and Woldekidan also suggested that measurement by occupation and consumption may be good indicators of the middle class (Hughes and Woldekidan 1994). Middle class occupation can be defined as professional, clerical, sales and services. The authors suggested ownership of alternative consumption goods for measuring the middle class. Among ownership of radios, televisions, cars and telephones, the latter two were preferred to describe the middle class in that era of the early nineties. However, as we know, this can also change with time as technology improves and these goods become cheaper and more easily available.

In more recent literature, being middle class is typically defined as having an income within some interval that includes the median. The interval has typically been symmetric in the income space around the median. The lower and upper bounds have been set in diverse and ad hoc ways. An influential early paper by Lester C. Thurow (Thurow 1987) focused on the interval from 75 to 125 per cent of the median (Ravallion 2009).

In recent decades, in Asian countries including India, economic growth has given rise to a new middle class with discretionary spending power. Recent literature in the context of developing countries has mainly focused on the role of the middle class in promoting economic development, such as through entrepreneurship, policy reform and institutional change.

Definitions and Estimation of the Middle Class in India

There is no official definition of the middle class in India, thus quantifying this demographic group yields varying results. A McKinsey Global Institute study using National Council of Applied Economic Research (NCAER) data estimated the size of this group to be around 50 million in 2005 (McKinsey & Company 2007), by using the definition of real annual household disposable incomes between Rs 200,000 and Rs 1,000,000 (Table 3.4). At the other end of the spectrum, a study by Martin Ravallion estimated the middle class at 264 million in 2005 using the median poverty line in 70 countries as a lower bound (daily income US$2) and the United States poverty line (daily income US$13) as an upper bound (Ravallion 2009). Ravallion stated that 'the developing world's middle class was defined as those who were not deemed "poor" by the standards of developing countries but were still poor by the standards of rich countries' (ibid.).

Another method employed by CNN-IBN in its middle class survey utilised a consumption-based criterion to count households that owned a car or scooter, colour television or a telephone, and estimated that the middle class equalled approximately 20 per cent of the population, or slightly over 200 million people. Nancy Birdsall defined the middle class in the developing world to include people with an income above $10 a day, but excluding the top 5 per cent of that country (Birdsall 2010). By this definition, urban India alone would have had no middle class in 2010, as everyone with an income over $10 a day (Rs 276 in 2010) would have been in the top 5 per cent by income. Credit Suisse's *Global Wealth Report 2015* estimated the middle class on the basis of their wealth rather than their income (Credit Suisse 2015). By this definition, India had 23.6 million adults who qualified as middle class in 2015 (Table 3.4).

The more relevant definition for the Indian context was given by Abhijit V. Banerjee and Esther Duflo (Banerjee and Duflo 2008), which was similar to Ravallion's definition (Ravallion 2008). In the context of developing countries, they considered the income range of $2 to $10 per day to be classified as being in the middle class (Banerjee and Duflo 2008). By using data from the World Bank's Living Standard Measurement Surveys, they arrived at an estimate of 233 million middle-class Indians in 1997 (ibid.).

Sandhya Krishnan and Neeraj Hatekar (Krishnan and Hatekar 2017) used the Banerjee and Duflo 2008 definition of the middle class (income $2 to $10 a day) and applied it to NSS Consumption Expenditure Survey (CES) data to arrive at an estimate of 604 million of what they termed the 'new middle class' in 2011–12. This new middle class almost doubled between 2004–05 and 2011–12, constituting nearly half of India's population in 2011–12 (Table 3.5).

Data, methodology and estimation of urban middle class

In order to capture employment-related aspects of economic class based on monthly per capita consumption expenditure (MPCE), we use the labour force survey, i.e. the NSSO's Employment and Unemployment Survey (EUS) for 2004–05 and 2011–12 (NSS 61st and 68th Rounds). The labour force survey captures the MPCE

TABLE 3.4: Definitions and estimates of size of the middle class, India

Study	Year	Definition (US$/PPP)	Conversion (year)	Estimated middle-class population in millions (% of total)
McKinsey & Company	2005	$4,376 to $21,881 (45.7=$1 in Real 2000)*	Annual household Income: Rs 2 lakh to Rs 10 lakh (Real 2000)*	50 in 2005)
CNN-IBN	2007	—	Household ownership of car or scooter, colour television or telephone	200
Nancy Birdsall	2010	Income >= $10 per day, excluding the top 5%		No middle class in India
Abhijit V. Banerjee and Esther Duflo	2008	Income >$2 and <$10 (PPP): $2 to $4 $6 to $10	38% to 12% 22% to 10% 4% to 1%	233 (20%) 181 (15%) 29 (2%)
Martin Ravallion	2008	Above $2 and below $13 (2005 PPP)		263.7 in 2005
Credit Suisse	2015	Wealth >= $13,662	Rs 737,748 and above	23.6

Note: *Real 2000 means adjusted for inflation using year 2000 as the base year

Source: McKinsey & Company 2007; Birdsall 2010; Banerjee and Duflo 2008; Ravallion 2008; and Credit Suisse 2015

TABLE 3.5: Percentage of middle class all-India in 2004–05 and 2011–12, using Banerjee and Duflo 2008 definition

Class	MPCE (Rs) (2011–12)	Percentage of population (population in millions)	
		2004–05	2011–12
Poor (<$2)	<39.5	71.4 (777.3)	47.8 (574.8)
New middle class ($2–10)	39.5–197.3	27.9 (304.2)	50.3 (604.3)
Lower middle: ($2–4)	39.5–78.9	21.8 (237.8)	37.1 (446.3)
Middle middle ($4–6)	78.9–118.4	4.2 (45.4)	9.0 (108.5)
Upper middle ($6–10)	118.4–197.3	1.9 (21.0)	4.1 (49.5)
Affluent (>$10)	>197.3	0.7 (7.5)	1.9 (22.9)

Source: Krishnan and Hatekar 2017

of each household by a shorter survey module than the CES used by Krishnan and Hatekar (2017). Hence, our estimates differ slightly from theirs and we discuss this in the next section. For a comparative perspective, we estimate the middle class in India based on the two different approaches.

Median Based Definition: According to this criterion, middle class is defined in the range of 75 and 125 per cent of the median MPCE (Birdsall 2010). We apply this method to EUS data for 2004–05 and 2011–12. First, we calculate median and decile classes based on the MPCE for urban India. The population below 75 per cent of the median MPCE is considered poor (lower class) and the population above 175 per cent of the median are considered rich (upper class). The middle class falls between these two groups, which is further classified into lower and upper middle class. Lower middle class is above the lower class but less than the median decile, whereas upper middle class falls between the median decile and upper class.

Table 3.6 presents the application of our estimation process using the median-based definition of the middle class. The range of MPCE in Indian rupees (INR) in each class for 2004–05 and 2011–12 and the estimated population based on the definition is presented.

TABLE 3.6: Size estimation of urban Indian middle class by median-based definition, 2004–05 and 2011–12

Class	Range MPCE (Rs)		Estimated population (%)	
	2004–05	2011–12	2004–05	2011–12
Lower class	529	1,222	30.4	32.7
Middle class	529–1,804	1,222–3,985	59.6	57.3
Lower middle class	529–835	1,222–1,630	29.6	17.3
Upper middle class	835–1,804	1,630–3,985	30	40
Upper class	1,804	3,985	10	10

Source: Authors' own estimation based on unit level data from NSS 61st and 68th Rounds

As we are applying a distribution-specific measure (median decile), the MPCE ranges in INR are taken at the current rate and not at the real (deflated) rate. The size of the middle class declines slightly from nearly 60 to 57 per cent of the population between 2004–05 and 2011–12 with this definition. However, we see a movement across the lower and upper middle class. The proportion of the lower middle class decreased to 17.3 per cent in 2011–12 (from 29.6 per cent in 2004–05), which is reflected in the increased size of the upper middle class by around 10 per cent and marginal increase of the lower class.

These estimations need to be read with caution. Firstly, there might be underestimation of the upper class due to low representation of rich and elite households in NSS data. Secondly, by definition, the median-based indicator is sensitive to the distribution and can only provide relative ranges of income or consumption classes.

Banerjee-Duflo Definition: This definition is applicable to developing countries and classifies households with daily per capita income range of $2 to $10 in terms of 2005 PPP (Banerjee and Duflo 2008). As discussed earlier, Krishnan and Hatekar applied this definition to the Indian context using NSS Consumption Expenditure Survey (CES) data (Krishnan and Hatekar 2017). They categorised the middle class into three sub-classes: lower-middle, middle-middle and upper-middle class. We make use of the INR conversion of PPP in 2005 that they provided and estimate the MPCE range of various classes using the NSS labour force surveys. We merge middle-middle and upper-middle into upper middle class. Unlike the distribution-sensitive median-based measure, this measure is quite robust and objective. It is also useful for cross-country comparisons. We use the Banerjee-Duflo definition for our further analysis of incidence of entrepreneurship (self-employment) (Banerjee and Duflo 2008). Table 3.7 provides the estimated MPCE range of the middle class using the Banerjee-Duflo definition.

TABLE 3.7: MPCE range for economic classes, 2004–05 and 2011–12

Economic class (daily PPP $, 2005)	MPCE range (Rs)			
	2004–05		2011–12	
Poor (<$2)		741		1185
New middle class ($2–$10)	741	3702	1185	5919
Lower middle class ($2–$4)	741	1482	1185	2367
Middle-middle class ($4–$6)	1482	2220	2367	3552
Upper middle class ($6–$10)	2220	3702	3552	5919
Affluent (>$10)	3702		5919	

Source: Authors' own estimation based on EUS from unit level data, NSS 61st and 68th Rounds

Figure 3.1 shows the estimated size of urban economic classes. Along with our estimations based on EUS data, we also show the original estimates by Krishnan and Hatekar using CES data (Krishnan and Hatekar 2017). The computation based on the EUS estimated a larger share of the poor or lower class at nearly 31 per cent of the population in 2011–12, compared to 22 per cent using CES data (Figure 3.1). Estimates based on CES had slightly larger estimates of all the middle and upper classes, especially the lower middle class. The changes in proportion of the population in the different classes were, however, the same by either data set, with a rise in all segments of the middle classes.

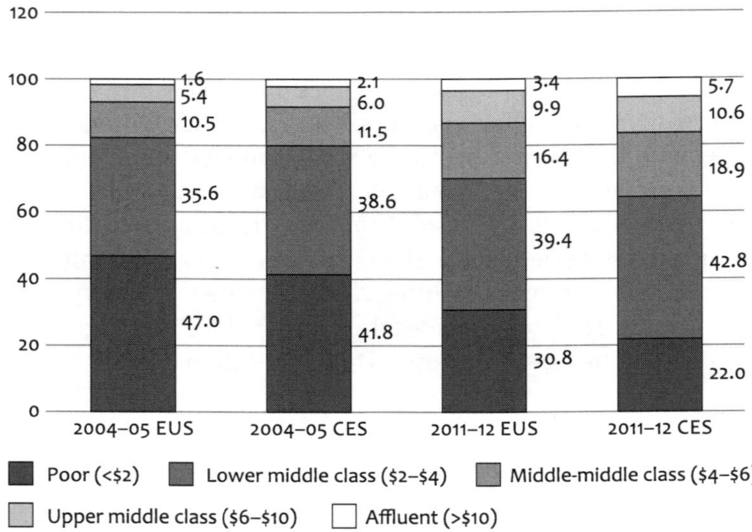

FIGURE 3.1: Urban economic classes, 2004–05, 2011–12

Note: EUS = Employment and Unemployment Survey; CES = Consumption Expenditure Survey

Source: Authors' own estimation based on EUS unit level data, NSS 61st and 68th Rounds; Krishnan and Hatekar 2017

According to estimations based on the EUS, the percentage of the lower class population (poor) dropped by nearly 5 per centage points, from 47 to 42 per cent during 2004–05 to 2011–12 (Figure 3.1). The largest percentage of the population was the lower middle class in 2011–12, 39 per cent. However, the largest increase in share of population was noted in the middle-middle class with a daily PPP of $4–6 (6 percentage points) and upper middle class with a daily PPP of $6–10 (4 percentage points) during the period. This clearly confirms the perception that there was an increase in the middle classes, particularly the upper middle class. For this analysis, we combined the middle-middle and upper middle classes to constitute the upper middle class, with a daily PPP of $4–10, which constituted about 17.5 per cent of the population. In 2011–12, the middle class constituted

57 per cent of the population in India, but there was a marked difference in the characteristics of the lower middle and upper middle classes, as we shall describe below.

Entrepreneurship among the Middle Class

The NSSO's EUS data describes workers by employment status, that is, self-employed, regular salaried and casual workers. The self-employed can be considered the entrepreneurial class. Albert Shapero and Lisa Sokol classified entrepreneurs as opportunity-based or necessity-driven (Shapero and Sokol 1982). This has particularly become popular in describing women entrepreneurs. The NSSO category of self-employed workers would include both opportunity-based entrepreneurs who start an enterprise in response to an opportunity, and necessity-driven ones who start a business due to push factors. In a later chapter, we also analyse the drivers of growth of informal enterprises that were expanding and likely opportunity-oriented, and those that were stagnant or contracting and likely necessity-driven.

The proportion of self-employed male workers was more or less stable at 42 per cent, while female self-employed workers rose from 46 per cent in 2004–05 to 49 per cent in 2011–12 (Table 3.8a). Self-employment among the poor and lower middle class rose considerably for both men and women during this period. The proportion of self-employed declined among the upper middle and affluent class, while the proportion of regular salaried employment rose. Poor and lower middle class self-employed workers were more likely to be necessity-driven entrepreneurs. In the literature review in the first chapter, we noted studies that argued that the middle class was different from the poor in that they were more likely to work in stable, regular salaried employment (Banerjee and Duflo 2008). Here, we note that the upper segment of the middle class does exhibit this characteristic of increase in regular salaried work.

The NSSO data further divides self-employed workers into own account workers (OAWs), employers and unpaid family

TABLE 3.8A: Distribution of workers by status of employment and among self-employed, by gender, urban, 15+ years, principal + subsidiary, 2004–05 and 2011–12

All	2004–05					2011–12				
	Poor	Lower-middle	Upper-middle	Affluent	Total	Poor	Lower-middle	Upper-middle	Affluent	Total
Male										
Self-employed	19.8	28.3	41.0	46.6	43.4	43.2	44.2	40.2	35.5	42.4
Regular salaried	55.5	42.8	36.8	47.2	43.0	24.1	38.2	53.7	62.7	39.7
Casual work	24.6	28.9	22.3	6.1	13.6	32.8	17.6	6.1	1.8	17.8
Total	100.0	100.0	100.0	100.0	100.0	100.0	100.0	100.0	100.0	100.0
Female										
Self-employed	39.6	39.4	48.2	45.2	46.2	53.6	54.3	40.5	29.2	49.2
Regular salaried	43.7	35.5	31.8	49.8	40.7	23.6	33.1	55.3	69.5	37.8
Casual Work	16.7	25.1	20.0	5.0	13.1	22.9	12.6	4.2	1.4	13.0
Total	100.0	100.0	100.0	100.0	100.0	100.0	100.0	100.0	100.0	100.0

Source: NSSO, EUS, 2004–05 and 2011–12

workers (UFWs) or helpers. OAWs are those who do not employ hired workers on a regular basis. They operate either alone or with the help of family members or UFWs. Employers hire at least one worker on a regular basis. The latter are most likely to be opportunity-based entrepreneurs, as suggested by Arnaud Daymard (2015).

A majority of self-employed workers were OAWs—nearly three-quarters of the men and more than half of the women. Among self-employed women, the proportion of OAWs rose and that of contributing UFWs declined during the period 2004–05 to 2011–12, which is a good sign (Table 3.8b). However, when looked at in terms of class, we find that the proportion of female OAWs declined among the poor and middle class, while the number of UFWs rose. Female OAWs rose among the upper middle and affluent classes. It appears that poor and lower middle-class women were losing out on independent employment opportunities. Among men, the proportion of employers rose in the upper and affluent classes. Self-employed males were improving their status both as regular salaried workers and as opportunity-driven entrepreneurs. Poor and lower middle-class OAWs who were most likely to be necessity-based entrepreneurs appeared to be losing even this status.

More than half of the self-employed women and less than one-fifth of self-employed men were in the manufacturing sector, though the share of both declined by about 2 percentage points during 2004–05 to 2011–12 (Table 3.9). Trade was the next largest industry group, accounting for nearly 43 per cent of self-employed workers among men and 27 per cent among women (having grown from 22 per cent). Among women, real estate and business services rose from 1 to 7 per cent while social and personal services fell. This is a positive sign. In terms of class, real estate and business services grew in the middle and affluent class among women entrepreneurs. Women entrepreneurs in trade also grew among the upper middle class during this period. Both these are positive features of growth of women entrepreneurship.

TABLE 3.8B: Distribution of self-employed workers by status, gender, urban, 15+ years, principal + subsidiary, 2004–05 and 2011–12

Self-employed	2004–05					2011–12				
	Poor	Lower-middle	Upper-middle	Affluent	Total	Poor	Lower-middle	Upper-middle	Affluent	Total
Male										
OAW	99.1	95.1	86.2	68.2	75.9	80.7	80.7	76.5	65.5	79.1
Employer	0.0	1.6	2.0	9.8	6.6	0.9	3.2	10.5	24.1	5.2
UFW	0.9	3.3	11.7	21.7	17.4	18.4	16.1	13.0	10.4	15.7
Total	100.0	100.0	100.0	100.0	100.0	100	100	100	100	100
Female										
OAW	88.1	69.4	53.2	53.6	54.5	57.6	63.5	65.9	67.5	62.1
Employer	0.0	1.2	0.3	2.8	1.5	0.2	0.6	1.2	7.3	0.8
UFW	11.9	29.4	46.5	43.6	44.0	42.2	36.0	32.9	25.1	37.1
Total	100.0	100.0	100.0	100.0	100.0	100	100	100	100	100

Source: NSSO, EUS, 2004–05 and 2011–12

TABLE 3.9: Distribution of self-employed workers by industry, gender, urban, 15+ years, principal + subsidiary, 2004–05 and 2011–12

Industry	2004–05					2011–12				
	Poor	Lower-middle	Upper-middle	Affluent	Total	Poor	Lower-middle	Upper-middle	Affluent	Total
Male										
Mining-quarrying	0.0	0.1	0.1	0.1	0.1	0.2	0.2	0.3	0.0	0.2
Manufacturing	13.6	16.0	20.8	19.1	19.6	20.7	17.4	15.2	15.1	17.6
Electricity, etc.	0.0	0.0	0.0	0.0	0.0	0.8	0.3	0.1	0.0	0.4
Construction	0.0	6.8	6.2	5.7	5.9	5.7	6.5	6.1	8.3	6.2
Trade	24.3	31.6	41.0	47.5	44.7	39.0	45.1	45.9	37.0	43.4
Hotel-restaurants	13.4	4.1	4.9	3.6	4.2	6.1	5.7	4.3	4.1	5.4
Transport-communication	42.5	27.7	15.8	8.1	11.6	13.6	10.4	7.9	4.1	10.4
Financial intermediation	0.0	0.0	0.8	1.5	1.2	0.7	1.3	2.2	3.0	1.4
Real estate, business services	0.9	0.6	2.0	6.6	4.7	3.0	5.6	10.7	18.6	6.7
Public administration, defense	0.0	0.0	0.0	0.1	0.1	0.0	0.0	0.1	0.3	0.0
Social, other services	5.4	12.9	8.5	7.3	7.9	10.2	7.7	7.2	9.7	8.4
Total	100.0	100.0	100.0	100.0	100.0	100	100	100	100	100

(Contd)

Table 3.9 (Contd)

Industry	2004–05					2011–12				
	Poor	Lower-middle	Upper-middle	Affluent	Total	Poor	Lower-middle	Upper-middle	Affluent	Total
Female										
Mining-quarrying	1.5	0.0	0.0	0.0	0.0	0.0	0.2	0.0	0.0	0.1
Manufacturing	62.7	49.1	57.4	46.2	51.9	63.7	50.3	34.5	22.0	50.5
Electricity, etc.	0.0	0.0	0.0	0.0	0.0	0.8	0.3	0.0	0.0	0.4
Construction	0.0	0.0	0.1	0.5	0.3	0.2	0.2	0.1	1.2	0.2
Trade	26.4	29.3	22.7	22.1	22.8	21.5	29.5	33.9	22.0	27.6
Hotel-restaurants	7.6	7.3	6.2	4.0	5.3	4.5	5.6	4.5	6.0	5.0
Transport-communication	0.0	1.4	0.9	1.5	1.2	0.1	0.0	0.6	0.0	0.2
Financial intermediation	0.0	0.0	0.4	1.1	0.7	0.4	1.0	2.6	6.0	1.3
Real estate, business services	0.0	0.0	0.2	2.4	1.2	3.1	5.6	13.4	24.4	7.0
Public administration, defense	0.0	0.0	0.0	0.0	0.0	0.0	0.0	0.1	0.0	0.0
Social, other services	1.8	12.9	12.2	22.1	16.7	5.5	7.3	10.3	18.5	7.7
Total	100.0	100.0	100.0	100.0	100.0	100.0	100.0	100.0	100.0	100.0

Source: NSSO, EUS, 2004–05 and 2011–12

Nearly three-fourths of self-employed women workers were home-based, while only one-fourth of self-employed men were home-based (Table 3.10). The men mainly had units of their own away from home, though this declined slightly to 43 per cent in 2011–12, while only about 14 per cent of women had their own units away from home. The other major and growing location of work for men was on the street without a fixed location, amounting to 14 per cent, while 6 per cent were on the street with a fixed location and 5 per cent worked on construction sites. About 7 per cent of women self-employed workers were on the street, both mobile and with a fixed location.

Overall, there has been an increase in mean years of education of self-employed and regular salaried workers over the period 2004–05 to 2011–12 (Table 3.11). While both categories showed improvement in years of education among men, among women only the regular salaried employed showed improvement. However, both self-employed men and women among the lower classes showed an increase in mean years of education.

When self-employed workers are disaggregated into employer, OAW and unpaid family helper/worker (UFW), an interesting gender differential appears (Table 3.12). Employers among both men and women (a very small proportion) showed an increase in mean years of education. However, while male OAWs improved their education level, women OAWs, mainly in the upper classes, seem to have lost out.

CASE STUDIES OF WOMEN ENTREPRENEURS

In this section we present case studies of two Indian middle-class women entrepreneurs. The first case is of Vivam Agrotech, initially a sole proprietorship firm. The women entrepreneur started Vivam by supplying vermicompost (natural fertiliser made using earthworms to decompose waste), made from a small unit on her own terrace, to women in villages nearby. Gradually, she expanded her business to manufacturing biogas and waste-processing products for rural and urban areas in India.

TABLE 3.10: Self-employed by location of work, urban, 15+ years, non-agriculture, principal + subsidiary, 2004–05 and 2011–12

	2004–05					2011–12				
	Lower	Lower-middle	Upper-middle	Upper	Total	Lower	Lower-middle	Upper-middle	Upper	Total
Male										
Own dwelling	33.1	28.1	24.8	19.8	21.8	24.1	24.8	21.5	20.1	23.5
Own unit away from dwelling	21.5	18.1	35.2	59.9	49.7	31.3	42.4	54.8	63.0	43.4
Employer's dwelling	0.4	1.3	0.9	0.4	0.6	0.9	0.8	0.4	0.5	0.7
Outside employer's dwelling	0.7	1.4	2.9	3.1	3.0	3.3	3.7	3.9	5.5	3.7
Street fixed location	25.3	7.0	10.2	4.0	6.3	9.2	5.8	2.7	1.4	5.7
Street without fixed location	13.1	28.3	16.6	5.7	10.2	20.9	13.7	9.3	4.5	14.2
Construction site	0.2	8.2	4.9	3.7	4.2	4.3	4.9	4.4	3.8	4.6
Others	5.8	7.7	4.3	3.1	3.7	5.9	4.0	2.9	1.3	4.2
Total	100.0	100.0	100.0	100.0	100.0	100.0	100.0	100.0	100.0	100.0

(Contd)

Table 3.10 (Contd)

	2004–05					2011–12				
	Lower	Lower-middle	Upper-middle	Upper	Total	Lower	Lower-middle	Upper-middle	Upper	Total
Female										
Own dwelling	65.0	63.5	72.3	70.3	70.9	77.7	73.8	69.4	59.6	73.7
Own unit away from dwelling	10.6	9.2	11.9	19.3	15.2	9.3	13.8	21.4	32.2	14.5
Employer's dwelling	1.0	1.8	1.8	1.1	1.5	0.9	1.1	0.4	0.0	0.9
Outside employer's dwelling	4.2	1.0	0.6	1.3	1.0	1.3	1.5	1.5	3.5	1.5
Street fixed location	4.0	7.9	4.7	2.4	3.8	3.8	3.0	2.8	0.0	3.1
Street without fixed location	11.4	15.3	6.2	2.1	4.8	5.0	4.7	2.8	2.3	4.3
Construction site	0.0	0.2	0.1	0.3	0.2	0.4	0.2	0.1	0.0	0.2
Others	3.8	1.1	2.5	3.1	2.7	1.6	1.8	1.7	2.3	1.7
Total	100.0	100.0	100.0	100.0	100.0	100.0	100.0	100.0	100.0	100.0

Source: NSSO, EUS, 2004–05 and 2011–12

TABLE 3.11: Mean years of education by employment status and gender (years)

Workers	2004–05					2011–12				
	Lower	Lower-middle	Upper-middle	Upper	Total	Lower	Lower-middle	Upper-middle	Upper	Total
Male										
Self-employed	8	10	12	14	9	9	10	11	13	10
Regular salaried	8	11	13	14	11	9	11	13	14	12
Casual work	7	7	8	10	7	7	7	8	7	7
Total	8	10	12	14	10	8	10	12	14	10
Female										
Self-employed	7	9	11	15	9	8	9	10	13	9
Regular salaried	9	12	14	14	12	9	12	14	15	13
Casual work	6	7	10	4	6	7	7	8	12	7
Total	8	11	13	14	10	8	10	13	14	11
Persons										
Self-employed	8	10	12	14	9	8	10	11	13	10
Regular salaried	8	11	13	14	11	9	11	13	15	12
Casual work	7	7	9	9	7	7	7	8	8	7
Total	8	10	12	14	10	8	10	12	14	10

Source: NSSO, EUS, 2004–05 and 2011–12

TABLE 3.12: Mean years of education among self-employed workers (years)

Self-employed	2004–05					2011–12				
	Lower	Lower-middle	Upper-middle	Upper	Total	Lower	Lower-middle	Upper-middle	Upper	Total
Male										
OAW	8.0	10.0	12.0	13.0	9.0	8.0	10.0	11.0	13.0	10.0
Employer	8.0	10.0	12.0	14.0	11.0	9.0	10.0	12.0	14.0	12.0
UFW	8.0	10.0	12.0	12.0	10.0	9.0	11.0	12.0	14.0	11.0
Total	8.0	10.0	12.0	14.0	9.0	9.0	10.0	11.0	13.0	10.0
Female										
OAW	8.0	9.0	12.0	15.0	9.0	8.0	9.0	11.0	12.0	9.0
Employer	8.0	10.0	11.0	13.0	11.0	8.0	12.0	16.0	14.0	14.0
UFW	7.0	8.0	11.0	15.0	8.0	8.0	9.0	10.0	13.0	9.0
Total	7.0	9.0	11.0	15.0	9.0	8.0	9.0	10.0	13.0	9.0
Persons										
OAW	8.0	10.0	12.0	14.0	9.0	8.0	10.0	11.0	13.0	10.0
Employer	8.0	10.0	12.0	14.0	11.0	9.0	10.0	12.0	14.0	12.0
UFW	8.0	10.0	12.0	14.0	9.0	9.0	10.0	11.0	14.0	10.0
Total	8.0	10.0	12.0	14.0	9.0	8.0	10.0	11.0	13.0	10.0

Source: NSSO, EUS, 2004–05 and 2011–12

The second case is of Bambooz, a bamboo products manufacturing company which also began as a sole proprietorship firm. Initially, Bambooz was a small manufacturing unit. The woman entrepreneur later expanded her business and launched another company, Fern Bamboo Private Limited, with her husband.

The two cases bring forward insights from the entrepreneurial journeys of two women who started their businesses as small proprietorship firms in the informal sector after marriage, then registered private limited companies in the formal sector as their businesses grew. Family background played an important role in their career choices. In both cases, we find that a private limited company became a natural means of progression for a woman proprietorship firm to scale and grow. Also, the role of husbands as mentors and co-founders was evident in both cases. In addition, recommendations for aspiring women entrepreneurs are highlighted in the case studies.

CASE STUDY 3: **Producing Electricity from Garbage**

Entrepreneur: Nirmala Khandalgaonkar
Company: Vivam Agrotech
Industries: Sustainable Products, Solid Waste Management

Nirmala Khandalgaonkar was born in Parbhani, in the state of Maharashtra in India. She lost her father at the very young age of eight. Her mother, who worked as a teacher in a district education board school, brought up all her six children alone. Nirmala completed her school education in her village and later obtained a Bachelor of Science degree in Aurangabad city. After graduation, Nirmala did some social work for the Rashtriya Sevika Samiti at the district and taluka level.

After marriage, Nirmala did not work as she and her husband had an understanding that he would earn and she would take care of the family. Her husband, a mechanical engineer, was the breadwinner. After her children grew up, Nirmala had spare time in hand. The idea of launching Vivam was conceived when she started working again as a social worker in villages in Kandhar taluka, Nanded district, Maharashtra. She saw that most of the local people were involved in agriculture and were using chemical fertilisers, which affected the soil adversely. Nirmala thought that if vermicompost units were installed in the villages, the villagers would be able to process their agricultural waste in-house and also produce natural fertiliser for their crops. She started by building a vermicompost unit on her own terrace, using earthworms she purchased. She then gave the compost to the women in the nearby village to test it in their fields. From vermicomposting, she expanded to biogas products, waste-processing plants and waste-management solutions for urban and rural areas. Nirmala calls herself 'the first Indian woman to produce electricity from garbage'.

On 5 June 2001, World Environment Day, Nirmala launched her sole proprietorship firm, Vivam Agrotech. Subsequently, she saw an opportunity in large tenders from nagarpalikas and mahanagarpalikas (urban local bodies). Nirmala's proprietorship firm was not eligible to apply for such tenders because they were open only to private limited companies. Therefore, she incorporated another company Vivam Solid Waste Management Private Limited along with her husband in 2011. Nirmala was the founder CEO and majority shareholder, with 51 per cent share. Nirmala has had mostly informal mentors in the form of family and friends. She considers her mother as her greatest mentor and inspiration.

The initial investment to launch Vivam was around Indian rupees (INR) 50,000, which Nirmala got from her own family funds. A major part of that was directed toward research and development costs and travelling to various agricultural universities across India to gather technological inputs from academia. In 2006, the Bhabha Atomic Research Centre in Mumbai provided Vivam Agrotech the technology for biogas manufacturing through a technology-transfer collaboration. This helped Vivam Agrotech achieve scale. Vivam Solid Waste Management Private Limited was partly financed through bank loans and partly though Nirmala's own funds.

The company also manufactures municipal solid waste treatment plants for power generation in Pune and Aurangabad. Nirmala Khandalgaokar is also a consultant to 125 municipal councils in Maharashtra. The company plans to expand its business abroad in countries like Kenya and South Africa.

Recommendations for women entrepreneurs

Tap the sustainable green business opportunity: 'As Indian citizens, we are still not trained to dispose waste at the home level. We just don't have that kind of training or even that mental capacity... we are not mentally geared for it and we don't have the instruments,' says Nirmala. She highlights the 'huge sustainable business opportunity in waste'. Such businesses can help manage waste and eradicate landfills to make India greener. She also recommends that one should be concerned not only with the company's turnover, but also see how the idea behind it reaches and impacts the maximum number of people.

Build awareness through education: There is a casual attitude towards waste management in society. For a waste management business to succeed, Nirmala suggests that people first need to be educated on the basic principles of waste management. Her company tries to build awareness and educate people with the help of non-governmental organisations.

Address the challenge of growth: Nirmala wanted to grow her company from state level to national level and later expand to international markets. To achieve this, she faced the challenge of building a motivated team of managers and employees who could successfully lead projects. She recommends allocating a substantial budget for the training and development of managers.

CASE STUDY 4: **Sustainability-driven Bamboo Products and Design Solutions**

Entrepreneur: Indrani Mukherjee
Company: Bambooz

Industries: Sustainable Products, Bamboo Products, Construction and Design

Indrani Mukherjee was born in Kolkata, and her early childhood years were spent in Northeast India. Her father worked with Oil and Natural Gas Corporation Limited, and her mother was a homemaker. Indrani studied in public Kendriya Vidyalaya schools, which offered a multicultural learning environment and had students from diverse middle-class backgrounds. Indrani was good in academics, and her parents wanted her to pursue a professional course like engineering. Therefore, she graduated with a degree in Civil and Environmental Engineering.

Growing up in a service-oriented family, Indrani had no plans of becoming an entrepreneur initially. She worked in several corporations for thirteen years. Her industry experience also included working as a project officer in a United Nations Children's Emergency Fund project in the Siliguri-Jalpaiguri Development Authority, West Bengal for six–seven years. Indrani's work in Northeast India exposed her to the use of bamboo as raw material for construction, which later inspired her to launch her own firm, Bambooz. She says, 'Having been in the field of conventional construction for so long, deep in my heart, I always wanted to create green and sustainable solutions that last'.

Being a civil engineer, Indrani knew that bamboo structures were feasible. However, she was also skeptical of leaving her secure job to pursue the idea of using bamboo to make plywood for use in construction and design. Indrani continued to explore the idea and researched bamboo-based work done in India and abroad. She even wrote to the National Bamboo Mission of India, seeking feedback on the feasibility of her idea.

Finally, in 2010, Indrani co-founded Bambooz in Bengaluru with her husband Samrat R. Saha, also a civil engineer, who heads operations. They chose Bengaluru because they had existing support systems in the city and were well-networked there. During her entrepreneurial journey, Indrani mainly had informal mentors. Her mother had a great influence on her. She learnt soft skills like how to be patient, compassionate and stay grounded from her mother. Bambooz got its first project in 2010, which involved introducing bamboo floor boards in Karnataka State Road Transport Corporation (KSRTC) and Bengaluru Metropolitan Transport Corporation buses.

Indrani used both informal and formal sources of finance for her firm. Initially, she and Samrat used their personal money, but later applied for a bank loan for the manufacturing unit. Indrani got a term loan of Rs 10 lakh from the Central Bank of India for machinery.

Bambooz started as a sole proprietorship firm. Initially, Bambooz was mainly a manufacturing unit. Later, Indrani and her husband realised the need to expand the business and launched another company called Fern Bamboo Private Limited in January 2016. Indrani is the majority shareholder in the company. Her firm now consists of a team of highly skilled artisans, designers and engineers. The artisans are trained under a Government of India scheme for bamboo structures and products. They undertake turnkey projects for bamboo-based structures. Her firm also manufactures and supplies bamboo boards, roofing sheets and utility products like skewers and handicraft items.

Indrani and Samrat had a fair idea of the procedures to be followed for incorporating a venture due to prior work experience. They first registered the company for Value Added Tax in the Commercial Taxes department. Next, they registered the company under Micro, Small and Medium Enterprises (MSME) and the District Industry Corporation (DIC). For the initial paperwork, they hired a charted accountant (CA), but not a lawyer because most technical information was available online. For instance, the DIC website had information on all required forms and they could easily make a Part One form application on their own. For the Part Two form, they took the CA's help. Indrani got the Part One approval for her company very fast. For the Part Two approval, government officials visited her manufacturing unit for inspection. On the whole, Indrani was able to deal with legal matters comfortably.

Recommendations for women entrepreneurs

Getting orders throughout the year: Initially, Indrani's firm received orders for building structures and also orders from state government departments. But these were few and there was no continuous business throughout the year. She felt that it was not a sustainable model. 'Creating awareness [about bamboo-based products and structures], approaching big institutions and government agencies to invest in their firm and believe in their solutions was itself a huge problem to overcome,' she recalls.

Growth through trial and error: Indrani realised that construction work alone was not sustainable and subsequently diversified into manufacturing and furniture. 'But the big question was: what to manufacture with very limited funds?' she said. Bamboo is an excellent material for making sticks of any kind. Therefore, they started manufacturing *agarbattis* (incense sticks), kebab sticks and chopsticks. Then, they graduated to manufacturing furniture. They grew by trial and error and gradually improved their processes.

Avail benefits of government schemes: Indrani and her husband created a project report and submitted it to the Central Bank of India. They were aware of a CGT Scheme through which a woman entrepreneur could get collateral-free loans. Indrani's application was accepted and she also registered her company with the National Small Industry Corporation of India (NSIC). In the process, she met many government officials and felt that they were supportive towards her as a woman entrepreneur. Indrani got a Rs 10 lakh term loan from the Central Bank of India for machinery. She also registered her firm online on e-retailers Amazon and Flipkart, which connected her firm to a large network of online buyers.

CONCLUSION

We noted a rise in informal enterprises compared to formal ones during the period 2005–2013. It is possible that the global economic crisis led to reduction in employment in the formal enterprises. A large proportion of informal enterprises, before and after the recession were small scale, own account enterprises being operated from home. These enterprises were likely to be operated by the lower middle classes, a very large component being women-owned.

A brief review of definitions of the middle class in India led us to adopt the Banerjee and Duflo definition of daily per capita income range of $2 to $10 in terms of 2005 PPP as an appropriate one (Banerjee and Duflo 2008). We divided this group into the lower middle $2–4 and upper middle $4–10 groups. The lower middle class constituted nearly 39 per cent while the upper middle was nearly 18 per cent of the population. We consider the self-employed as the entrepreneurial class, while recalling that this segment could be either opportunity-based or necessity-driven. Those in the poor and lower middle classes were more likely to be necessity-driven, while the self-employed in the upper middle and upper classes were chasing a business opportunity.

The proportion of all self-employed women rose by three percentage points to 49 per cent in 2011–12. The majority of the self-employed were own account workers (OAWs) among both men and women. However, the proportion of women OAWs fell and that of contributing family workers rose in the poor and lower middle classes. Women OAWs rose in the upper middle and upper classes. There was a major class difference where upper middle-class women were perhaps taking up business opportunities, while poor and lower middle-class women were losing their independent status in business.

The upper-middle and upper-class women employers also recorded an increase in their levels of education. While employers form a very small proportion of self-employed men, their improved education might have helped them in their entrepreneurial enterprise. The lower class OAWs did not see any improvement in their level of education, while the upper middle and upper class had reduced mean years of education over the period. This might have caused further deterioration in their independent status of business on average.

More than half of all self-employed women were in the manufacturing sector, much of this being undertaken at home, perhaps as sub-contracted homeworkers. Trade was the next largest economic activity among self-employed women, with growth occurring among the upper middle class. In terms of class, a positive feature was growth of self-employed women in the real estate and business services, mainly in the upper middle and upper classes. Hence, we note a definite class difference among self-employed women with the poor and lower middle classes engaged in home-based manufacturing and trade, while the upper middle and affluent women were venturing into real estate and business services.

NOTES

[1]An earlier version of this section of the chapter was published by Unni and Naik as a background paper titled 'Gender Differentials in Expansion of Informal Enterprises', for the *State of Working India Report 2018*, Azim Premji University (Unni and Naik 2018).

[2]Excluding public administration, defense and compulsory social security activities.

IV

Low Return Entrepreneurship and Small Business

Do Behavioural Traits Matter?[1]

There were 58 million enterprises operating in India in 2013 (Central Statistical Office 2016), of which 72 per cent were own account enterprises (OAEs) operating with no hired workers and 36 per cent of all enterprises were home-based or located within household premises, as noted in the previous chapter. The overwhelming proportion of own account and home-based enterprises tells us that the scale of operation of the majority of enterprises was very small, irrespective of whether they were owned by men or women. In this context the characterisation of entrepreneurship in the management literature which emerged in the seventies, mainly regarding women, as being opportunity-based or necessity-driven becomes crucial.

This chapter critically discusses the extant empirical literature on entrepreneurship from a behavioural perspective. Adam Oliver (2015) argued that besides behavioural devices being used to nudge people into desired behaviour, insights from behavioural economics can also be used to inform possible regulation or policy. In this chapter, we seek to understand how behavioural motivations influence entrepreneurship and self-employment with low returns using *Global Entrepreneurship Monitor* (GEM) data from India.

We present a brief review of the literature on entrepreneurship using the behavioural perspective. We then use a regression-based analysis model to address the questions: what behavioural traits and motivational factors are associated with necessity-driven and opportunity-based entrepreneurship? Do these behavioural traits differ by gender of ownership? This line of enquiry will help researchers and policy-makers formulate appropriate 'nudge' techniques to encourage productive entrepreneurship. We present the specification of the model including the data and specification of variables, the variables on behavioural traits that possibly influence the choice of entrepreneurship, and the results of the influence of the quantitative analysis. We also illustrate two case studies of women whose behavioural traits of risk-taking and self-confidence allowed them to pursue entrepreneurial opportunities in hitherto unexplored areas of a multi-brand pet store and teleradiology, and establish successful businesses. Lastly, we discuss our findings and the contribution of this chapter to the literature on women entrepreneurship.

INSIGHTS FROM BEHAVIOURAL ECONOMICS

In the review of literature in chapter 2, we noted that behavioural economics seeks to explain the puzzle of entry into low return entrepreneurship through three main factors. These are preference for risk that attracts entrepreneurs to the possibility of large gains from risky ventures; overconfidence in his or her abilities and optimism about the business environment; and the non-pecuniary benefits of entrepreneurship, such as the advantages of being one's own boss, envisaged through observing a role model.

In the typical neo-classical model, the choice of becoming an entrepreneur is based on the expected utility gained from incomes and working conditions (Eisenhauer 1995). Evan Douglas and Dean Shepard (2000, 2002) used the same framework but distinguished between entrepreneurial attitudes and entrepreneurial abilities. They developed the choice of being self-employed based on a utility maximisation model of human behaviour. The individual's behaviour considered in this choice was attitude toward work, risk, independence and income. They found that positive attitude to risk and feeling of independence (being one's own boss) were the most important behavioural traits that influence the choice of self-employment or entrepreneurship (Douglas and Shepard 2002).

The emergence of the strands of literature on women entrepreneurship and behavioural economics challenges the primacy of goals related to economic gain in the prevailing conception of entrepreneurship. In the entrepreneurial management literature, these women can be seen to work out of necessity. Behavioural economics questions the construction of an entrepreneur as only driven by a desire to seize opportunity and chase profit, and seeks to answer the puzzle of low returns and high variance.

Behavioural Traits Impacting Entrepreneurship

In the extensive literature on entrepreneurship, women and men are compared by their distinctive entrepreneurial characteristics, e.g. motivations, personality traits, experience (Ahl 2002; Verheul et al. 2004; Masters and Meier 1988; Sexton and Bowman-Upton 1990; Mroczkowski 1997; Catley and Hamilton 1998; Anna et al. 2000) or features of their firms, e.g. size, goals and strategy, management and performance (Gundry and Welsch 2001; Watson 2014; Watson and Robinson 2003).

The fear of failure (usually operationalised through the individual's risk aversion) was a particularly critical issue for entrepreneurs due to little separation between business and personal risk in an entrepreneurial venture (Watson and Robinson 2003). Research comparing women entrepreneurs' risk aversion with that of their male counterparts tends to hypothesise that women were more risk averse than men (Powell and Ansic 1997). The presence of a role model for women entrepreneurs was considered a factor that facilitated their decision to start their businesses (Dhaliwal 2000; Levent et al. 2003). However, as women have historically formed a minority of the entrepreneurial population, they lack close role models, or at least were less likely to have a role model compared to men (Delmar and Holmquist 2004: 42).

A growing number of studies also consider significant gender differences between entrepreneurs vis-a-vis aspects of personal and business profile, such as how they start and run businesses, have different experiences and backgrounds, aim for different goals, and structure their businesses in different ways (Verheul et al. 2006). Some studies found that businesses led by women tend to underperform in several areas (Verheul et al. 2003) and were characterised as smaller in size compared to those led by men (Carter et al. 1997; Hill et al. 2006). This can be related to the sector of businesses that women enter, which was more likely to have low entry barriers, low profit margins and high competition (Verheul and Thurik 2001). Women tend to have less business experience (Fischer et al. 1993) and their businesses were usually under-capitalised (Carter 2000; Marlow and Patton 2005). In terms of business age, companies led by women were generally younger than those led by men (Hill et al. 2006). Moreover, several studies indicated that women preferred to grow their businesses slowly and were less likely to target growth, which is reflected in the size of their businesses (Jennings and Cash 2006).

The business model of women enterprises showed that women entrepreneurs had more personal commitment than male entrepreneurs. Regarding organisational structure, women's perspective was more open and less secretive. Women entrepreneurs often required longer time in decision-making control systems (Zhang et al. 2014).

The family's emotional or instrumental support was a crucial factor in the success of women entrepreneurs (Lee and Choo 2001). Marriage or parental obligations may have an effect on a woman's decision to become an entrepreneur. For married women, domestic responsibilities left less time for business-related activities. 'In other words, the married women entrepreneurs face more problems in balancing their work and family. Family and household ties leaves women with less time to spend on the growth and expansion on their business. In general, work-family conflicts are experienced more by female entrepreneurs than male entrepreneurs' (Jennings and Brush 2013).

RESEARCH QUESTIONS AND MODEL

We employ regression-based analysis to address the following questions:

1. Do behavioural traits of the entrepreneur influence whether she undertakes opportunity-based and necessity-driven entrepreneurship?
2. Do behavioural traits have a differential impact on the nature of entrepreneurship?

The Model

To estimate the parameters of the model, we specify a multinomial logit regression model which deals with a probability of an event taking place with more than two possible outcomes. For the specification of the multinomial regression, we divided all the respondents into three groups: opportunity-based entrepreneurs, necessity-driven entrepreneurs and those who were not entrepreneurs, the last being used as the reference category.

$$\text{Logit}\,[P\,(y = 1)]_{ij} = \alpha_{ij} + \beta_1 \chi_{ij} + \beta_2\, Y_{ij} + E_{ij}$$

The regression constant term is represented by α, χ represents a vector of owner characteristics, Y is a vector of behavioural traits, i is the individual firm, j is gender and E is the error term.

Data and Specification of Variables

GEM Data

We base our analysis on the pooled sample for India from the *Global Entrepreneurship Monitor*[2] (GEM) pooled data for the years 2012, 2013 and 2014. GEM data defines 'early stage entrepreneur' (Total Early-Stage Entrepreneurial Activity or TEA) as an individual involved in setting up a new business (nascent entrepreneur), or as owner or manager of a current business less than five years old, including self-employment. We have defined an entrepreneur of the age 18–64 years as one starting a new business and owner-managers of existing firms, irrespective of age of firm. Of a total pooled sample of 8,360 respondents, there were 4,100 male and 4,260 female respondents. Of these, there were 624 male and 263 female entrepreneurs. We analyse male- and female-owned enterprises separately to see whether and how gender matters in the pursuit of entrepreneurship in India. Table 4.1 presents the descriptive statistics.

TABLE 4.1: Descriptive statistics-GEM variables

Variables		Male	Female	Persons
Owner characteristics	**Level of education**			
	No education	269 (6.56)	600 (14.08)	869 (10.39)
	Primary	852 (20.78)	1,031 (24.2)	1,883 (22.52)
	Secondary	1,408 (34.34)	1,497 (35.14)	2,905 (34.75)
	Post-secondary	1,488 (36.29)	1.078 (25.31)	2,566 (30.69)
	Graduate	83 (2.02)	54 (1.27)	137 (1.64)
	Total	4,100 (100)	4,260 (100)	8,360 (100)
	Household income			
	Lowest 33 percentile	1,375 (33.54)	1,514 (35.54)	2,889 (34.56)
	Middle 33 percentile	1,190 (29.02)	1,241 (29.13)	2,431 (29.08)
	Upper 33 percentile	1,394 (34)	1,345 (31.57)	2,739 (32.76)
	Missing	141 (3.44)	160 (3.76)	301 (3.6)
	Total	4,100 (100)	4,260 (100)	8,360 (100)
	Age			
	18–24	960 (23.41)	659 (15.47)	1,619 (19.37)
	25–34	1,210 (29.51)	1,332 (31.27)	2,542 (30.41)
	35–44	949 (23.15)	1,165 (27.35)	2,114 (25.29)
	45–54	616 (15.02)	701 (16.46)	1,317 (15.75)
	55–64	365 (8.9)	403 (9.46)	768 (9.19)
	Total	4,100 (100)	4,260 (100)	8,360 (100)

(Contd)

Table 4.1 (Contd)

Variables		Male	Female	Persons
Behavioural traits	**Role model**			
	No	2,638 (64.34)	3,362 (78.92)	6,000 (71.77)
	Yes	1,399 (34.12)	786 (18.45)	2,185 (26.14)
	Missing	63 (1.54)	112 (2.63)	175 (2.09)
	Total	4,100 (100)	4,260 (100)	8,360 (100)
	Alertness to opportunity			
	No	2,401 (58.56)	2,851 (66.92)	5,252 (62.82)
	Yes	1,546 (37.71)	1,138 (26.71)	2,684 (32.11)
	Missing	153 (3.73)	271 (6.36)	424 (5.07)
	Total	4,100 (100)	4,260 (100)	8,360 (100)
	Self-confidence			
	No	1,915 (46.71)	2,726 (63.99)	4,641 (55.51)
	Yes	2,111 (51.49)	1,446 (33.94)	3,557 (42.55)
	Missing	74 (1.8)	88 (2.07)	162 (1.94)
	Total	4,100 (100)	4,260 (100)	8,360 (100)
	Fear of failure			
	No	2,566 (62.59)	2,602 (61.08)	5,168 (61.82)
	Yes	1,378 (33.61)	1,398 (32.82)	2,776 (33.21)
	Missing	156 (3.8)	260 (6.1)	416 (4.98)
	Total	4,100 (100)	4,260 (100)	8,360 (100)
	Types of entrepreneur			
	Non-entrepreneur	3,342 (81.5)	3,948 (92.7)	7,290 (87.2)
	Entrepreneurs	624 (15.2)	263 (6.2)	887 (10.6)
	Opportunity	371 (9)	146 (3.4)	517 (6.2)
	Necessity	253 (6.2)	117 (2.7)	370 (4.4)
	Mixed	106 (2.6)	41 (1)	147 (1.8)
	Missing	28 (0.7)	8 (0.2)	36 (0.4)
	Total	4,100 (100)	4,260 (100)	8,360 (100)

Source: GEM 2012, 2013, 2014

Dependent variable

Dependent variable was defined by three statuses of entrepreneurship: opportunity-based entrepreneurship, necessity-driven entrepreneurship and not being an entrepreneur. GEM data defined those respondents as 'opportunity-based entrepreneurs' who stated that the main or partial motivation was to take advantage of a business opportunity, or who were seeking better opportunities than the current jobs. Those respondents were defined as 'necessity-driven entrepreneurs' who indicated that the main motivation behind setting up or owning a business entity was due to no better choices for work. In the sample, there were a few entrepreneurs who gave mixed responses. Since their income distribution was closer to the necessity-driven entrepreneurs in our model, we included them in this category.

Distribution of household income for types of entrepreneurs

We present the distribution of entrepreneurs by their household income in Figures 4.1a and 4.1b. We found that both women

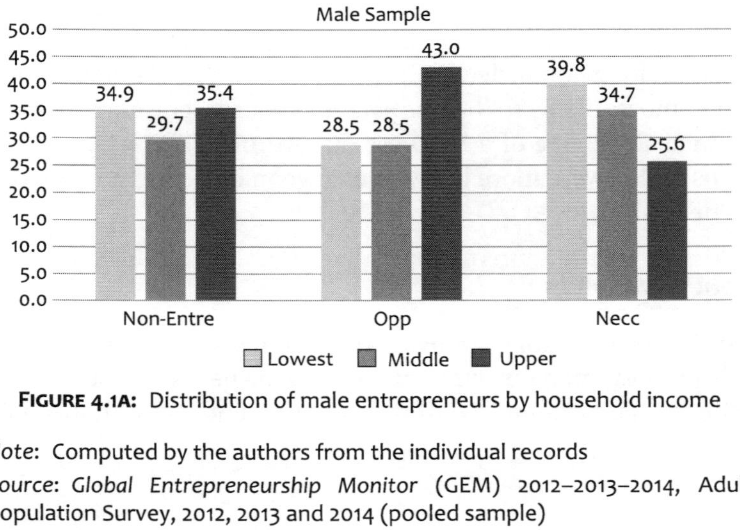

FIGURE 4.1A: Distribution of male entrepreneurs by household income

Note: Computed by the authors from the individual records

Source: *Global Entrepreneurship Monitor* (GEM) 2012–2013–2014, Adult Population Survey, 2012, 2013 and 2014 (pooled sample)

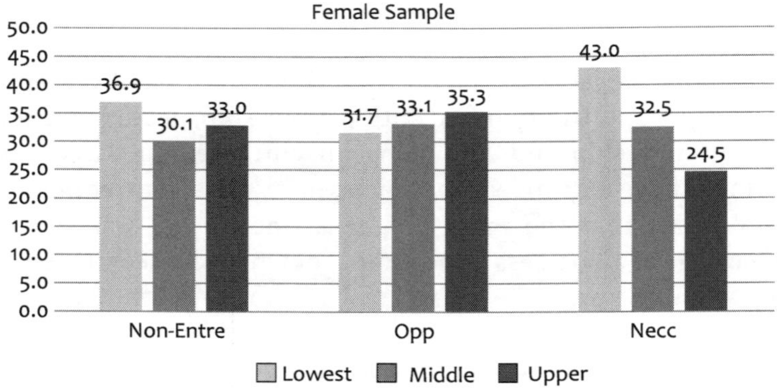

FIGURE 4.1B: Distribution of female entrepreneurs by household income

Note: Computed by the authors from the individual records

Source: *Global Entrepreneurship Monitor* (GEM) 2012–2013–2014, Adult Population Survey, 2012, 2013 and 2014 (pooled sample)

and men opportunity-based entrepreneurs were more likely to be in the top 33 percentile of household income, with male entrepreneurs more likely to be so (43 per cent of male and 35 per cent of female). The opposite was found to be true for the necessity-driven entrepreneurs, with 40 per cent of the men and 43 per cent of the women entrepreneurs being in the bottom household income decile. That is, the better-off households were more likely to be motivated towards entrepreneurship to take advantage of a business opportunity. The least well-off households were more likely to engage in entrepreneurship due to necessity.

Control variables

The control variables, individual and household characteristics of the entrepreneur, were age of the owner; highest level of educational attainment of the owner; and total household income.

BEHAVIOURAL TRAITS FOR CHOICE OF ENTREPRENEURSHIP

We use behavioural traits of the entrepreneur from the GEM data as explanatory or independent variables. These are mainly psychological traits and motivation of the individual entrepreneur. We specify four variables to define three behavioural traits of the entrepreneur based on prior literature.

Risk Taking

The capacity of the entrepreneur to take risk motivates him/her to undertake business activity that may not have very high returns (Astebro 2014; Douglas and Shepard 2002). We defined the obverse, risk averseness of the respondent by the variable fear of failure, defined as having fear that would prevent one from starting a new business.

Fear of failure was hypothesised to be negatively related to opportunity entrepreneurship. That is, entrepreneurs who are risk-taking will seize an opportunity and choose to be an entrepreneur. Those who suffer from fear of failure were less likely to be opportunity entrepreneurs, but may still set up an enterprise due to necessity.

Overconfidence

We define two variables to proxy for overconfidence as a reason for undertaking entrepreneurship (Moore and Healy 2008). The belief that there were excellent opportunities for a business in the area where the respondent lived was defined by the variable alertness to business opportunities. Another variable to proxy for overconfidence was self-confidence, defined as the perception of having the required knowledge, skill and experience to run a business.

Alertness to opportunity and self-confidence were hypothesised to be positively related to being an opportunity entrepreneur. She had confidence in the environment for business and presumed she had the knowledge and skill to take up entrepreneurship. Necessity entrepreneurs may be less confident of their ability.

Non-pecuniary Benefit of Feeling of Independence

A non-pecuniary behavioural motivation to take up entrepreneurship suggested in the literature was the feeling of independence and autonomy. Having a role model who was an entrepreneur motivated the budding entrepreneur. The entrepreneur saw the role model as being independent and being in the role model's company reduced uncertainty and increased confidence (Bandura 1978; Indrawati et al. 2015). A proxy for non-pecuniary benefit used in the analysis was having a role model. A role model was defined as someone who started a business in the recent two years and was known to the respondent.

Persons having a role model were hypothesised to undertake opportunity entrepreneurship as she perceived less uncertainty. However, it is possible that knowing someone in the field also encouraged persons to take up entrepreneurship in circumstances of necessity, as the role model could be viewed as social capital that can be harnessed to undertake and continue business.

RESULTS

We present four specifications of the model adding each of the four behavioural traits/motivations variables in each subsequent specification. We run this model separately for male and female entrepreneurs. We only present the log of odds-ratios and not the β coefficient. If the coefficient of a simple logistic regression is 1.17, then in terms of log odds, with a one unit increase in the predictor we can expect to see a 17 per cent increase in the odds of the firm being innovative. If the coefficient is 0.17, there is a 17 per cent chance of the firm not being innovative. This increase or decrease does not depend on the value of the predictor variable. The results of the logistic regression model are presented in Table 4.2.

TABLE 4.2: Log odds of opportunity-based and necessity-driven entrepreneurship[1] (GEM data)

	Opportunity				Necessity			
	Model 1	**Model 2**	**Model 3**	**Model 4**	**Model 1**	**Model 2**	**Model 3**	**Model 4**
Male sample								
Fear of failure	1.162 (0.14)	1.204 (0.14)	1.191 (0.15)	1.154 (0.14)	1.376* (0.16)	1.436* (0.17)	1.430* (0.18)	1.400* (0.18)
Self-confidence		2.666* (0.34)	2.050* (0.27)	1.797* (0.24)		3.101* (0.41)	2.446* (0.33)	1.990* (0.28)
Role model			3.971* (0.49)	3.302* (0.43)			4.083* (0.51)	3.090* (0.41)
Alertness to opportunity				1.794* (0.23)				2.771* (0.38)
Age								
25–34	2.012* (0.36)	1.870* (0.34)	1.727* (0.32)	1.699* (0.32)	1.639* (0.30)	1.560* (0.29)	1.432+ (0.28)	1.402+ (0.27)
35–44	2.331* (0.43)	2.116* (0.39)	2.007* (0.38)	2.047* (0.40)	2.166* (0.41)	1.974* (0.37)	1.808* (0.35)	1.811* (0.36)
45–54	2.002* (0.41)	1.979* (0.41)	1.952* (0.42)	1.887* (0.41)	1.855* (0.38)	1.831* (0.38)	1.785* (0.38)	1.708* (0.37)
55–64	1.553+ (0.39)	1.459 (0.38)	1.445 (0.38)	1.531 (0.41)	1.487 (0.37)	1.459 (0.36)	1.377 (0.35)	1.458 (0.38)
Household income								
Middle 33pctile	1.169 (0.18)	1.161 (0.18)	1.010 (0.16)	1.096 (0.17)	1.134 (0.16)	1.134 (0.16)	0.977 (0.14)	1.087 (0.16)
Top 33pctile	1.460* (0.21)	1.392* (0.20)	1.274 (0.19)	1.322+ (0.20)	0.798 (0.12)	0.774+ (0.12)	0.717* (0.11)	0.802 (0.13)

(Contd)

Table 4.2 (Contd)

	Opportunity				Necessity			
	Model 1	Model 2	Model 3	Model 4	Model 1	Model 2	Model 3	Model 4
Education								
Primary	1.492 (0.44)	1.407 (0.42)	1.509 (0.46)	1.548 (0.47)	0.928 (0.20)	0.892 (0.19)	0.975 (0.22)	1.004 (0.23)
Secondary	1.441 (0.42)	1.509 (0.44)	1.610 (0.47)	1.612 (0.48)	0.706+ (0.15)	0.735 (0.16)	0.782 (0.17)	0.801 (0.18)
Post-secondary	1.425 (0.42)	1.353 (0.40)	1.376 (0.41)	1.397 (0.42)	0.410* (0.09)	0.402* (0.09)	0.418* (0.10)	0.434* (0.11)
Graduate	1.428 (0.67)	1.504 (0.71)	1.793 (0.86)	1.978 (0.95)	0.291* (0.18)	0.298+ (0.19)	0.361 (0.23)	0.432 (0.28)
Female sample								
Fear of failure	1.456* (0.26)	1.449* (0.26)	1.409+ (0.26)	1.465* (0.28)	1.386+ (0.24)	1.360+ (0.24)	1.337 (0.24)	1.279 (0.24)
Self-confidence		6.331* (1.28)	5.136* (1.07)	4.229* (0.91)		5.940* (1.14)	4.350* (0.87)	3.536* (0.74)
Role model			3.099* (0.58)	2.392* (0.47)			4.026* (0.74)	3.231* (0.63)
Alertness to opportunity				2.771* (0.55)				2.863* (0.57)
Age								
25–34	2.268* (0.77)	2.262* (0.78)	2.194* (0.76)	2.305* (0.84)	1.386 (0.41)	1.405 (0.42)	1.370 (0.43)	1.434 (0.48)
35–44	2.660* (0.91)	2.621* (0.91)	2.469* (0.86)	2.655* (0.97)	1.160 (0.36)	1.168 (0.36)	1.050 (0.34)	1.123 (0.39)
45–54	1.757 (0.68)	1.744 (0.69)	1.635 (0.66)	1.550 (0.66)	1.288 (0.42)	1.393 (0.47)	1.349 (0.47)	1.386 (0.51)
55–64	1.194 (0.57)	1.369 (0.67)	1.381 (0.68)	1.523 (0.77)	0.891 (0.36)	1.008 (0.41)	1.046 (0.44)	1.034 (0.47)

(Contd)

Table 4.2 (Contd)

	Opportunity				Necessity			
	Model 1	**Model 2**	**Model 3**	**Model 4**	**Model 1**	**Model 2**	**Model 3**	**Model 4**
Household income	1 (.)	1 (.)	1 (.)	1 (.)	1 (.)	1 (.)	1 (.)	1 (.)
Middle 33pctile	1.264 (0.28)	1.195 (0.27)	1.045 (0.24)	1.179 (0.28)	0.977 (0.20)	0.942 (0.19)	0.820 (0.18)	0.859 (0.19)
Top 33pctile	1.213 (0.27)	1.178 (0.27)	1.071 (0.25)	1.139 (0.28)	0.760 (0.17)	0.733 (0.17)	0.657+ (0.16)	0.694 (0.17)
Education	1 (.)	1 (.)	1 (.)	1 (.)	1 (.)	1 (.)	1 (.)	1 (.)
Primary	0.723 (0.22)	0.622 (0.20)	0.677 (0.22)	0.538+ (0.18)	0.679 (0.17)	0.594* (0.15)	0.688 (0.19)	0.661 (0.18)
Secondary	0.880 (0.25)	0.820 (0.24)	0.860 (0.26)	0.830 (0.25)	0.671 (0.16)	0.632+ (0.16)	0.690 (0.18)	0.683 (0.19)
Post-secondary	0.930 (0.29)	0.815 (0.26)	0.824 (0.27)	0.807 (0.27)	0.304* (0.10)	0.282* (0.09)	0.317* (0.11)	0.293* (0.11)
Graduate	0.509 (0.53)	0.373 (0.39)	0.422 (0.45)	0.503 (0.54)	0.314 (0.32)	0.231 (0.24)	0.293 (0.31)	0.383 (0.41)

Notes: [1]The base variable for the multinomial is not being an entrepreneur. [2]Base age category is 18–24 years. [3]Base household income is the lowest 33 percentile. [4]Base education category is no education. [5]Number of observations in the multinomial regression under each column is as in Table 4.1. With a few missing observations the total sample is 8,360, with 4,100 male and 4,260 female respondents. Total male entrepreneurs are 624 and female entrepreneurs are 263.

Source: Authors' own estimation (GEM 2012, 2013, 2014)

Among the control variables, we found that younger men and women in the age group 25 to 44 years were most likely to engage in opportunity entrepreneurship. Men from the top 33 percentile of household income were more likely to be opportunity entrepreneurs, while the household income class did not make any difference to women taking up any kind of entrepreneurship. Overall, the level of education did not have any effect on entrepreneurship, though men and women with post-secondary education were more likely to take up entrepreneurship out of necessity.

TABLE 4.3: Diagnostic results of the four specifications for male and female models

	Model 1	Model 2	Model 3	Model 4
Male sample				
Log likelihood	−2222.14	−1679.05	−1545.95	−1490.67
LR chi2(21)	120.03	211.12	444.63	500.00
Pseudo R2	0.03	0.06	0.13	0.14
Mean VIF	2.13	2.03	1.96	1.91
Hosmer-Lemeshow Chi2	143.07	289.78	584.27	950.89
Hosmer-Lemeshow P	0.26	0.07	0.00	0.00
Female sample				
Log likelihood	−994.04	−887.95	−828.87	−770.87
LR chi2(21)	30.20	222.13	296.18	342.97
Pseudo R2	0.02	0.11	0.15	0.18
Mean VIF	1.79	1.72	1.68	1.65
Hosmer-Lemeshow Chi2	103.76	237.35	520.50	716.72
Hosmer-Lemeshow P	0.98	0.83	0.02	0.75

Source: Authors' own estimation (GEM 2012, 2013, 2014)

Diagnostic Test and Limitations

We presented four specifications of the model separately for each nature of entrepreneurship: opportunity and necessity. This helps to check the robustness of the model. In general, the four predictor variables provide consistent results for male and female entrepreneurs, adding confidence to our results.

We present the diagnostic results of the male and female model specifications in Table 4.3. The Pseudo R2 showed that the predictive power was higher in model specification 4 in both male and female samples. The Mean VIF test showed there was not much multicollinearity within the models' independent variables. According to the Hosmer-Lemeshow Chi2 Test, the model specification 1 with only one predictor fear of failure has the best fit for the male and female sample. However, the Hosmer-Lemeshow P value showed that the model seemed to fit the female sample better than the male sample. We are aware that the current model is very specifically trying to test for the association between the type of entrepreneurship with a limited set of behavioural variables only. In the review of literature, we noted there were a large number of institutional and other variables that would influence the choice of type of entrepreneurship. All these would add to the missing variables bias in our model. These are obvious limitations of the model.

In this chapter, we used the GEM data to explore behavioural traits of entrepreneurs that led to entrepreneurship. We would like to include family and other indicators of social reproduction characteristics that may inhibit or encourage women from setting up business. However, GEM data does not include such social reproduction variables. This remains a limitation of the analysis. The limitation of the regression exercise is that the results reported cannot capture and control all possible causes of the dynamism of the firms. Hence, the results are preliminary and can be considered characteristics associated with or factors that affect growth orientation and expansion of the business.

Interpretation of the Specifications of the Model

In specification 1 of the model, we included the behavioural variable fear of failure only; in specification 2, we added the variable self-confidence; in the third, we added having a role model; and in the fourth specification, we added being alert to opportunity. All four specifications were run for male- and female-owned enterprises separately, and all specifications included the three control variables age, level of education and household income of the household.

Risk taking

The first behavioural trait we considered was risk-taking capacity, which we proxied as the obverse, having fear of failure, specification 1. Fear of failure was not significant among the male opportunity entrepreneurs, while males with significant fear of failure were 1.4 times more likely to take up entrepreneurship due to necessity. This is as hypothesised (Douglas and Shepard, 2002), that even with low returns to entrepreneurship, the optimistic males were opting for opportunity entrepreneurship. However, as noted in Figures 4.1a and 4.1b, the male opportunity-based entrepreneurs were more likely to belong to the upper 33rd percentile of household income. Those who venture into entrepreneurship due to necessity do so despite fear of failure, that is, they have no choice as they were more likely to belong to the lowest 33rd percentile of household income.

The situation, however, was different for women entrepreneurs. Women with significant fear of failure were 1.4 times more likely to opt for opportunity entrepreneurship, while the necessity entrepreneurs get into it without any significant fear. Women opportunity entrepreneurs do not follow the expected behavioural trait of entering this field due to risk-taking ability. However, those who feel the necessity to earn enter entrepreneurship despite the fear of failure.

Overconfidence

The second behavioural trait we considered was overconfidence. This was proxied by two variables, self-confidence and the perception that there was sufficient business opportunity and being alert to it, included in specification 2 and 4. Both men and women opportunity entrepreneurs showed significant positive self-confidence and alertness to opportunity. Women with self-confidence were nearly five to six times more likely to be opportunity entrepreneurs, while men were only about two times more likely to be so. This was as hypothesised. Similarly, women who were alert to business opportunity were 2.7 times more likely than men (1.8 times) to opt for opportunity entrepreneurship. The importance of this second behavioural trait of possible overconfidence among women overcomes the early trait of fear of failure, which was against the expected behaviour for opportunity entrepreneurs.

Non-pecuniary benefit of independence

The third behavioural trait included in specification 3 was the non-pecuniary benefit of being independent, which we proxied through knowing an entrepreneur role model which helped to reduce uncertainty. As hypothesised, both men and women having a role model were 2 to 3 times more likely to take up opportunity entrepreneurship. They were also more likely to take up necessity entrepreneurship. In the Indian context, where the institutional environment for small business is not very conducive, knowing someone in the field reduces uncertainty and becomes a crucial factor that encourages entering and continuing as an entrepreneur.

CASE STUDIES OF WOMEN ENTREPRENEURS

This section presents two case studies of confident women who exhibit risk-taking behaviour. They pursued entrepreneurial opportunities to launch their businesses. The first case is of a firm called Heads Up For Tails (HUFT) that manufactures, retails and sells high quality pet products in India. The idea behind HUFT was opportunity-driven entrepreneurship based on the founder's own experience with her pet dog. HUFT is also an example of user entrepreneurship, where the user felt the need for a product and created a firm to satisfy his or her own need (Goyal and Yadav 2014). The user innovation theory proposed by Eric von Hippel (1988) suggests that users develop important products and processes for their own use. For example, a surgeon invents a new medical device for self-use, or a sportsperson invents a new sports equipment for their own use. Later, these inventions are commercialised by the user-entrepreneur or by other manufacturing firms.

The second case is of an innovative healthcare firm, Teleradiology Solutions. This company was launched by two doctors (a husband and wife team) who call themselves 'accidental entrepreneurs'. It is a case study of a woman entrepreneur who exhibits behavioural traits like alertness to opportunity, risk-taking and self-confidence. Both case studies reveal challenges faced by these women while launching their enterprises in India. Important recommendations for aspiring women entrepreneurs are also presented in both cases.

CASE STUDY 5: **Woman User-Entrepreneur Launching Firms in Niche Area**

Entrepreneur: Rashi Narang
Company: Heads Up For Tails
Industry: Pet Products

Rashi Narang grew up in a business family with a homemaker mother and businessman father. Her parents encouraged Rashi and her brother to adopt a balanced approach in life. They preferred a middle path and their parenting style was neither too strict nor too liberal. Rashi spent her childhood and school years in New Delhi. She holds a Bachelor of Business Administration degree from Cardiff University, UK and a Master's in Human Resource Management from the London School of Economics. Rashi worked in a multinational bank after completing her education.

As a child, Rashi had grown up with pet dogs. After marriage, Rashi got a labrador retriever dog called Sara. But keeping a dog this time was different as she was directly responsible for Sara's upkeep. Rashi had travelled across the world and had seen not only high quality, but also variety in pet products. Unfortunately, choices in India were very limited and were of inferior quality. 'There was nothing "good" to buy for Sara!' Rashi recalled. She felt that she should do something to make high quality pet products available in India, for Sara and for other pet owners like her. Eventually, she launched her own firm that produced high quality pet products and also sold imported, high quality products from across the globe.

Heads Up For Tails is Rashi's own venture. She is founder and CEO of the company. She received informal mentoring support from her husband, who is a finance professional. She did not have formal business mentors but was open to the idea of a mentor to advise her formally in her entrepreneurial pursuit.

Rashi avoided external funding, and started her venture with her personal finances. 'Seeking funding from high net worth investors is not only exciting but also scary,' Rashi felt. She did not seek finances from venture capitalists because she found them too aggressive in their approach towards her business. She did hold meetings with venture capitalists, but eventually backed away. Rashi said, 'They wanted to just come in and take over, they wanted to change everything.'

As a result, she built up her company by bootstrapping. Everything she earned went back into the business. She did not draw any salary and there was no profit. Whatever came in went back in. These long years of struggle indicated self-confidence and clarity that there was a market for these products, which she could access. Her self-confidence paid off when in 2015, she was able to raise around a million Singapore dollars from angel investors to scale up her business. Angel investors were relatively softer in their approach than venture capitalists, she shared. They were 'demanding in terms of reporting but they don't micromanage the business.'

Initially, Rashi started by launching a sole proprietorship firm in 2008. Six years later, in 2015, she converted the proprietorship into a private limited company, Precious Pet Services Private Limited. In order to grow her business and seek funding from external investors, she felt the need to launch a private limited company. She also got directors and other professionals onboard. Precious Pet Services has three directors, including Rashi's husband Samarth, who acts as the company's chief financial officer.

Heads Up For Tails is a brand name of Precious Pet Services. Rashi later acquired another firm called The Tail Lovers Company and has expanded her business in other cities like Bengaluru. This acquisition helped her build India's first multi-brand pet store, with merchandise and pet products from across the globe.

Rashi felt that incorporating a company in India was a tedious process and even the simplest of steps took forever. She often wondered, 'Why couldn't it be at the click of a button? In Singapore everything is at the click of a button. It takes one day to incorporate a company there. Here it is systems after systems after systems. There is so much paperwork to be done.' Rashi took the help of an accountant but still had to put together the entire documentation for submission.

Recommendations for women entrepreneurs

Passionately believe in your idea: Whenever Rashi shared her business idea with people, they would tell her that she was crazy! A lot of her friends liked the idea but were skeptical about Rashi selling pet products. Many could not even comprehend what she was trying to convey. However, she was self-confident, believed in her business idea and strongly felt that she must do something in the pet space. Rashi says, 'My parents and in-laws were very supportive even though they did not have a clear idea about what I was thinking.'

Continuously learn on-the-job: Rashi says, 'I didn't know anything when I started...everything was learnt on the job.' Initially, she had no knowledge of how to manage a startup, what it meant to be able to get systems in place, inventory management, pricing, managing finances, managing people and making sure the service was good. She felt that it had been a steep learning curve for her for more than six years.

Protect your company's intellectual property rights against copyright infringement and fake products: Rashi shares that one vendor had started copying and selling Rashi's product designs. She had to threaten the vendor to stop copying, and warned him that she would file a case against him in court for copying and cheating.

Create a new market for niche products: Rashi states, 'If one goes to a pet store [in India], it is not a very memorable experience.' Most pet stores in India are run by people who do not own a pet. These are usually small shops selling low-quality products. Most of the people running such shops lack empathy towards animals and have a poor understanding of the pet products business, she says. Rashi also revealed that the pet product industry in India was fragmented and outdated compared to global markets. Many people told Rashi that a dog-related business is not viable. She sensed that people could not comprehend what she was trying to do because the pet products market was not fully developed in India at that time. Despite the odds, Rashi pursued her vision of creating a multi-brand pet products marketplace in India due to her risk-taking behavioural trait.

Invest in technology to manage processes and inventory: Rashi's stores were maintaining a stock of more than 100 brands, and inventory management became a challenge as her firm lacked technology-enabled processes and systems. Lack of finances was the main reason for not having made investments in technology to manage backend processes and inventory. But with recent funding from investors, she plans to procure systems and hire people to automate systems and workflow.

CASE STUDY 6: **Technology-enabled Entrepreneurial Opportunities in Healthcare**

Entrepreneur: Sunita Maheshwari
Company: Teleradiology Solutions
Industry: Healthcare

Dr. Sunita Maheshwari was born to a Marwari Indian father and a Syrian American mother. She grew up in Hyderabad, where the social environment in the seventies was conservative. Her parents raised Sunita and her brother with egalitarian values. As a young girl, she often volunteered to work at the Mother Teresa home in Hyderabad. Her desire to serve people motivated her to join the medical profession.

She obtained an MBBS degree from Osmania Medical College and for postgraduate studies, joined the All India Institute of Medical Sciences (AIIMS) in Delhi. After AIIMS, she went to the USA for postgraduate degrees in Pediatrics and Pediatric Cardiology. Sunita worked for ten years as a pediatric cardiologist at various hospitals like Manipal and Narayana Hrudayalaya in India.

Sunita calls herself an 'accidental entrepreneur' as she does not have a business background. In 1999, Sunita and her husband moved back to India. She started working at a local hospital in Bangalore but her husband, Arjun Kalyanpur, did not get a job. Arjun had an MD from Cornell and Yale University, USA and an MBBS from AIIMS, New Delhi. Many local hospitals considered him overqualified and did not offer him a job. A professor at Yale told Arjun that they were facing difficulty in getting doctors to read and diagnose patient scans at night in the US. Arjun offered to do this job online from Bengaluru. The concept of a patient scan being sent from America to a doctor sitting in India for diagnosis and then sending the report back to America for treatment was totally new then. This assignment with Yale ended soon because many within the Yale University hospital raised concerns over outsourcing a US patient's diagnosis to a doctor in India.

Sunita recalls, 'It was like a door opened and you saw the opportunity, and the door closed...The *door* [a project with Yale] was now closed, but the opportunity was lying behind it, and what do we do?' This assignment gave birth to the idea of launching Teleradiology Solutions. Sunita and Arjun conceptualised the company jointly. Sunita calls herself an 'out-of-the-box thinker' and definitely a risk-taker who saw an opportunity and was willing to take the risk of starting a business.

Sunita's father was her formal as well as informal mentor. Her father taught her the importance of enjoying one's work and not to be driven by money. He inculcated moral values of honesty and integrity in Sunita and her brother. Since Sunita's father had academic specialisation in the management domain, he also acted as her business advisor and consultant. He would often advise Sunita on matters related to corporate ethics, financial planning, tax management, employee hiring and business strategy.

Teleradiology Solutions started with Sunita and Arjun's personal money. Whenever they made profits, they used the amount for scaling up the company and setting up new startups, such as RxDx Clinics, a chain of primary care clinics. They followed the 'growth via re-investment' model and decided 'not to take any VC funding and go crazy'. Their vision was to gradually grow by investing the profits back into the venture and create more clinics that were self-sustaining.

The entrepreneurial process of launching Teleradiology Solutions was through trial and error. They started by launching a website and saw people were visiting it. They also started getting work queries, which required a formal contract and a payment process. Sunita realised that to receive payment from clients, they needed to set up a company. Sunita and Arjun both were doctors and had little knowledge of the legal process of setting up a private limited company.

Sunita recalls how they came up with the name of the company. 'We went to the [registrar's] office and told the guy that we wanted to register our company. He asked, what's the name? We did not have a company name! We sat in the parking area and discussed what should we call this company...So we said we are doing radiology, we are doing tele and giving a solution. So, we came up with Teleradiology Solutions Private Limited.' As Teleradiology Solutions grew, Sunita and Arjun set up a support company for building teleradiology technology and registered it as Teleradtec. It employs software engineers and has its own CEO. Subsequently, Sunita and Arjun also launched the RxDx

Clinics. Their risk-taking behaviour and self-confidence had made them serial entrepreneurs.

Recommendations for women entrepreneurs

Avail government-sponsored schemes for women and entrepreneurs: Sunita recalls that she learnt about several beneficial government schemes till very late. She says, 'For three years we did not know [about the available schemes[3]]...For a company like us which basically does exports, we were eligible for the Software Technology Park of India (STPI), which gives you a seven-year tax-free window...When we got to know about this and applied... we got the benefit for about five years under STPI. That was a big help because we did not have to pay 30 per cent corporate tax and we used that money to pay for infrastructure.'

Manage infrastructure costs: Sunita shared that infrastructure costs in India were very high and that, 'To be honest, infrastructural challenges almost drove us to Singapore in the early years. I would say that in the first three–four years, we were killed in India because of infrastructure issues...There was no reliable electricity or internet bandwidth; the computers burned down because of a surge in electricity—all that kind of stuff. But we were very patriotic, and that is the reason we stuck on.' Sunita recommends that women entrepreneurs must understand the kind of infrastructure required to run their business and plan costs accordingly. Sunita's entrepreneurial journey highlights the importance of external institutional environment being crucial for women entrepreneurs to succeed. This we will further elaborate in the next chapter.

Manage finances and operational costs of shared resources: Sunita shared that they [the founding team] made many mistakes, and learned from them. The services between all her different companies and clinics were commonly shared and the cost of all the shared services was attributed to the main company, Teleradiology Solutions. As a result, it gave the impression that all the support companies and clinics were doing well; but in reality

Teleradiology Solutions was covering all their costs related to HR, finance, infrastructure and others. Sunita finally employed a chief financial officer (CFO), and after one week, he told Sunita, 'Doctor, I don't know how you managed without me...Really, God was looking after you all!'

DISCUSSION AND CONTRIBUTION TO ENTREPRENEURSHIP LITERATURE

The significant contribution of this chapter to existing literature on entrepreneurship is, adding a multidisciplinary context-specific view of what enables small businesses to be more entrepreneurial. We explored what encourages entrepreneurship from the perspective of behavioural economics. India's small business sector consists of an overwhelming number of self-employed, mainly own account enterprises, operated without hired workers. While their scale of operation was small, we argue that it is important to consider the section of such small business enterprises that are expanding operations as opportunity-based entrepreneurs to bring positive policy focus on them, as they created an opportunity for employment.

From the management literature, we borrowed the classification of entrepreneurship into opportunity-based and necessity-driven. From the behavioural economics perspective, we highlighted certain common as well as distinct behavioural motivations of these entrepreneurs. Three behavioural traits in the choice of the type of entrepreneurship, viz., risk-taking, overconfidence and non-pecuniary benefits such as independence, were analysed. We found that risk-taking was a trait among male opportunity driven entrepreneurs from better-off households. Women opportunity entrepreneurs did not follow the expected behavioural trait of risk-taking. However, if entrepreneurship is a choice of necessity then women enter it despite the fear of failure. The puzzle of low return entrepreneurship can be explained by necessity of individuals from low income households. Overconfidence and non-pecuniary benefits highlighted by role-models who help reduce uncertainty are behavioural motivations that further explain the predominance of low return entrepreneurship. We found that women with great self-confidence and who have a mentor or role model, helped them reduce uncertainties, overcome fear and enter the field. Such women small business owners are truly entrepreneurial and should be encouraged by policies that focus on their needs. This will help such businesses to expand and contribute further to the country's economic growth.

This chapter also suggests that available national data sets should capture more details regarding women-owned business activities and motivations for the same. Micro-data based case studies offer insights into how women deal with a wide range of issues related to the complex nature of entrepreneurship. Two case studies presented in this chapter offer insights from micro-data on the behavioural traits of risk-taking and self-confidence in overcoming the challenges faced by women. The chapter highlights the importance of a deeper understanding of behavioural traits behind entrepreneurship, such as attitudes, motivations and perceptions, in addition to the economic and operational characteristics. It implies that improving attitudes and motivation towards entrepreneurship and enabling institutions to provide a favourable business environment are vital in promoting entrepreneurship.

Women entrepreneurship today can address the current concerns of boosting job creation and economic growth. Zoltan Acs and José Ernesto Amorós suggested two-fold policy strategies: 'reducing necessity-driven entrepreneurship to achieve the efficiency-driven stage, and on the other hand, promoting innovative entrepreneurship to reach the innovation-driven stage' (Acs and Amorós 2008). To foster opportunity-based entrepreneurship, policy should emphasise opportunity creation, networking, skill and knowledge upgrade. This also applies to necessity-driven entrepreneurship, but the reduction of fear of failure is an additional policy measure to be considered for these businesses. While the policy framework should be able to sustain the opportunity-oriented enterprises, it should also promote the transition from necessity-driven activities to opportunity-seeking business activities.

Policies aimed at providing a better business environment also need to consider the underlying motivation for involvement in the business. As the feminist critique of the gendered entrepreneurial subject suggests, social reproduction role could be the reason for undertaking business. To enable women enterprises to grow, provision of child care and old age care facilities at the local level is an agenda for public policy. It would be interesting to examine whether there are productivity differentials among opportunity and necessity enterprises. Our future research will explore this dimension.

In this chapter, we have focused on the impact of behavioural traits on undertaking opportunity or necessity entrepreneurship and have also presented two real life case studies of women entrepreneurs. However, as discussed in the literature review section, the institutional environment of the country or the entrepreneurial ecosystem plays a major role in whether these small businesses can grow to scale or remain small with low returns. There is an evident need for future research to empirically examine this phenomenon in greater detail. The next chapter will analyse the impact of the institutional eco-system on enterprises in the formal and informal sector.

NOTES

[1]Earlier versions of parts of Chapters 4 and 5 were presented in the 20th Anniversary Conference of the Association of Heterodox Economics at Leicester, United Kingdom in June 2018. We are grateful for the comments received from reviewers and participants at these events.

[2]*Global Entrepreneurship Monitor* (GEM) 2012–2013–2014, Adult Population Survey (APS). Available at: https://www.gemconsortium.org/data/sets

[3]The interviewee gave examples of available government schemes and tax benefits; see https://www.stpi.in/home

V

Dualistic Structure of Industry and Growth of Firms

Do Institutions Matter?

Economic reforms were initiated in India in 1991. There was a slow deregulation of the economy beginning with removal of the 'license raj' with its over-emphasis on obtaining licenses for every economic activity, and reduction of tariffs. Gradually, sectors of the economy were opened up to allow foreign investment. Currently, the Indian economy is more or less open to the flow of capital, with restrictions only in a few key sectors. The Indian labour market has been dualistic, with a large proportion of enterprises and employment in the informal or unorganised sector. This was partly the reason for following a gradual process of liberalisation. The shock of liberalisation was expected to negatively affect this large sector and consequently impact economic growth.

The policy framework in India has provided support to micro and small enterprises located in both the formal and informal sectors. Prior to 1991, various commodities were reserved for the small scale industry (SSI) sector, leading to a form of dualism. Reservation for the SSI sector has been lifted, except for a few commodities. However, protection and support to small scale enterprises continue in some form till date. For example, the Micro, Small and Medium Enterprises (MSME) Act, 2006, aimed at promoting and developing MSMEs.[1] In India, the MSME sector's contribution to GDP was about 17 per cent in five years from 2004–05 to 2009–10. A comprehensive National Policy for

Skill Development and Entrepreneurship was introduced in 2015,[2] superseding the National Skill Development Policy, 2009. The new policy's vision statement was: 'To create an ecosystem of empowerment by skilling on a large scale at speed with high standards and to promote a culture of innovation based entrepreneurship which can generate wealth and employment so as to ensure sustainable livelihoods for all citizens in the country.' Recent policies such as demonetisation in 2016 and implementation of the Goods and Services Tax (GST) regime in 2017 created a setback for micro enterprises in the informal economy, which mainly operate with cash transactions.

In this chapter, we analyse the external institutional factors that create impetus for growth of firms in the informal and formal sectors of the economy using separate data sets, to address the questions of whether external institutional support helps entrepreneurs in the informal sector to expand, and what external institutional factors drive or inhibit entrepreneurs to respond to business opportunity through innovation in the formal sector. We further probe whether the gender of ownership of informal and formal enterprises influenced the response of firms to the external economic environment.

We first present a brief review of literature on institutional factors and the informal sector enterprises. We present the data, methodology, model and discussion of results for the informal sector using National Sample Survey Office's (NSSO) Unorganised Non-Agricultural Enterprises Survey data (National Sample Survey Office 2018), followed by the data, methodology, model and discussion of results for the formal sector using the World Bank Enterprise Surveys (WBES) data for India (World Bank 2013). We then present two case studies of women entrepreneurs, one each from the informal and formal sectors. Lastly, we conclude with a comparison of the growth impetus in industry within this dualistic structure of India's economy.

BRIEF REVIEW OF LITERATURE

Institutional Factors Affecting Women Entrepreneurs' Performance

The literature on women entrepreneurship included institutional factors, such as financial constraints or other challenges faced and support received by women at the start-up or development stages of their businesses (Orhan and Scott 2001; Anna et al. 2000). The ways of overcoming such barriers were suggested at an individual level (Ahl 2002). Research on gender and entrepreneurship included analysis of programmes fostering women's entrepreneurship (Weeks and Seiler 2001), impact of certain governmental policies on entrepreneurial activity (Lituchy and Reavley 2004) and the relationships that women entrepreneurs establish with governmental and non-governmental institutions (ibid.).

Access to finance: Women entrepreneurs face significantly greater challenges than men in gaining access to financial services. Lack of financial education can also limit women from gaining access to and benefitting from financial services. Further, not only do loan officers have negative perceptions about female entrepreneurs, but lack of collateral is also the main obstacle for female entrepreneurs to apply for any loans (Haq 2000).

Lack of collateral: The World Bank report showed that only 1 per cent of the world's property was owned by women, and the legal right of women declined with marriage in two-third of the countries (Makena, Kubaison and Njati 2014). In most of the cases, women were less likely to have land or other assets titled under their name (Agarwal 2003; Makena, Kubaison and Njati 2014). The lack of property ownership limited women entrepreneurs' capacity to secure loans due to lack of collateral.

Access to market: Women have limited knowledge and marketing skills, which are the main hindering factors for capturing new markets. There is also the fear of sexual harassment, which restricts women from travelling long distances in order to make new contracts (Ewoh 2014).

Access to training: Women had limited access to vocational and technical training in South Asia. In fact, women on average had less access to education and technical and vocational skills than men (Agrawal 2013). According to Carmen Niethammer (2013) limited access to skills and trainings were the main obstacles to achieve success and growth of the businesses run or managed by women.

Access to network: Women entrepreneurs faced many challenges in terms of building networks. Majority of the existing networks and contracts are male-dominated, and women frequently faced discrimination in terms of accessing those networks; for example, a major challenge women faced in terms of accessing networks is the unfavourable time for meeting. Lack of access to networks is the most hindering factor for the growth of women entrepreneurs (Ewoh 2014; Haq 2000).

Access to policymakers: According to Ethel R. Ewoh, women faced lack of information on various policies that are in favour of their business (Ewoh 2014). They also have very little access to policy makers and are unable to advocate the right policy which will be suitable for them. Additionally, in developing countries, very few women reach the leadership position in the business organisation. As a result women may not be able to contribute to any policy making which could be helpful for their own business.

Legal barriers: Study also indicates that in developing countries, taxation, law and regulations are serious hindrances for running successful business for women entrepreneurs (Vossenberg 2013).

Societal support: In developing countries, social attitudes on cultural and religious beliefs generally do not support women working or women becoming entrepreneurs (Vossenberg 2013). OECD (OECD 2002) and ILO (ILO 2006, 2008) added that the key factors that affect women entrepreneurs' performance, especially in developing continents, are: vulnerability of women to adverse effects of trade reform; restraints with regard to assets (land); lack of information to exploit opportunities; poor mobilisation of women entrepreneurs; lack of management skills; lack of awareness among young women of entrepreneurship as a career option; conflicting gender roles; gender inequality; inappropriate technology; and constraints at the legal, institutional and policy levels.

Informal Enterprises

The majority of entrepreneurs in India were own account, operating with family labour and having no employees. The proportion of entrepreneurs with workers, that is employers, was very small as we shall discuss. Using NSSO data on unorganised enterprises, Arnaud Daymard defined necessity-driven entrepreneurship as own account enterprises (OAEs) operating with the use of only family labour, and opportunity-based entrepreneurship as enterprises operating with at least one hired worker (Daymard 2015). In India, both categories also differ by their level of human capital and by their motivation, and might respond differently to the policy changes (ibid.). Women entrepreneurship was low, but growing in the category of own account workers, that is necessity-driven entrepreneurship (ibid.). The transition from entrepreneurs without workers to becoming entrepreneurs employing workers was quite low in India (Schoar 2009).

Daymard provided a detailed analysis of the nature and drivers of women entrepreneurship in India using data from the NSSO Unorganised Non-Agricultural Enterprises Survey (Daymard 2015). He argued that distinction between entrepreneurs with and without workers was crucial to understand the dynamics of women entrepreneurship in India. With the distinction based on employees, the study found that education and female labour force participation were the main factors driving female entrepreneurs. The study highlighted the importance of female human capital, both general human capital through education, and specific human capital through labour force participation as drivers of female entrepreneurship in India. It was noted that enterprises with hired workers were more likely to experience growth, maintain accounts, use a computer and operate from a premise designated for the purpose and not from home. Variables such as access to bank credit, provision of credit or income per capita, were not recognised as important barriers or facilitators to female entrepreneurship.

Ejaz Ghani, William Kerr and Stephen O'Connell provided a broad understanding of the issues that confront women entrepreneurs in India (Ghani, Kerr and O'Connell 2012). They noted that informal entrepreneurship provided opportunities as well as escape from the unpaid domestic work for women. Key factors that determine the extent of women entrepreneurship in India were insufficient family income, widowhood, ill-health of spouse or estrangement from spouse. The extent of opportunity-oriented entrepreneurship among women in India was low (Khokhar and Singh 2016).

Pinaki Das and Bhabasankar Das analysed the status of micro-enterprises in the unorganised sector in West Bengal using the NSSO, 67th Round, 2010–11, Survey of Unorganised Non-Agricultural Enterprises (Das and Das 2017). They estimated the probability of an enterprise expanding and found that productivity, profitability, location and nature of enterprises significantly and positively affected the status of growth. Larger enterprises were more likely to expand.

The limitation of using the NSSO data alone is that it may not provide a true picture of women entrepreneurs as this data set refers only to the unorganised/informal sector or unregistered units. Though this constitutes the large majority of enterprises in India, it would not be correct to judge the potential and need to encourage women entrepreneurship from such a truncated data set. Hence in this chapter we use data from both informal enterprises and formal enterprises to study growth impetus of firms.

Formal Enterprises

Studies that consider external institutional factors for the performance of firms, mainly formal, focus on the impact of business climate on economic growth and productivity at the cross-country level. Business climate variables found to have a positive effect on business performance were good infrastructure (Straub et al. 2010), legal institutions, improved court systems, government bureaucracy, formal financial markets and improved democracy (World Bank 2004), property rights and good governance (Dethier, Hirn and Straub 2011).

The literature was replete with studies on the impact of various external institutional variables on firm performance, expansion and growth, productivity and being export oriented. It was observed that firm productivity was affected by competitiveness and regulation. Further, financial constraint had a negative impact on firm growth and smaller firms were more affected by it. The probability of a firm being export oriented was positively affected by access to overdraft facility or overcoming the financial constraint (Dollar, Hallward-Driemeier and Mengistae 2005). Studies found that the probability of exporting had a negative and significant impact on losses from a power outage (ibid.).

There are various limitations to the approach of cross-country level analysis (Dethier, Hirn and Straub 2011). First, it does not capture the impact of heterogeneity of states, regions within the country or across firms. They mainly relate to formal firms at the country level. Secondly, business climate studies rely on de jure information or subjective judgment about relative weights of different components. Thirdly, most country-level indicators do not vary over time and hence act like fixed effect (of country or region), which may reflect features other than business climate (Commander and Svejnar 2007).

This view implied that econometric analysis at a more disaggregated level, such as the firm or enterprise, and sector or industry within a country would provide a better understanding of the drivers of entrepreneurship. Such a focus would also provide a better policy perspective on how to encourage innovative entrepreneurship in the country or region of study (Kessides 2004; Pande and Udry 2005). As suggested by Abhijit Banerjee and Esther Duflo (2005), an enterprise level study would help understand the behaviour of individual firms when the market or governments fail, or people, including women, have difficulty in taking advantage of opportunities. Firm-level studies provide a better understanding of the drivers of entrepreneurship than the macro-econometric literature. They have shown that within-country variations in the local business environment were essential in explaining differences in firm performance.

Studies use indicators of power outages, water outages, telephone connectivity, and roads to proxy for the efficiency of infrastructure. Unexpected losses due to power or water outages, telephone connectivity, poor roads would increase the cost of production and reduce international competitiveness (Seker 2011). Firm-level productivity and infrastructure studies may suffer from 'reverse causality'. 'More infrastructure can cause the efficiency of firms to improve, but better economic performance may also attract more infrastructure' (Aterido, Hallward-Driemeier and Pagés 2007). Reverse causality can be countered by the use of a more generic variable such as location so that all firms in the area are equally affected by the variable power or water outages. Location and industry variables can help remove endogeneity due to reverse causality. One can use an interaction variable such as business climate and firm size to take care of reverse causality (ibid.). In our study of formal firms we use interaction terms to remove impact of reverse causality on certain variables.

EXPANSION OF INFORMAL ENTERPRISES, NSSO DATA

Data and Methodology

The study uses unit level data of the Unorganised Non-Agricultural Enterprises Survey conducted by the NSSO, India for the year 2015–16 (73rd Round). This consists of unit level records of about 270,400 sole proprietary enterprises in both manufacturing and services in the unorganised sector. Of these approximately 235,800 were male proprietary and 34,600 were female proprietary enterprises. That is, about 13 per cent of the sole proprietors were women.

Dependent variables and limitation of data: The 73rd Round Survey (2015–16) enquired of all enterprises older than 3 years as to whether the enterprise was expanding, stagnant or contracting. Nearly 31 per cent of the male proprietors and 25 per cent of the female proprietors felt their operations were expanding. Nearly half, 45 and 48 per cent of men and women owned enterprises respectively, were stagnant and about 12 per cent were contracting.

The dependent variable was a dummy for informal enterprises that were expanding (Expanding =1, otherwise =0). We excluded the enterprises that were less than 3 years old from the regression analysis.

Since this data set consists of enterprises in the unorganised sector only, any measure of expansion will be limited. It excludes the well-to-do and financially better off entrepreneurs who were more likely to operate formal enterprises. We must bear in mind that we were exploring the possibility of small, mainly OAEs that were able to see and siege a business opportunity which allowed them to expand. The characteristics of enterprises by gender of ownership are presented in Table 5.1.

TABLE 5.1: Characteristics of male and female proprietary non-agricultural enterprises, NSSO, 2015–16 (percentage)

Enterprises	Male	Female	Total
Status of enterprise			
Expanding (opportunity based)	30.8	24.9	29.6
Stagnant	45.1	48.5	45.8
Contracting	11.9	11.5	11.8
<3 years old	12.2	15.2	12.8
Total	100.0	100.0	100.0

(Contd)

Table 5.1 (Contd)

Enterprises	Male	Female	Total
Type of enterprises			
OAE	81.4	96.1	84.4
Establishment (with at least one hired worker)	18.6	3.9	15.6
Total	100.0	100.0	100.0
Whether registered with any statutory body, Yes	35.1	8.3	29.6
Whether book of accounts maintained, Yes	11.5	3.6	9.9
Located within household premises	33.4	84.7	43.8
Age of firm			
<5 years	39.5	45.5	40.7
6–10 years	25.7	26.5	25.9
11–20 years	25.2	22.1	24.6
>20 years	9.6	5.9	8.9
Total	100.0	100.0	100.0
Social group of wwner			
SC-ST	16.1	19.4	16.8
OBC	50.4	49.7	50.2
General	33.6	30.9	33.0
Total	100.0	100.0	100.0
With current outstanding loan	13.6	5.9	12.0
Getting government assistance	0.8	0.6	0.8
Enterprise used computer	5.5	1.3	4.7
Enterprise used internet	4.4	1.2	3.7
Value of asset per enterprise (Rs)	435594	274821	414996
Value added per worker (Rs)			
Expanding	10805	7136	10637
Stagnant	9088	4846	8620
Contracting	8009	3844	7642
<3 years old	8963	4637	8324
Total	9579	5370	9191

Source: Computed by authors from unit records of the National Sample Survey, 73rd Round (National Sample Survey Office 2018)

The vast majority of women-operated enterprises (96 per cent) were own account, i.e. run with family labour, while 20 per cent of male owned enterprises were operated with at least one hired worker. The characteristics of the independent variables are presented in Table 5.1 and highlighted below. While 35 per cent of male proprietors were registered with a statutory body, only 8 per cent of female proprietors were registered. A small proportion (11 per cent) of men and an even smaller per cent of women (3) proprietors maintained books of accounts of the enterprise. Adding to this, 85 per cent of women proprietors operated from their homes, while about one-third of men did so. These characteristics of the firm mean that the women-operated enterprises were smaller in size and scale, perhaps with limited reach, compared to those operated by men, which were definitely larger in scale. However, the gross value added per worker for expanding enterprises was not very different across gender of ownership, compared to stagnant and contracting enterprises.

The age of the firms and social group of the entrepreneur did not differ much by gender, though a slightly larger proportion of women-owned proprietary firms were less than five years old. Only about 13 per cent of men and 6 per cent of women proprietors had current outstanding loans, implying that these enterprises mainly operated with their own funds, or funds borrowed from family and friends. Less than 1 per cent of male and female proprietors received any assistance from the government. About 4 to 5 per cent of men- and a little over 1 per cent of women-owned informal enterprises used computers or had an internet connection. Overall, one can see that the scale of operation of the informal enterprises was small, women enterprises even more so. However, what we highlight in this chapter is that nearly 25 to 30 per cent of them expanded their operations despite the small scale.

RESEARCH QUESTIONS AND MODEL

We use three control variables, industry of the enterprise using the NIC classification, and location in an urban area and district of the enterprise; these variables control the characteristics of the industry and the location of the enterprise.

Research questions: What characteristics of the firm and external support drive entrepreneurs in the informal sector to expand? Further, are the drivers of opportunity entrepreneurship different by gender of ownership?

Methodology

Model 1: In the first model we estimate the probability that the expanding firm is owned by a woman, given the characteristics of the firm and institutional factors. The sample consists of all expanding firms.

$$\text{Probit}\,[P\,(y = 1)]_{ij} = \alpha_{ij} + \beta_1 \chi_{ij} + \beta_2 E + \beta_3 C_{ij} + \mu_{ij} \qquad (1)$$

Where $[P\,(y = 1)]$ is the probability of expanding enterprise being owned by a woman, i is the individual firm, j is gender; α is the regression constant; β_1, β_2, β_3 is estimate for the regression coefficients, χ_{ij} being vector of the firm and location characteristics; E being a vector of institutional variables, C being vector of the control variables; and μ is the estimate for error term.

Model 2: The second model is a logistic regression to estimate the impact of institutional factors and characteristics of the firm on the log odds that the firm expands. The model consists of all the firms in the sample. The binary logistic model for categorical dependent variable, the expanding firm, separately by gender of ownership is specified as follows:

$$\text{Logit}\,[P\,(y = 1)]_{ij} = \alpha_{ij} + \beta_1 \chi_{ij} + \beta_2 E + \beta_3 C_{ij} + \mu_{ij} \qquad (2)$$

Where $[P\,(y = 1)]$ is the log odds ratio that the firm is expanding separately by gender of ownership, i is the individual firm, j is gender; α is the regression constant; rest are similar to equation 1.

Results and Discussion

Model 1 estimated the probability of expanding firms with a female owner among all expanding firms in the sample (89,662 firms). Women-owned enterprises that were expanding were more likely to be younger and belong to scheduled class households compared to male-owned ones. Among expanding enterprises, women proprietors were more likely to be home-based, have lower value of assets and lower gross value added per worker, compared to their male counterparts. They were also less likely to hire workers on a regular basis. That is, the scale of operation of women-owned firms was smaller than male-owned ones even if they were expanding. Expanding women-owned enterprises were more likely to utilise computers, have an internet connection and be a beneficiary of some government assistance. However, women-owned enterprises that were expanding were less likely to be registered with a statutory authority.

Model 2 investigates the gender differential in drivers of expansion of firms through a logistic regression model separately for male and female proprietors. Being located in the household premise did not inhibit expansion of male or female enterprises. Among social groups, compared to the Scheduled Castes and Scheduled Tribes (SC-ST), proprietors belonging to the upper castes in the general category were less likely to be expanding enterprises. It is possible that the upper castes with their better educational status were more likely to get good formal sector jobs and operating enterprises in the informal sector may be their secondary source of income, hence less competitive.

Enterprises that were expanding were more likely to be relatively more recently set up. Firms with a larger scale of operation, higher gross value added per worker, value of fixed assets and establishments with at least one hired worker were more likely to expand, irrespective of gender of ownership. Units that maintained books of accounts, indicating better organisation skills, were also more likely to expand.

The surprising result was that male proprietors that had a current loan liability were less likely to be expanding. Current

TABLE 5.2: Probability of women-owned firm expanding and log odds ratio of expanding firms by gender of ownership, NSSO, 2015–16

	Probit woman entrepreneur	Log odds ratio	
		Male	Female
	Sample of expanding enterprises	All firms	
	Model 1	Model 2	
Location within household premise	0.567***	1.174***	1.165***
Social group: OBC	−0.242***	1.006	0.933*
Social group: General	−0.239***	0.944***	0.779***
Age of firm 6–10 years	−0.145***	2.318***	2.286***
Age of firm 11–20 years	−0.262***	2.191***	2.175***
Age of firm >20 years	−0.389***	1.755***	1.830***
GVA per worker (log)	−0.321***	1.380***	1.581***
Log value of assets	−0.0387***	1.033***	1.036***
Unit maintains accounts	0.138***	1.076***	1.057
With at least one hired worker	−0.187***	1.189***	1.143*
Current taken loan	−0.032	0.899***	0.967
Unit used computer	0.127***	0.981	0.847
Unit used internet	0.156***	1.115***	1.220*
Received government assistance	0.189***	1.140**	1.374**
Registered with statutory authority	−0.0814***	1.172***	1.169***
Control: Urban	0.335***	0.827***	0.910***
Control: Industry	−0.00000510***	1.000***	1.000***
Control: District	−0.0124***	1.011***	1.004***
N	89662	235825	34680

Source: Computed by authors from unit records of the National Sample Survey, 73rd Round (National Sample Survey Office 2018)

loan or credit did not have any significant effect on female entrepreneurship, a result similar to that noted by Daymard (2015).

The drivers of expansion of enterprises were the use of internet and registration with any statutory authority. Further, informal enterprises that received some form of government assistance had higher log odds of expanding. This indicated the importance of government support for such informal enterprises.

Thus, we see that external institutional factors like availability of internet, being registered and receiving government assistance all helped the informal enterprises to expand, irrespective of gender of ownership.

INNOVATION AMONG FORMAL FIRMS, WBES DATA

Data and Methodology

The study used data from the Enterprise Surveys conducted by the World Bank (WBES) for India for the year 2013. WBES consists of unit-level data of around 9,000 firms, in both the manufacturing and service sector. This survey provides qualitative and quantitative information on the external institutional factors that affect firm dynamics. Information is collected on innovation, infrastructure, trade, finance, regulations, taxes and business licensing, corruption, crime, informality, finance and labour. We used this data to analyse whether there were gender differentials in the probability of the firm being innovative, given the characteristics of the firm and its location. We further explore how objective factors such as the economic and business ecosystem affect the odds of the firms being innovative, by gender of ownership.

Specification of Variables and Limitation of Data

In the WBES data, a male-owned enterprise was one where all owners are male. The survey does not identify all female-owned enterprises. In fact, it identifies enterprises where there was at least one female owner. Hence, we use the term mixed ownership and female ownership interchangeably. This was a limitation of our model where the impact of female proprietary was only partial.

The enterprises surveyed were mainly registered firms in the formal sector and were relatively large, with a size of five workers and above. Hence, we have to keep in mind that we are studying innovation of firms in the large, registered sector. We are not addressing the question of gender differences among opportunity-driven and necessity-based entrepreneurship in this data set. However, by defining innovation as product and process innovation, as discussed below, we are exploring gender differentials in the entrepreneurial mindset, or grabbing a business opportunity given the institutional environment.

The key variable we wish to explore is the innovative behaviour of entrepreneurial firms. WBES collected information on innovation regarding product, process and organisational changes brought about by the firm. We constructed the variable on innovation based on product and process innovation only. The firm was considered to be innovative if it answered 'Yes' to any of the three following questions:

1. During the last three years, has this establishment introduced new or significantly improved products or services (Yes=1, No=0)
2. Were any of the new or significantly improved products or services also new for the establishment's main market? (Yes=1, No=0)
3. During the last three years, has this establishment introduced any new or significantly improved methods of manufacturing products or offering services? (Yes=1, No=0)

The dependent variable was specified as enterprises that were innovative, as defined above, by gender of ownership, i.e. male-owned or mixed ownership enterprises.

The specification of the control variables and the descriptive statistics are presented in Table 5.3. Some characteristics of enterprises by gender of ownership are highlighted here as they have a bearing on the results of the model. About 45 per cent of all firms were medium sized, with 20–99 workers. However, about 30 per cent of enterprises with female owners were large, with more than 100 workers, while 20 per cent of male-owned firms were large. In fact, one-third of male-owned firms were small, with 5–20 workers, opposed to a quarter of mixed firms.

Regarding age of firms, about 41 per cent of enterprises with a female owner was more than 20 years old, while only 33 per cent of male-owned firms were so. Nearly 40 per cent of male-owned firms were in large towns, compared to 30 per cent of female-owned firms. Finally, the most striking gender differential was in

TABLE 5.3: Specification of independent variables: Firm-level characteristics (percentage)

Variable	Specification	Male owners	Mixed ownership	Total
Gender of ownership	1 if there are female/s amongst the firm owners, and 0 if owned by only males.			
Characteristics of firm				
Legal status of firm*	1 = Shareholder company with shares traded in stock market	2.0	3.0	2.2
	2 = Shareholder company with shares not traded or traded privately	6.8	17.3	8.3
	3 = Sole proprietary	53.2	13.7	47.4
	4 = Partnership	17.8	28.5	19.4
	5 = Limited partnership	17.8	31.0	19.8
	6 = Other	2.4	6.5	3.0
Size of firm	1 = Small = 5–19 workers	34.7	27.1	33.6
	2 = Medium = 20–99 workers	44	42.7	43.8
	3 = Large = >= 100 workers	21.3	30.2	22.6
Age of firm	1 <= 5 years	13.6	10.2	13.1
	2 = 6–10 years	21.4	19.9	21.2
	3 = 11–20 years	31.9	28.7	31.5
	4 = >20 years	33.1	41.2	34.3
Location: Size of town	1 = <50000	5.4	7.1	5.6
	2 = 50000–250000	22.6	27.8	23.4
	3 = >250000 to 1 million	31.6	35.8	32.3
	4 = > 1 million	40.4	29.3	38.8
Industry	Two digit industry codes			
Growth of sales per worker	Growth of sales per worker over a period of three years			

Note: *Nested columns add up to 100 for each category.

Source: Computed by the authors from Enterprise Surveys, The World Bank (World Bank 2013).

the legal status. More than half the male-owned firms were sole proprietary, while mixed (with female) ownership firms were mainly partnership (60 per cent) and share-holding (20 per cent) firms. Clearly, the inclusion of female owners came at a later stage in the life of the enterprise so that mixed ownership enterprises were older, larger and in a partnership or limited companies. This would clearly make a difference to their behaviour in innovation, as we shall see below.

The objective institutional factors or independent variables considered were power outages as a proxy for infrastructure, time spent by the manager on regulatory issues as a proxy for regulation, lack of support from the local chamber of commerce or industry association as a proxy for the private eco-system, sole use of internal funds as capital as a proxy for capital constraint, and competition faced from unregistered/informal firms (Table 5.4).

TABLE 5.4: Specification of independent variables: Institutional factors (percentage)

Variable	Specification	Male owners	Mixed ownership	Total
Power outages	No obstacle (0)	36.3	30	35.3
	Obstacle (1)	63.7	70	64.7
	Total	100	100	100
Competition	No obstacle (0)	58.3	61.9	58.8
	Obstacle (1)	41.7	38.1	41.2
	Total	100	100	100
Regulation	No obstacle (0)	58.3	42.2	55.9
	Obstacle (1)	41.7	57.8	44.1
	Total	100	100	100
Private ecosystem	No obstacle (0)	49.5	51.6	49.8
	Obstacle (1)	50.5	48.4	50.2
	Total	100	100	100
Credit constraint	No obstacle (0)	51	68.2	53.5
	Obstacle (1)	49	31.8	46.5
	Total	100	100	100

Source: Computed by the authors from Enterprise Surveys, The World Bank (World Bank 2013).

Research questions: What drives or inhibits entrepreneurs to respond to business opportunity through innovation? How do external institutional factors drive or inhibit innovative entrepreneurship by gender of ownership?

The Model

Model 1 and 2: We specify two models to identify the innovative behaviour of male-owned firms and enterprises with female owners separately. We estimate a logistic regression to analyse the likelihood of a firm being innovative by gender of ownership and the influence of the characteristics of the firm, control variables only, in Model 1. We estimate a logistic regression separately by gender of ownership to estimate the impact of external institutional factors on innovative behaviour of the firm in Model 2. The variables in Model 1 were used as control variables in Model 2. The binary logistic model for the categorical dependent variable for innovation is specified as follows:

$$\text{Logit } [P\ (y = 1)]_{ij} = \alpha_{ij} + \beta_1 \chi_{ij} + \beta \text{ Control Variables}_{ij} + E_{ij} \quad (1)$$

$$\text{Logit } [P\ (y = 1)]_{ij} = \alpha_{ij} + \beta_1 \chi_{ij} + \beta_2 \text{ Power outages}_{ij} + \beta_3 \text{ Competition}_{ij} + \beta_4 \text{ Private Ecosystem}_{ij} + \beta_5 \text{ Regulation}_{ij} + \beta_6 \text{ Credit constraint}_{ij} + \beta_7 \text{ Competition*location}_{ij} + \beta_8 \text{ Power outages* location}_{ij} + \beta \text{ Control Variables}_{ij} + E_{ij} \quad (2)$$

Where $[P\ (y = 1)]$ is the log odds ratio that a firm is innovative, i is the individual firm, j is gender; α is the regression constant; χ_{ij} being vector of the individual and location characteristics, β estimates for the regression coefficient of predictors and the interaction effect of location of the firm with respect to power outages and competition from informal units, and a vector of the control variables. E is the estimate for error term.

The results of the logistic regression model are presented in Table 5.5 We only present the log of odds-ratios and not the β coefficient. If the coefficient of simple logistic regression is 1.17, then regarding log odds, with a one unit increase in the predictor we can expect to see a 17 per cent increase in the odds of the firm being innovative. If the coefficient is 0.17, there is a 17 per cent chance of the firm not being innovative. This increase or decrease does not depend on the value of the predictor variable.

We believe that the impact of external variables such as power outage and competition from informal enterprises may vary with the size of the town where the firm is located. We expect power outages to be greater and competition from informal firms to be more intense in smaller size towns. It is useful, therefore, to add an interaction term to the model to test the hypothesis of whether location (size of the town) affected the relationships of these independent variables on the firm's innovativeness. We did test for the interaction effect of location on the other external factors, but it did not appear to have a significant impact on the result.

RESULTS AND DISCUSSION

Model 1 and 2

Gender differential in drivers of innovativeness were analysed through logistic regression models. Our results showed that innovative behaviour of firms with female owners was inhibited by external factors of poor regulatory environment (manager spent more time on regulatory issues), while male-owned firms were not. A poor private eco-system (with no support from the local chamber of commerce) inhibited firms with both male and female owners. Credit constraint did not significantly inhibit innovation in these firms (Table 5.5).

Infrastructure deficiency like power outage and competition from informal enterprises appeared to encourage innovation in both male- and female owned firms. Both these relationships were counterintuitive and may suffer from reverse causality. That is, power outage may be greater in smaller size towns. Similarly, informal firms may be flocking to regions with innovative firms, where they expect to find a market. To test for reverse causality and the impact of the size of the town, we included two interaction variables in the logistic regression. The variables experiencing competition from informal enterprises and power outages were interacted with the size of town variable. No clear relationship was noted of the interacted term with power outage.

TABLE 5.5: Log odds ratio: Innovative male and mixed (female) ownership by objective business environment factors, interaction with location and by firm and location characteristics (WBES data)

	Male		Mixed/Female	
	Model 1	**Model 2**	**Model 1**	**Model 2**
Firm characteristics				
Size of firm: Medium	1.573*** (0.09)	1.554*** (0.09)	1.618** (0.25)	1.676** (0.27)
Size of firm: Large	2.173*** (0.17)	2.051*** (0.17)	2.618*** (0.49)	2.462*** (0.50)
Location 2: 50K–250K population	1.622*** (0.19)	3.255*** (1.17)	1.547 (0.39)	6.025 (6.17)
Location 3: 250K–1 million population	2.007*** (0.23)	4.798*** (1.70)	1.975** (0.50)	5.850 (5.93)
Location 4: 1 million population	0.844 (0.10)	1.637 (0.57)	0.815 (0.21)	2.936 (2.94)
Legal status: Company with non-traded shares	0.650* (0.14)	0.467** (0.12)	0.350 (0.20)	0.355 (0.21)
Legal status: Sole proprietorship	0.637* (0.13)	0.482** (0.11)	0.387 (0.22)	0.364 (0.22)
Legal status: Partnership	0.866 (0.18)	0.586* (0.14)	0.391 (0.22)	0.344 (0.20)
Legal status: Limited partnership	1.162 (0.24)	0.831 (0.20)	0.398 (0.22)	0.376 (0.22)
Legal status: Other	0.551* (0.14)	0.430** (0.12)	0.285* (0.17)	0.337 (0.21)
Firm age: 6–10 years	0.880 (0.08)	0.918 (0.08)	1.309 (0.31)	1.409 (0.36)
Firm age: 11–20 years	0.961 (0.08)	1.039 (0.09)	1.282 (0.28)	1.186 (0.28)
Firm age: above 20 years	1.212* (0.10)	1.317** (0.11)	1.539* (0.33)	1.599* (0.37)

(Contd)

Table 5.5 (Contd)

	Male		Mixed/Female	
	Model 1	**Model 2**	**Model 1**	**Model 2**
Institutional factors				
Regulation: Time spent by manager		0.981 (0.05)		0.620** (0.09)
Private ecosystem		0.775*** (0.04)		0.728* (0.10)
Credit constraint		0.954 (0.05)		0.783 (0.12)
Competition from informal units		4.802*** (1.14)		20.05*** (12.47)
Infrastructure: Power outages		1.631 (0.57)		1.605 (1.63)
Competition*Location 2		0.267*** (0.07)		0.0861*** (0.06)
Competition*Location 3		0.132*** (0.03)		0.0830*** (0.06)
Competition*Location 4		0.166*** (0.04)		0.0553*** (0.04)
Power outage*Location 2		0.731 (0.27)		0.482 (0.51)
Power outage*Location 3		0.901 (0.33)		0.713 (0.75)
Power outage*Location 4		1.481 (0.53)		0.716 (0.75)
N	**7183**	**6756**	**1234**	**1155**

Note: *Control variable industry and growth of sales per worker not reported in table.

Source: Computed by the authors from Enterprise Surveys, The World Bank (World Bank 2013).

The inclusion of the interaction variable with competition from informal enterprises reverses the result, and it is found that competition mainly in middle-sized towns in comparison to very small towns significantly inhibited innovation in male- and female-owned firms. The location interaction variable apparently removed reverse causality and helped obtain a more meaningful explanation for the impact of the external business environment on innovation in firms. That is, in medium-sized towns in particular, competition from informal firms inhibited innovativeness of formal firms.

CASE STUDIES OF WOMEN ENTREPRENEURS

This section presents two cases of women, one launching an informal and one a formal enterprise in India. The first case is of a rural tourism venture called Travel Another India (TAI). This firm is an example of an informal sector enterprise that started at home as a project by the female entrepreneur. It grew when members of the village community and support workers joined TAI as collaborative stakeholders or partners. Later, three to four people were employed informally to manage the village destinations, and the founder's sister helped design the TAI website. This is important as it highlighted the case of an informal enterprise graduating to becoming a formal, registered company. This was a unique case of how a woman entrepreneur aspired to skill people in villages to set up and run their own enterprises. It was partly inspired by the training in rural management that she received from the Institute of Rural Management, Anand (IRMA). The entrepreneur then moved on to formalise her company and set up many more such rural tourism ventures with the participation of the local population.

The second case is of a formal sector enterprise called LimeRoad. This is a professionally managed e-commerce firm that was set up by a team of three professional co-founders, including the woman entrepreneur. It is a classic case of a woman entrepreneur observing and seizing a business opportunity and growing to scale. It was registered as a private limited company and gradually scaled up to employ more than 400 workers. The company had successfully raised a series of venture capital funding to finance the venture. This case is an example of a successful woman entrepreneur in the formal sector of the economy.

CASE STUDY 7: Empowering Rural Communities through Tourism

Entrepreneur: Gouthami
Company: Travel Another India (TAI)
Industry: Rural Tourism

Gouthami hails from Chennai. She holds a postgraduate degree in Rural Management from IRMA, India. Before starting TAI, Gouthami had worked for more than 17 years in the development sector with many non-governmental organisations (NGOs) like Actionaid, Christian Aid, Kutch Mahila Vikas Sangathan (KMVS), the United Nations Development Programme (UNDP) and the Ministry of Tourism.

During her work with NGOs across India, Gouthami had often expressed her desire to undertake a rural tourism project. She wanted to work in the rural tourism sector as every travel experience across rural India had left her inspired. She felt that travelling across rural India was a beautiful experience and rural people were very hospitable. Further, there were many things to do in rural areas like exploring the natural beauty of the villages, seeing historical unexplored places, and understanding the architecture in rural areas. 'From childhood I remember travelling, either by car or by train, at least once in three months. This fascination with travel was fortunately fostered by the kind of jobs that I took up with international and national development agencies in India, East Timor, the Philippines and Bangladesh,' she shared.

Gouthami's interest in this area and work on a community tourism project in Hodka, Kutch with UNDP, Ministry of Tourism and KMVS resulted in the idea of starting her rural tourism venture. Gouthami used her own resources and started working out of her parents' home. The costs she incurred were mainly travel costs to the villages. These trips were primarily to coordinate, collaborate and train rural communities for acting as hosts for urban travellers, and to set up the entire experience with guests. Most of the communication with travellers willing to explore rural destinations was done using email and phone.

Members of the participating rural communities became her partners and earned money for working at the guest house or offering services like a special meal, selling craft items and tour guide services for urban guests.

During her entrepreneurial journey, Gouthami's alumni friends from IRMA acted as mentors. She also received formal mentoring support upon being awarded the Cartier Women's Initiative award. This helped her refine her business plan. Gouthami could not legally register the name of her company as 'Travel Another India' because it contained the word 'India' in it. Therefore, she finally registered her company as TAI Responsible Tourism Consultants Private Limited on 16 April 2009. Gouthami co-founded TAI with two friends, Vinay Raj, a senior at IRMA and childhood friend Meera Menon, a chartered accountant. It took them six months just to get an appropriate name. Both co-founders later left the venture, and Gouthami mostly managed TAI single-handedly thereafter.

Recommendations for women entrepreneurs

For a startup social enterprise, build relationships for community mobilisation: Gouthami said community mobilisation was her biggest challenge. She felt that one needs to invest in building relationships with all partners in a travel venture. She was offering a village life experience to urban customers, and her key partners were the village community that acted as hosts. She tried very hard in terms of selling and explaining her idea of rural tourism to the village community. 'Because they [villagers] need to understand, they need to get in [be a partner in business] and they need to see that there is some money happening here. They would say, "Who will come here [to a village]? Why do you think people will come here?"' she shared. She recalled that the first year was very frustrating. It was a big challenge to explain her idea to the village community and to get them on board.

Invest in training (soft skills and sensitisation): Gouthami shared that in a rural tourism venture, one needed to train and sensitise not only the rural host community but also the urban customers/guests. Both come from different cultures, and it was her responsibility to sensitise them to ensure they had an enriching experience and avoided miscommunication. For example, one guest had asked for tea at 6:45 a.m., and the guest house manager had politely said yes. But instead of 6:45 a.m., the *chai* [tea] was brought at 8 a.m. On inquiring about the delay, the guest was told that the milk used in preparing tea only arrived by around 8 a.m. When asked, 'Then why did you agree to 6:45?' the manager replied, 'We do not say no to our guests!'

Passionately believe in your social enterprise idea: Gouthami shared that one has to be mission-driven to launch a social enterprise. The objective of a social enterprise is to generate social values that would go beyond mere profits. Gouthami's education and more than a decade of work experience in the development sector motivated her to work with rural communities.

CASE STUDY 8: **Launching a Professionally Managed E-commerce Firm**

Entrepreneur: Suchi Mukherjee
Company: LimeRoad
Industry: E-commerce

Suchi Mukherjee was born in Bengal and grew up in Delhi. She graduated in economics from St. Stephen's College, Delhi University. She was awarded the British Chevening Scholarship in 1994 to pursue a Master's in Finance and Economics at the London School of Economics.

Prior to launching LimeRoad in India, Suchi had worked for more than 16 years in the UK with companies like Skype, eBay and Gumtree in different capacities. She was a member of the executive management team at Skype. Later, she became managing director and CEO of Gumtree, the UK's largest online classified business.

Suchi shared that the idea of LimeRoad was born 'out of a moment of utter frustration'. While reading a magazine in London, she saw a piece of jewellery that she wanted to buy. But it was not feasible because it was from a store in Mumbai and one had to physically travel to Mumbai to purchase it. She reflected on this thought and realised two things: 'There was no existing consumer technology that made it possible to discover products in an easy and entertaining manner, like reading a magazine and buying a product if one likes and, more importantly, there was no existing platform that could enable global access to a variety of products manufactured in India.' To address this opportunity, Suchi launched LimeRoad as an e-commerce firm offering products from all across India.

Suchi co-founded LimeRoad with Prashant Mallik and Ankush Mehra. The legal name of the company was A.M. Marketplaces Private Limited and 'LimeRoad' was the brand name. They took the help of legal and finance professionals to incorporate the venture. It was a professionally managed firm, with a board of directors. LimeRoad was launched with funding support from investors and had secured many rounds of funding. Tiger Global Management, Lightspeed Venture Partners and Matrix Partners India were some of the investors.

Suchi believed that family, household help, friends and board members act as critical support systems/network for a woman entrepreneur. This support network she felt was different from a mentor network.

Recommendations for women entrepreneurs

Convince your family first: Suchi's major challenge was convincing her parents, especially her mother. When she got to know that Suchi was planning to start her own business, Suchi recalls her mother exclaiming, '*Shorbonash!* [What a catastrophe!] And on top of that you are a woman!' Suchi was an academically bright child, and her parents felt that 'Bengali middle-class families do not necessarily go into business...one does a regular job, does secure things'.

Solve a real-world problem with passion: Suchi believed that the important challenge was to address a real-world problem. Suchi was very passionate about what she wanted to do and considered

LimeRoad as her third child. She said, 'You have to be passionate, and to know that you are super passionate, you need to be very sure that what you are planning to build is really solving somebody's problem.' She felt that 'Most people forget to ask: what problem would the company be solving? Why does it need to exist? Is the world any different because the company exists?'

Build a support network: Suchi's core thesis is that a woman entrepreneur does not need a social network; what she needs is a support network, and that a business mentor is not a part of that network. In this support network, according to her there are five key players of utmost importance.

Suchi's first support network was her husband. She feels that most women tend to underestimate the importance of having a supportive spouse. Her second support network was the house-help. Suchi shares that she would not have been able to focus on her work without the help of her housekeeper, who assisted in managing her house and looking after her two children (a little baby and a five-year-old). She strongly felt that a woman needs the critical support system of house-helps to manage both work and home responsibilities together. Her third support network was parents. Suchi recommended that a woman entrepreneur with small children should select a house that was in close proximity to either parents' or parent-in-laws' homes. She said her only concern while searching for a house was: 'whether she was 10 minutes away from her parents or from her in-laws' home, and that if all hell breaks loose...they can come and take over her house'. This was not something that books or people will advocate, she added, but she felt that as a woman, 'that's the only thing that matters in house selection'.

The first set of board members was Suchi's fourth support network. Distinguishing between a board member and a mentor, she explained that a board member was someone with whom one could have a heart-to-heart conversation and challenge each other's beliefs. At the same time, there should be mutual respect and space for individual decision-making. 'Most people forget that and just appoint people who are unconcerned or indifferent on the board', Suchi said, adding that this was something absolutely 'not to be done', at least when the firm was a small startup.

Invest in technology to manage processes and lower costs: Suchi strongly recommended the use of technology-enabled systems as a good business strategy. Her firm had the entire workflow automated. As far as possible, they tried to implement technology to lower operational costs.

CONCLUSION

Twenty-seven years after the introduction of economic reforms in India, we are still faced with a dualistic structure of industry. The small scale of operation of informal enterprises is a cause for concern as it inhibited economic growth in the country. However, these small enterprises can address the current concerns of boosting job creation and economic growth. In this chapter, we analysed the response of male- and female-owned firms to the external environment in both the formal and informal sector using nationally representative data.

Informal Firms

We used the latest available 2015–16, unit level data of Unincorporated Non-Agricultural Enterprises Survey, NSSO, to explore the gender differential of male and female proprietors in the informal sector. The female proprietors were more likely to be home-based and have smaller scale operations than male proprietary firms. Despite small size and scale, a quarter of women entrepreneurs in the informal sector were found to be expanding their operations. Though operating under many constraints, these women can be recognised as being entrepreneurial.

The main drivers of expansion of informal firms were the use of internet and registration under any statutory act. Another important driver of expansion of informal enterprises was having received government assistance. This highlights the importance of government support for enterprises in the informal sector to expand their business and grow to scale. All these three main drivers of expansion of informal enterprises were positive for both male and female proprietors. Though smaller in scale of operation, the responses of women owners of small informal enterprises to external incentives were similar to those of male proprietors.

The case study of TAI was of a woman entrepreneur setting up a tourism enterprise in the informal sector, at first by convincing and training villagers to run their own enterprise. This was an entrepreneur who found a business opportunity and was driven by the passion to create and solve various problems of employment and lack of entrepreneurship skills in rural areas. It has many lessons for entrepreneurship, including how to build collective enterprises and address the challenges of doing so. The model of collective enterprise was a useful model for scaling up small and tiny enterprises that are deficient in capital, skills and technology.

Formal Firms

Formal firms with women owners tended to be larger and older in this sample. While half of male-owned firms were sole proprietors, firms with women owners were more likely to be partnership and share-holding companies. It appeared that incorporation of women owners into the firm occurred at a later stage, when the firm had matured. The realities of the economic institutions affect the innovative behaviour of firms with women owners, given the characteristics of the firm and its location. Innovation in firms with female owners was inhibited by a poor regulatory environment, but male-owned firms do not report so. The perception of poor infrastructure and a poor court system inhibited innovative behaviour among all firms, irrespective of gender of ownership. Lack of support from the local private ecosystem hindered innovative behaviour among all firms. Use of an interaction term, competition from informal firms with location, showed that innovation in men- and women-owned enterprises was mainly inhibited in medium-sized towns.

The second case study of a woman entrepreneur in the formal sector suggests that policies aimed at providing better business environments also need to consider the underlying motivation of involvement in the business. As the feminist critique of the gendered entrepreneurial subject suggested (Boeri 2018), social reproduction role could be the reason for undertaking business among women-owned firms. The case study of LimeRoad highlights that provision of child-care facilities at the local level are essential to enable women enterprises to grow and should be an agenda for public policy.

Zoltan Acs and José Ernesto Amorós suggested two-fold policy strategies: 'reducing necessity-based entrepreneurship to achieve the efficiency-driven stage, and on the other hand, promoting innovative entrepreneurship to reach the innovation-driven stage' (Acs and Amorós 2008). To foster growth-oriented entrepreneurship, policy should emphasise opportunity creation, networking, skill and knowledge upgrades. A friendly regulatory environment was crucial, particularly for women-owned firms, and government assistance for informal firms. While the policy framework should be able to provide an enabling entrepreneurial ecosystem for formal enterprises, it should also promote the transition of informal enterprises from stagnancy to the expansion phase.

NOTES

[1]See http://msme.gov.in (accessed 22 June 2021).

[2]Available at: https://www.nsdcindia.org/sites/default/files/files/National-Policy-on-Skill-Development.pdf (accessed 22 June 2021).

VI

Attitudes and Perceptions of Youth towards Women Entrepreneurship

Several researchers have attempted to identify the characteristics of an entrepreneur. Following the *trait approach* to entrepreneurship, studies from the USA, Russia, Spain, Singapore and Turkey have linked personality traits like locus of control, tolerance for ambiguity, need for achievement, innovation and risk-taking propensity to entrepreneurs (Armstrong and Hird 2009; Marques et al. 2012). Prior literature also focuses on the effect of psychological factors on entrepreneurial success. Many studies report that women score differently than men on personal characteristics, such as fear of failure (Wagner 2007), risk attitudes (Caliendo et al. 2009, and 2014; Fossen 2012), self-confidence (Koellinger et al. 2013), or the willingness to compete (Bönte and Piegeler 2013). However, the reasons for the gender gap in entrepreneurship are still not fully understood.

This chapter contributes to entrepreneurship literature by considering a group of personality traits among college students that can be matched to attributes of the entrepreneur. Specifically, personality traits like self-efficacy, internal locus of control, proactiveness, autonomy, innovativeness, optimism, risk tolerance and competitiveness are considered among college-going youth in the National Capital Region (NCR) in India. A micro perspective on how the youth view entrepreneurship is examined through a first-time survey of men and women final-year students in public and private undergraduate and postgraduate institutions, including technical and non-technical courses, in the NCR. Our survey research focused on the role of individual characteristics in becoming an entrepreneur. We compute an index of the summed up scores of task-matched personality traits called the Individual Entrepreneurial Aptitude (IEA) score. Further, we use an ordered probit model to compute the relationship between the willingness to become an entrepreneur among current students and their IEA score, along with other socio-demographic variables. Our aim is to assess the attitudes and perceptions towards entrepreneurship among final year students in the NCR. We also assess gender dimensions related to entrepreneurial intentions among these students.

There is a growing number of educated unemployed youth in developing countries like India. Therefore, there is a need to assess attitudes and perceptions towards entrepreneurship among students in higher education institutions in developing countries. Addressing this need, we present an interesting perspective for examining gender differences in attitudes towards pursuing entrepreneurship among youth studying in colleges and universities.

This chapter begins with a review of literature on entrepreneurial intentions, motivations and the theory of planned behaviour. Findings from national and international studies examining entrepreneurial intentions of youth are discussed. We then present the method and results of our survey research. And lastly, we present two case studies of successful women entrepreneurs.

LITERATURE REVIEW

Entrepreneurial Intentions and the Theory of Planned Behaviour

Entrepreneurial intention is a mainstream concept in new business formation literature (Thompson 2009). In recent years, researchers have used the theory of planned behaviour (TPB) to examine the motivation to predict entrepreneurial intentions under various contexts (Malebana 2014; Fatoki 2014; Otuya et al. 2013; Fitzsimmons and Douglas 2011; Engle et al.

2010; Fatoki 2010). In this sense, an individual's entrepreneurial intention reflects his or her level of interest in starting a business (De Clercq et al. 2013; Fitzsimmons and Douglas 2011; Krueger et al. 2000) and, therefore, a subsequent positive influence in employment creation. Along these lines, TPB has been widely adopted as one of the most powerful tools to test consumers' behavioural intentions (Ajzen 2001). Icek Ajzen (2011) provides a generic definition of intention as a person's readiness to perform a given behaviour (Kautonen et al. 2013).

Ajzen's theory of planned behaviour states that a person's intent toward an activity is the best predictor of the activity occurring in future (Ajzen 1991). Ajzen explained that the underlying factors that influence a behaviour are motivational factors (ibid.). It is assumed that these motivational factors influence and shape the behavioural intention such as the individual's attitude toward the behaviour, subjective norm and perceived control. These factors are included in the TPB model.

Attitude is developed from behavioural beliefs. It is assumed that an individual with higher attitude towards the behaviour will be more likely to take action that is being monitored (Ajzen 2002). Subjective norms are an individual's perceptions of the values and beliefs of influential people including his/her family members, teachers, friends and other entrepreneurs that impact and shape that individual's desire to comply with those norms. It is believed that subjective norms can shape the formation of an individual's entrepreneurship intentions. Norris F. Krueger, Michael D. Reilly and Alan L. Carsrud report intention as the single best predictor of planned behaviour (Krueger et al. 2000). Further studies have also shown that personal attitudes and perceived behaviour positively influence the student's intention to choose entrepreneurship as a career (Maes et al. 2014; Mumtaz et al. 2012; Altinay et al. 2012).

Motivation to Become Entrepreneur

The motivation for entrepreneurship is seemingly complex and involves the dynamic interaction of a number of factors

(Edelman et al. 2010). It is the core of biological, cognitive and social regulation (Ryan and Deci 2000). Studies have shown that attitudes toward behaviour, subjective norms and perceived behavioural control significantly increase the likelihood of students reporting the formation of entrepreneurial intentions. This indicates that social norm is a strong and consistent predictor of intentions to become an entrepreneur (Engle et al. 2010). Further, Ng Kim-Soon et al. argue that we need to first identify youths who are really serious about starting and owning a business as would-be entrepreneurs (Kim-Soon et al. 2013), and then target these youth to develop entrepreneurial skills through government entrepreneurship interventions. Another study suggests that policy-makers and educators should consider the factors influencing desirability of self-employment to energise the intention towards self-employment (Ummah 2009). *Global Entrepreneurship Monitor* reports (GEM 2003; 2004) indicate that for the general population, the choice of an entrepreneurial career is dictated more by push (or necessity) than pull (or opportunity) factors.

Role of Entrepreneurship Education

Entrepreneurship education can create a capacity for imagination, flexibility, creativity, willingness to think conceptually, and the art of seeing change as an opportunity. This should ideally be in addition to the basic skills of starting and managing a business (Timmons and Spinelli 2004).

Entrepreneurship education using formal courses is likely to be correlated to entrepreneurial intentions. This is due to three possible reasons. First, entrepreneurship education helps students learn and identify new business opportunities. Such knowledge enhances the number and innovativeness of opportunities that are linked with technology (Shepherd and De Tienne 2005). Students who learn and acquire entrepreneurial skills and competencies are likely to develop new venture ideas (Krueger et al. 2000; Zhao et al. 2005). Second, there is a positive association between social desirability and entrepreneurship career intention (Tkachev and Kolvereid 1999). Third, through entrepreneurship courses, one can acquire knowledge on starting a new business in a better and faster way (Zhao et al. 2005).

Hessel Oosterbeek, Mirjam van Praag and Auke Ijsselstein (Oosterbeek et al. 2010) reported a negative impact of entrepreneurship education on entrepreneurship intentions. They find the impact of entrepreneurship education on entrepreneurial skills and traits significantly zero or negative. They suggest that such results may be because of students acquiring 'realistic perspectives' about themselves through entrepreneurship education. In other words, students learnt what was required to be an entrepreneur, and assessed themselves accordingly. Georg von Graevenitz, Dietmar Harhoff and Richard Weber found the effect of entrepreneurship education on entrepreneurial intentions decreasing to a certain extent (Graevenitz et al. 2010). However, they report that entrepreneurship education had a significantly positive impact on students' entrepreneurial skills.

Empirical Evidence from National and International Studies

Lars Kolvereid and Øystein Moen (1997), and Sizong Wu and Wu Lingfei (2008) revealed that there is disparity in entrepreneurial intention of students from different disciplines. Further, they illustrate that the time anticipated to start a firm is longer for those studying science and/or technical disciplines than those studying humanities. According to Gulruh Gurbuz and Sinem Aykol, the determinants of entrepreneurial intention among educated youth in Turkey are gender, entrepreneurial parents, subjective norms, perceived behavioural control, attitudes, favourable environmental conditions, and academic support (Gurbuz and Aykol 2008). Their studies used 324 respondents among third- and fourth-year students from the departments of economics, administrative sciences and engineering at a state university in Istanbul.

Zahariah Mohd. Zain, Amalina Mohd. Akram and Erlane K. Ghani studied Malaysian undergraduate business students in a public university using survey research (Zain et al. 2010). They had a sample of 230 respondents selected through systematic sampling. Their study revealed that graduating students had a greater desire to pursue entrepreneurship. The graduating students were also influenced by entrepreneurial courses taken, family members who were entrepreneurs and academics in business-related disciplines. Zain et al.'s findings reveal that personality traits influence intention (ibid). In other words, how a person thinks and behaves influences their decision to become an entrepreneur. Akhtar Ali, Keith J. Topping and Riaz H. Tariq explored entrepreneurial attributes among students of the Islamic University of Bahawalpur, a public sector university in Pakistan, using multistage sampling of 521 graduate students (Ali et al. 2010). Their results indicate that self-efficacy, efficiency, commitment, and entrepreneurial inclinations are entrepreneurial attributes. Most of the respondents in their study showed positive entrepreneurial attributes (ibid.). Further, they found that demographic variables like gender, parental income and profession do not affect entrepreneurial attributes significantly.

Yeboah A. Samuel, Kumi Ernest and Jacob B. Awuah explored motivators and obstacles to entrepreneurial intentions among students of polytechnic marketing in Ghana (Samuel et al. 2013). They found that demographic variables such as gender, age, religion and parents' work sector affect student response related to entrepreneurial intentions. There was significant difference between genders and in the access to means of overcoming obstacles to become entrepreneurs, such as lack of collateral security and lack of opportunities in the market. There were significant gender differences in terms of reasons to choose entrepreneurship, such as prestige and status.

Chalchissa Amentie and Emnet Negash compared attitudes and perceptions of students towards entrepreneurship development in public and private universities in Ethiopia (Amentie and Negash 2014). They report that female undergraduate students had different attitudes towards self-employment because different factors influence women's decision to start their own small business. Family plays an important role in female entrepreneurship. Families in Ethiopia do not encourage female students to start their own businesses. Female students in both public and private university colleges expressed the need for more entrepreneurship education. They also found that students in public universities who expressed their desire to start a business were not different from female students studying in private universities who also wanted to start their own small business.

In the Indian context, Narendra C. Bhandari investigated entrepreneurial intentions of Indian students (Bhandari 2006). A 62-item questionnaire was administered to first-year students of the faculty of commerce and management studies at Jai Narain Vyas University, Jodhpur. Bhandari found that luck and 'to lead other people' were significant factors related to starting one's own business. Further, he found that to lead other people, to 'be my own boss', to 'put my innovative ideas into practice', determination and personal challenge had significant influence on the decision to start a business.

S. A. Vasantha Kumara and C. Sahasranam (Kumara and Sahasranam 2008a, 2008b, 2009) found no significant influence of demographics on the intentions to become entrepreneurs among engineering as well as business students. Kumara and Y. Vijaya Kumar examined entrepreneurial competencies among engineering students from Visvesvarayya Technological University, Karnataka (Kumara and Kumar 2010). They found negligible demographic influence on students' soft skills. Self-employment intentions among the students surveyed did not match well with their entrepreneurial competencies. This suggests that it should be possible to train many students, regardless of background, for an entrepreneurial career.

Hem Chandra Kothari examined various factors shaping entrepreneurial intentions of students using a sample of 880 graduating final-year students in conventional and professional courses from different colleges in Uttarakhand (Kothari 2013). This study found that female respondents were less inclined to choose an entrepreneurial career than male respondents. Further, types of education (professional and traditional) and educational streams (science, commerce, arts etc.) were not significantly associated with entrepreneurial career intentions. This suggests that the students with professional education do not have the motivation to become an entrepreneur. Students with moderate academic performance are more likely to opt for an entrepreneurial career than students with good or bad academic performance. Father's occupation was reported as a significant factor and students with entrepreneurial family backgrounds were more enthusiastic about pursuing an entrepreneurial career.

Nimitha Aboobaker studied intentions of entrepreneurship among postgraduate management and non-management students in Kerala (Aboobaker 2015). The study found that management students possessed higher intention of pursuing entrepreneurship as compared to students from the arts and science streams. The study emphasised the importance of building and sustaining social relationships. Thus, the social capital of potential entrepreneurs, such as the social network provided by extended family, community, or organisational relationships complements the effects of education, experience and financial capital. Further, having parents, close friends or neighbours in business and encouragement from friends and family was strongly associated with the probability of becoming an entrepreneur.

SURVEY OF YOUTH STUDYING IN HIGHER EDUCATIONAL INSTITUTIONS IN NCR, INDIA

Methodology

We designed a survey to assess the gender dimensions related to entrepreneurial intentions among a total sample of 940 final-year students from 28 higher education institutions in the NCR. These included students studying both technical and non-technical courses in public and private educational institutions.

The survey design and pilot survey was conducted in 2017. Based on the findings of the pilot survey, we designed and conducted the final survey data and undertook our analysis in 2017–18.

Research Model and Scales

We computed an IEA score to study the relation between personality traits and who wants to become an entrepreneur based on prior study/studies on IEA scores (Bönte and Jarosch 2011). The items of the IEA score were autonomy, general self-efficacy, innovativeness, internal locus of control, optimism, proactiveness, and risk tolerance (Appendix Table 6A.1). All these items were measured on a five-point Likert-type scale, with 5 being 'strongly agree' and 1 being 'strongly disagree'. The index was computed as the unweighted sum of scores of all indicators, as all items are positively directed; the higher the summed score, the higher the IEA. This IEA-Index ranged between the value 8 at minimum and 40 at maximum. We divided the IEA scores into four categories: 8–20, 21–25, 26–30 and 30–40.

The strengths of motivation and obstacle variables were also measured using a five-point Likert-type scale. Mean score and factor analysis was used to identify the motivations and obstacle factors to becoming entrepreneurs. A higher mean score indicated greater importance. Cronbach's Alpha was used to check the reliability of the instrument used for the study. A widely acceptable criteria is that Alpha is 0.7 or higher (Nunnally 1978; Streiner 2003). In our study, the Cronbach's Alpha was within 0.84 to 0.93 ranges, which suggests high reliability of the instrument. A factor analysis was conducted to group the motivations and obstacles variables. Keiser-Meyer-Olkin measure of sampling adequacy was 0.675 and Bartlett's test of Sphericity was significant at 1 per cent, which showed that factor analysis was appropriate for the data. Factors were determined based on Eigen values via principal component factor analysis with vari max rotation. In addition, a summated scale or score for each factor, which was the average of variables included in that factor, was generated to find out which factor has greater effect on entrepreneurship.

To investigate the determinants of willingness to become entrepreneurs, we used an ordered probit model. Willingness to become an entrepreneur is an ordered multinomial variable with three values:

0 = I am not interested in taking up entrepreneurship as a career option.
1 = I am interested in taking up entrepreneurship as a career option but I do not have any business idea.
2 = I am interested in taking up entrepreneurship as a career option and I do have the business idea.

Thus, the more developed a person's business idea, the higher is the value of the variable 'willingness'. However, we do not consider the variable to be metric but only rank-ordered, which means we will use ordered probit regression (Wooldridge 2003). Ordered probit can be used when the choice is between more than two options, but the options are ordered. Probabilities of choices are linked to areas under probability distribution functions. Further, we need to identify the cutoff points to define the areas determining probability of making each choice. However, in ordered probit model, coefficient of the variable has no direct interpretation; it only gives the significance and sign of relation between dependent and independent variables.

Let y be an ordered response taking on the values {0; 1; 2; :::; J}: We derive the ordered probit from a latent variable model.

$$y^* = \beta_1 x_1 + \beta_2 x_2 + \beta_k x_k + \epsilon,$$

Where, ϵ is a normally distributed variable with the variance normalised to one.

In this model, y^* is the unobserved latent variable, and there are cutoffs α_1 and α_2 that determine what we observe:

Here y takes three values: 0, 1 or 2. We then have

$$\begin{aligned} y &= 0 \text{ if } x'\beta + \epsilon \leq \alpha_1 \\ &= 1 \text{ if } \alpha_1 < x'\beta + \epsilon \leq \alpha_2 \\ &= 2 \text{ if } \alpha_2 < x'\beta + \epsilon \end{aligned}$$

Estimation is done by maximum likelihood. The latent variable y^* can be interpreted as a single propensity measure of willingness to become an entrepreneur. The cutoff points (threshold parameters) are estimated to help match the probabilities associated with each discrete outcome.

RESULTS OF THE SURVEY RESEARCH STUDY

Demographics of the Sample

Our sample consisted of a total of 940 respondents, 504 males and 436 females. Of 570 respondents from public institutions, 336 were male and 234 female. Of 370 respondents from private institutions, 168 were males and 202 were females. Out of the total sample, 268 were pursuing technical courses and 672 were pursuing non-technical courses. Out of the 268 who were pursuing technical courses, 114 were male and 154 were female. Out of 672 respondents pursuing non-technical courses, 390 were male and 282 were female. Among our respondents, 578 were in final year of graduation and 362 were pursuing postgraduation; 294 male and 284 female respondents were pursuing graduation degrees and 210 male and 152 female were pursuing postgraduation degrees.

The majority of the respondents were in the age group 18–23 years (65 per cent). Some were pursuing higher education after having some work experience. About 25 per cent were in the age group of 24–30 years, followed by 10 per cent in the age group of 30–35 years. A majority of the respondents were from the 'others' or forward castes (76.2 per cent), followed by Scheduled Tribes (ST) (12.4 per cent) and Scheduled Castes (SC) (10.4 per cent). Only 2 per cent of the respondents were from Other Backward Classes (OBC).

To understand the relationship between attitudes and perceptions of women entrepreneurship with family background, we collected information on the education and occupation of the respondent's father. Fathers of a majority of respondents had graduate degrees (43.4 per cent), followed by postgraduate degrees (26.7 per cent). Only 11 per cent of the fathers of respondents had a professional degree. Fathers of a majority of respondents had their own business (38.2 per cent) followed by government jobs (34.5 per cent) and private jobs (18.4 per cent; see Appendix Table 6A.2).

More than one-third of the respondents came from affluent families with monthly income of more than 1 lakh Indian rupees (INR). About 33 per cent of respondents had family monthly income between Rs 50,000 to 1 lakh. Nearly 12 per cent reported monthly income being less than Rs 25,000. The rest 19 per cent had monthly income of Rs 25,000–50,000 (Table 6A.3)

Career Plan

In our sample, more than half of the respondents aspired for a salaried job after completion of their present education. However, the percentage of students aspiring for a salaried job was higher for men than for women (55.4 per cent and 46.1 per cent respectively). Further, aspiration for a salaried job was higher among the postgraduate respondents as compared to the graduate respondents (78.55 per cent and 34.25 per cent respectively). We found that interest to continue with further studies was higher for female and graduate respondents (Figure 6.1).

Only 5.3 per cent of respondents wanted to pursue entrepreneurship immediately after completion of their present education (Figure 6.1), while 62 per cent wanted to consider entrepreneurship as a career option after five to ten years (Figure 6.2). Entrepreneurship as a career option among the female respondents was quite high (59 per cent). Further, inclination to be an entrepreneur was higher among respondents from private institutions as compared to respondents from public institutions (66 per cent and 58 per cent). However, there was no significant difference between graduate and postgraduate students in their inclination to be an entrepreneur.

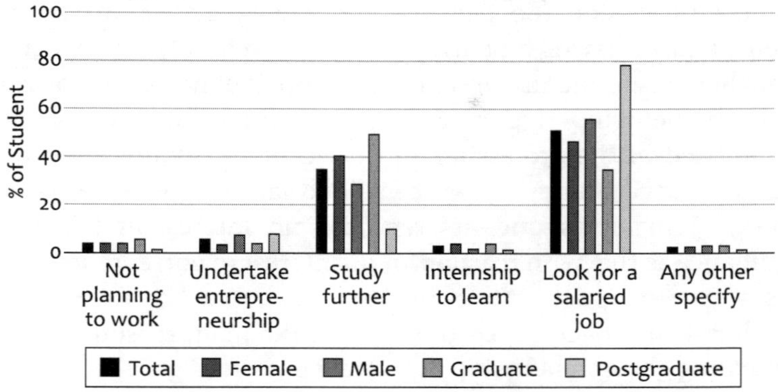

FIGURE 6.1: Career work planning (in percentage)

Source: Based on primary data collected by authors

Respondents in technical courses were less likely to report inclination to be an entrepreneur compared to respondents from non-technical courses. A possible explanation is that persons with technical degrees were more likely to find jobs since their employability was greater. Hence, they were less inclined to pursue entrepreneurship.

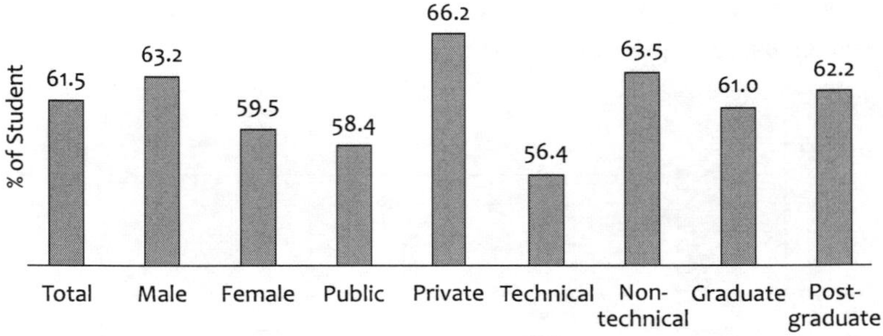

FIGURE 6.2: Entrepreneurship as a career option after five to ten years (in percentage)

Source: Based on primary data collected by authors

Respondents reported that the main reason for their interest in entrepreneurship as a career option (Figure 6.3) was dynamics of the profession (60 per cent), monetary attraction (20 per cent) and/or having an entrepreneur in the family (15 per cent). Further, respondents who reported no inclination to pursue entrepreneurship (Figure 6.4) mainly cited reasons like 'not interested in the profession' (40 per cent), risky (20 per cent), requires seed money (17 per cent) and lack of guidance (15 per cent). Female respondents reported no interest and lack of guidance as the main reasons for disinterest in entrepreneurship as a career option. Male respondents reported no interest, high risk and need for seed money as the main reasons for not pursuing entrepreneurship as a career option (Figure 6.5).

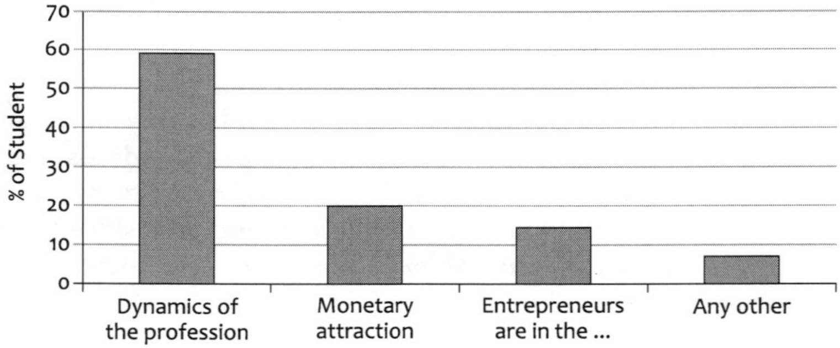

FIGURE 6.3: Reasons for interest in entrepreneurship as a career option
Source: Based on primary data collected by authors

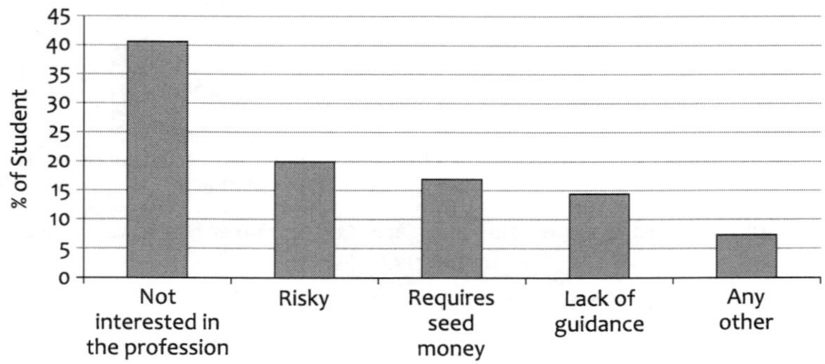

FIGURE 6.4: Reasons for disinterest in entrepreneurship as a career option
Source: Based on primary data collected by authors

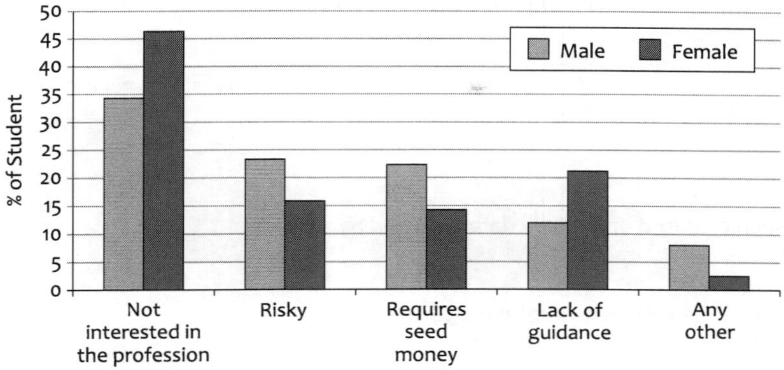

FIGURE 6.5: Reasons for disinterest in entrepreneurship as a career option, by gender

Source: Based on primary data collected by authors

TABLE 6.1: Source of motivation to pursue entrepreneurship, by gender (percentage)

Source of motivation	Male	Female	Total
Self	59.2	56.4	60.4
Family member	16.0	25.6	18.0
Professor/teacher/education counsellor	14.4	9.0	7.7
Relatives/friends	5.6	9.0	10.4
Any other (specify)	4.8	0	3.5

Source: Based on primary data collected by authors

About 60 per cent of respondents wanted to pursue entrepreneurship as a profession due to self-motivation. One-fourth of female respondents reported that they wanted to pursue entrepreneurship as a family member encouraged to them to do so (Table 6.1). Both male (68.8 per cent) and female (73.4 per cent) respondents from families with an entrepreneur were more inclined to pursue entrepreneurship (Table 6.2)

TABLE 6.2: Entrepreneurship as a career option by family background (percentage)

Respondents inclined to pursue entrepreneurship	Entrepreneurs in family	Entrepreneurs not in family
Male	68.83	60.88
Female	73.45	46.23

Source: Based on primary data collected by authors

Entrepreneurship-related Courses

Only 29 per cent of respondents stated that their institutes offered separate courses on entrepreneurship. About 82 per cent reported that their institute invited speakers and entrepreneurs from industries; however, female students (69 per cent) were less likely to participate in entrepreneurship-related events compared to male students (78 per cent). About 78 per cent of respondents reported that their institute encouraged extracurricular activities related to entrepreneurship. Only 9 per cent of respondents had undertaken any course or training on entrepreneurship in their own institute or outside. However, 69 per cent expressed their willingness to pursue entrepreneurship-related education in future (Appendix Table 6A.4). Existence of entrepreneurship courses in colleges provides awareness and encourages students to pursue entrepreneurship as a career.

We conducted informal interviews with 24 faculty members from 28 participating institutions who were either in charge of entrepreneurship-related courses or the entrepreneurship cell. We found that students organised most of the entrepreneurial activities. In some institutions, there was an entrepreneurship cell and a business incubation centre. However, entrepreneurial-related activities occurred only when students themselves took the initiative. Also, there was no regular activity or formal coursework on entrepreneurship in these institutions. The institution's role was primarily to facilitate student interest in entrepreneurship through funding or support in organising events. Some of the institutes felt that there was a need to undertake formal initiatives for promoting entrepreneurship among the students as there were few concrete activities within the institutions.

Individual Entrepreneurial Aptitude (IEA)

We found that respondents who wanted to be entrepreneurs had high IEA scores (61.79 per cent had score 30–40) compared to those who did not want to be entrepreneurs (57.26 per cent had score 30–40). This suggests that IEA score can be considered a plausible predictor of a respondent's interest in entrepreneurship (Table 6.3).

TABLE 6.3: Choice of entrepreneurship as a career option by IEA score

	IEA score 8–20	IEA Score 21–25	IEA score 26–30	IEA score 30–40
Want entrepreneurship as a career (%)	3.82	11.93	22.46	61.79
Don't want entrepreneurship as a career (%)	4.36	12.46	25.92	57.26

Source: Based on primary data collected by authors

Distribution of IEA score illustrates that a majority of individuals had an IEA score ranging from 30 to 40 (Figure 6.6).

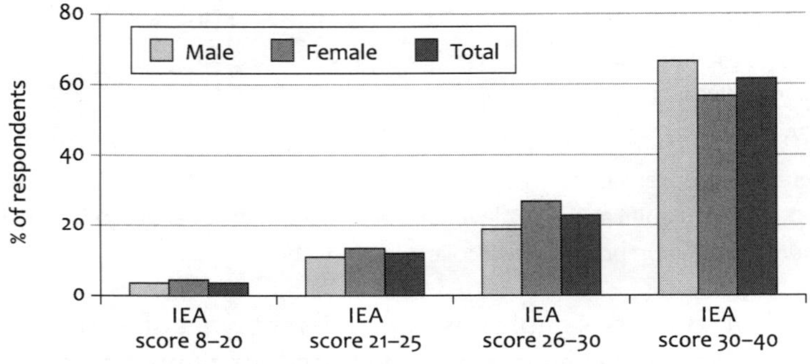

FIGURE 6.6: Distribution of IEA score by gender

Source: Based on primary data collected by authors

Only a small fraction of individuals in our sample belonged to the group of lowest scores (IEA score of 8 to 20). The average IEA score of women respondents was lower than the average for men. Compared to men, women were overrepresented in the lower IEA score categories and underrepresented in the higher IEA score categories. In other words, young women in our survey sample had relatively lower inclination to become entrepreneurs.

We examined whether the gender differences in task matched with personality traits. Gender-specific average scores were computed for each of the eight personality traits and the average scores of IEA. IEA components mean scores for female respondents were lower than that of male respondents, except in proactiveness. The gender mean difference was highest for internal versus external locus of control and lowest for autonomy (Table 6.4). Overall, the IEA scores did not show significant differences by gender. However, female students felt less in control of their life choices as compared to male students.

TABLE 6.4: Mean difference in IEA components, by gender

IEA components	Male	Female	Mean difference
Risk-taker	3.79	3.70	0.13**
General self-efficacy	3.83	3.7	0.13**
Internal vs. external locus of control	3.90	3.70	0.19***
Proactiveness	3.53	3.65	-0.12*
Autonomy	3.76	3.65	0.10**
Innovativeness	3.74	3.60	0.14**
General optimism	4.00	3.89	0.11*
Competitiveness	3.92	3.80	0.12**
IEA	30.53	29.68	0.85*

Note: Difference: mean (male)–mean (female), Test H0: difference in means=0
***1% level of significance, **5% level of significance, *10% level of significance
Source: Based on primary data collected by authors

Our students' sample was from different types of institutions and disciplines. Therefore, we also tested for significant gender differences in task-matched personality traits by type of institution (public or private), and by type of discipline (technical or non-technical). IEA scores were more or less the same in private institutions, while women had lower overall scores in public institutions (Appendix Table 6A.5). Gender differences in public institutions were observed for internal versus external control, being a risk-taker, general optimism, competitiveness and innovativeness. Here, the male students had higher scores than the female students. But in private colleges, there was very little significant gender difference. Two significant gender differentials were noted in private institutions: female students had higher mean scores for proactiveness and competitiveness. A plausible explanation could be that most students in private institutions come from upper-class/high-income families, where usually girls were equally encouraged and motivated as boys, unlike students in public institutions who came from lower income families.

Gender difference in IEA score was significant for technical and non-technical courses, with female students having lower scores (Appendix Table 6A.6). However, in terms of personality traits, only two were significantly different, namely control over life and innovativeness, where male students had higher scores. In the non-technical colleges, seven out of the eight variables were significantly different, with female students having lower scores. A possible explanation could be that premier technical institutions in India usually enroll the brightest students through a highly selective admission process. As a result, both male and female students who clear the selection process are inherently motivated and very hardworking. Therefore, the gender variation in personality traits is low.

We also computed average scores for each personality trait at graduate and postgraduate levels to see whether there was any significant difference in the task-matched personality traits. For each personality trait, respondents at postgraduate level had a higher mean score than respondents at graduate level. As a result, overall average IEA score at the postgraduate level was higher than at the graduate level (Appendix Table 6A.7).

Motivations and Obstacle Factors

Motivations: We found that important motivations for youth to start entrepreneurship were to create something innovative, focus on technology of interests and to satisfy a need in the market (Table 6.5). Among the less important factors were entrepreneurial family culture, job creation and gaining social status. However, there was a gender difference in mean score for motivation factors. For male respondents, the mean score was high for 'focus on a technology that interests them', followed by 'satisfies a need in a market' and 'create something innovative'. However, for female respondents, the mean score was high for 'have more free time', followed by 'have more flexibility', 'independence' and 'create something innovative'.

TABLE 6.5: Mean score for motivation

	Male	Female	Total
Focus on a technology that interests you	4.24 (0.97)	3.91 (0.84)	4.08 (0.92)
Satisfy a need in a market	4.11 (0.86)	3.95 (0.82)	4.03 (0.84)
Create something innovative	4.11 (0.92)	4.14 (0.81)	4.13 (0.87)
Have more flexibility and independence	3.95 (0.85)	4.15 (0.84)	4.05 (0.85)
Have more free time	3.34 (1.12)	4.36 (1.11)	3.85 (1.1)
Make more money	4.01 (0.98)	3.88 (0.92)	3.95 (0.95)
Head an organisation	3.92 (1.00)	3.76 (0.96)	3.84 (0.98)
Manage people	3.88 (0.96)	3.92 (0.86)	3.90 (0.92)
Create jobs	3.90 (1.00)	3.44 (0.82)	3.67 (1.1)
Entrepreneurial family culture	3.33 (1.16)	3.80 (1.04)	3.57 (1.02)
Gain high social status	3.76 (1.05)	3.75 (0.97)	3.76 (1.01)
To realise own dream	4.04 (0.83)	3.71 (0.82)	3.88 (0.83)

Note: ***1% level of significance, **5% level of significance, *10% level of significance; values in parenthesis are the standard deviation of the Likert score.

Source: Based on primary data collected by authors

We used factor analysis separately by gender to identify factors for motivation. Factor analysis led to four factors that account for 69.92 per cent of the cumulative variance (Appendix Tables 6A.8 and 6A.9). These factors can be interpreted as business development, independence, own success and family. The first factor referred to as 'business development' consisted of: focus on technology of interests, satisfy a need in a market, create something innovative and create jobs.

For male respondents, 'business development' was the first important factor, and explained 21 per cent of the cumulative variance. The second important factor was 'independence', which meant having more flexibility and independence, more free time, heading an organisation and managing people. 'Independence' was the second important motivational factor for male respondents, explaining 20 per cent of the cumulative variance. The third factor, 'own success', consisted of making more money, gaining high social status and realising one's dream. 'Own success' accounted for 15 per cent of cumulative variance and was the third important motivational factor for male students. Finally, 'family' was the fourth factor, which consisted of the variable entrepreneurial family, and accounted for nearly 14 per cent of the cumulative variance.

For female respondents, the most important factor was 'independence' that explained 21 per cent of the cumulative variance. The second most important factor was 'business development', which explained 18 per cent of the cumulative variance. The third most important factor was 'family', accounting for 14 per cent of the cumulative variance. The last important factor for female respondents was 'own success', accounting for 12 per cent of the cumulative variance. These four factors explained nearly 66 per cent of the cumulative variance in female respondents.

Mean score for motivational factors by gender was generated using factor analysis (Table 6.6). For male respondents, the mean score was highest for 'business development' whereas for female respondents the mean score was highest for 'independence'.

TABLE 6.6: Mean score for motivation factors by gender

Whole sample	Male	Female	T test for significance
Business development	4.09	3.92	7.45***
Independence	4.07	4.11	−6.54***
Own success	4.03	3.78	6.55***
Family	3.33	3.80	−6.54***
Who actually wants to be an entrepreneur			
Business development	4.07	4.01	0.15
Independence	3.87	3.81	0.12
Own success	4.1	4.02	0.16
Family	3.39	3.51	−0.19

Note: ***1% level of significance, **5% level of significance, *10 % level of significance

Source: Based on primary data collected by authors

When we considered the whole sample, there was a significant difference between male and female respondents in terms of the mean score for motivational factors. However, when we considered the sample of those who actually want to become an entrepreneur, there was no significant gender difference in the mean score for motivational factors. Therefore, we came to the conclusion that when the student is clear about the ambition to become an entrepreneur, gender does not matter.

Obstacles: Our study reports difficulty in obtaining bank finance, lack of business skill, lack of family support and lack of business experience as major obstacles perceived by youth for starting a business. Male respondents had higher mean scores for lack of savings, difficulty in obtaining bank finance and lack of assets for collateral. However, the mean scores for difficulty in convincing others and lack of family support were lower. For female respondents, difficulty in obtaining bank finance, lack of business skills and lack of business experience had higher mean scores, while difficulty in convincing others and unwillingness to leave a job had lower mean scores. Our results reveal that both male and female respondents perceived difficulty in obtaining

TABLE 6.7: Mean score for obstacles by gender

Obstacles	Male	Female	Total
Lack of savings	3.87	3.74	3.81
Difficulty in obtaining bank finance	3.78	4.78	4.28
Lack of assets for collateral	3.73	3.75	3.74
Lack of business skills (financial, marketing)	3.51	4.63	4.07
Do not have an idea	3.49	4.49	3.99
Lack of business experience	3.55	4.51	4.03
Lack of information on funding agencies	3.63	3.58	3.61
Ability to take risk	3.64	4.07	3.86
Future uncertainty	3.87	3.82	3.85
Lack of family support	3.59	4.48	4.04
Difficulty in convincing others that it is a good idea to carry on	2.61	2.67	2.64
Irregular income	3.69	3.61	3.65
Target market and market size	3.81	3.57	3.69
Unwillingness to leave a job	3.71	3.55	3.63

Source: Based on primary data collected by authors

bank finance as the biggest obstacle to entering entrepreneurship (Table 6.7).

Factor analysis was used to identify obstacles by gender. For male respondents, the first obstacle factor was 'finance', comprising 'lack of savings', 'difficulty in obtaining bank finance' and 'lack of assets for collateral', accounting for 31.34 per cent of the cumulative variance (Appendix Table 6A.10). The second obstacle factor was 'market and job opportunities', comprising 'irregular income', 'target market and market size', and 'unwillingness to leave a job', which explained 18.3 per cent of the cumulative variance. The third obstacle factor was 'risk', which included 'ability to take risk' and 'future uncertainty', and explained 12.1 per cent of the cumulative variance. The fourth and the fifth obstacle factors for male respondents were 'skill' and 'support', respectively. The obstacle factor 'skill' included 'lack of business skills', 'do not have an idea' and 'lack of business experience', explaining 10.1 per cent of the cumulative variance. The obstacle factor 'support' explained 9.2 per cent of the cumulative variance, and included 'lack of information for funding agencies' and 'lack of family support'. These five obstacle factors together explained 81 per cent of the cumulative variance for male respondents.

For female respondents, the most important obstacle factor was 'finance', which explained 25.3 per cent of the cumulative variance (Appendix Table 6A.11). The second most important obstacle factor was 'market and job opportunities', which explained 19.3 per cent of the cumulative variance. The third obstacle factor was 'skill', which explained 15.2 per cent of the cumulative variance. The fourth and fifth factors were 'risk' and 'support', which explained 11.2 and 8.4 per cent of the cumulative variance, respectively. These five obstacle factors together explained 79 per cent of the cumulative variance for female respondents.

Mean scores for each obstacle factor by gender were generated using factor analysis. Mean score was the highest for 'finance' and the lowest for 'support', irrespective of gender (Table 6.8). When we considered all obstacle factors together for all respondents, there was a significant difference by gender in the mean scores. However, when we considered all obstacles for only those respondents who wanted to be entrepreneurs, there was no significant gender difference in the mean score for obstacle factors. Thus, we concluded that once the student clearly aspires to become an entrepreneur, the perceptions of girls and boys about motivational factors and obstacles were similar.

TABLE 6.8: Significance of mean score for obstacles, by gender

	Male	Female	T test for significance
Finance	4.26	4.54	−3.12***
Market and job opportunities	4.15	4.08	3.15***
Risk	4.11	3.99	3.56***
Skill	3.52	4.03	−4.03***
Support	3.78	3.80	−3.56***

(Contd)

Table 6.8 (Contd)

Who wants to be an entrepreneur			
Finance	3.81	3.79	0.14
Market and job opportunities	3.69	3.67	0.14
Risk	3.67	3.60	0.34
Skill	3.62	3.64	0.32
Support	3.47	3.57	0.16

Note: ***1% level of significance, **5% level of significance, *10% level of significance

Source: Based on primary data collected by authors

Problems and Awareness

We explored the problems faced by women entrepreneurs as perceived by female as well as male respondents. We found 'family obligation' was perceived as the most important problem, followed by prevailing perceptions relating to individual abilities. Of the female respondents, 11 per cent perceived lack of adequate guidance as an important problem faced by women entrepreneurs (Table 6.9). We also examined reasons why young women were not being inspired to become entrepreneurs (Table 6.10). Young men felt that women preferred a salaried job, had less knowledge about starting a business and faced an environment that was non-conducive to becoming an entrepreneur. Young women reported 'lack of training', 'no idea about business' and

TABLE 6.9: Problems faced by women entrepreneurs as perceived by young male and female respondents (percentage)

Problems	Male	Female	Total
Family obligations	76.33	67.78	72.39
Prevailing perceptions relating to abilities	10.91	17.18	13.86
Lack of adequate guidance	7.41	11.22	9.20
Lack of monetary support	4.73	2.63	3.67
Any other	0.62	1.19	0.88

Source: Based on primary data collected by authors

non-conducive environment for women as the major challenges faced in starting a business.

TABLE 6.10: Reasons for women not pursuing entrepreneurship as perceived by young male and female respondents (percentage)

Reasons	Male	Female	Total
No idea about business	29.11	26.58	27.91
Preference for salaried job	29.58	18.99	24.93
Non-conducive environment for women to be in business	22.07	24.69	23.31
Lack of training	15.96	25.94	20.33
Any other	3.29	3.80	3.52

Source: Based on primary data collected by authors

In our survey we also asked young students how they thought the government could provide support to prospective women entrepreneurs. Young men and women felt that the government can support awareness-generation programmes on profitable business opportunities, set up institutions that can help tap innovative ideas of women students, and provide low-cost skill-training programmes for women entrepreneurship (Table 6.11). Both men and women felt the need for specialised training programmes for women interested in pursuing entrepreneurship

TABLE 6.11: Provision of government support for prospective women entrepreneurs (percentage)

Government support	Male	Female	Total
Awareness generation programmes on profitable business opportunities	42.58	45.74	44.09
Low-cost training programmes for developing entrepreneurial skills	19.92	16.30	18.07
Easier access to credit facility	15.68	11.44	13.75
Set up institutions/organisations to help tap innovative ideas of women students	21.61	24.82	23.18
Any other	0.21	1.7	0.91

Source: Based on primary data collected by authors

as a career, mentoring by professionals and separate courses in educational institutions to develop entrepreneurial skills among women students (Table 6.12).

TABLE 6.12: Educational institute support for entrepreneurial skill development in women (percentage)

Entrepreneurial skills	Male	Female	Total
Separate courses	23.56	21.19	22.38
Separate subjects within existing curriculum	14.58	10.33	12.46
Professional guidance on subject	24.37	24.21	24.29
Special training programmes for those who want to pursue it as a career	37.49	43.23	40.36
Any other (specify)	0	1.04	0.51

Source: Based on primary data collected by authors

Willingness to become Entrepreneurs

We used an ordered probit model to assess what factors affect willingness to become a woman entrepreneur. In Model 1, the dependent variable was willingness to become an entrepreneur and independent variables were age of the respondent, education and occupation of the respondent's father, monthly income of the respondent's household, respondent's current institute type, type of courses and degree being pursued by respondent, whether the institute had any separate courses for entrepreneurship, whether any family members were entrepreneurs, and IEA score (Table 6.13a). Model 2 had the same dependent variables and independent variable, but instead of the IEA score, we included eight items of IEA score, i.e., risk-taker, general self-efficacy, internal versus external locus of control, proactiveness, autonomy, innovativeness, general optimism and competitiveness (Table 6.13b).

The result from our models confirms that the willingness to become an entrepreneur depends on many factors, and that gender differentials exist (Table 6.13a and Table 6.13b). We used age and age square as a proxy for experience and as control variables to examine its impact on the willingness to become entrepreneurs. We found that willingness to become an entrepreneur rose with age in both models. Further, affluence and high household monthly per capita income level had a significant positive impact on willingness to become entrepreneur irrespective of gender, with lower significance for female respondents. Youth from lower middle-income households showed no association to respondent's willingness to become entrepreneurs and those from upper middle-income households showed a definite negative association. Household level income had an impact on the monetary resources that a household could contribute to entrepreneurial startups (Gentry and Hubbard 2004).

For male respondents, having a father with postgraduate and professional degrees tended to increase the willingness to become an entrepreneur. For female students, a father with only a professional degree increased willingness to become an entrepreneur. The father's occupation also affected the willingness to pursue entrepreneurship. The father's occupation as a business owner generally influenced willingness to become an entrepreneur for both male and female respondents. In general, for female respondents, entrepreneurs in the family mostly increased the willingness to become entrepreneurs. Studying in private institutions and non-technical courses tended to increase willingness to become an entrepreneur for female respondents. If the educational institute had separate courses on entrepreneurship, this influenced the willingness to become an entrepreneur with a higher level of significance for female students. The IEA score had a positive effect on willingness. Among the IEA variables, willingness to become an entrepreneur was positively significant for being a risk-taker, general self-efficacy, internal versus external locus of control, proactiveness, autonomy, innovativeness, general optimism and competitiveness. The effect of proactiveness and competitiveness was more significant for female students as compared to male.

TABLE 6.13A: Who wants to be an entrepreneur?

	Whole sample	Male	Female
Household monthly family income (Rs)			
25,000–50,000	0.11	0.12	0.09
50,000–75,000	0.28	0.34	0.19
75,000–1 lakh	−0.53***	−0.63***	−0.43***
Above 1 lakh	0.56***	0.86***	0.1 6*
Father's education			
12th standard	−0.29	−0.29	−0.29
Graduate	−0.08	−0.07	−0.04
Postgraduate	0.13*	0.24*	0.05
Professional	0.60*	0.50*	0.70**
Father's occupation			
Private job	0.19**	0.29**	0.39*
Business	0.15***	0.45***	0.35***
Retired and others	−0.57**	−0.37**	−0.67**
Age	0.14**	0.18**	0.20**
Age2	−0.002	−0.003	−0.004
Entrepreneurs in the family	0.16**	0.18**	0.26***
Pursuing postgraduation degree	0.14*	0.17**	0.08
Studying in private institutions	0.12*	0.12	0.19***
Pursuing non-technical courses	0.06*	0.06	0.07**
Institute has separate courses on entrepreneurship	0.11**	0.15**	0.21***
IEA score	0.57***	0.52***	0.63***
α_1	3.78		
α_2	5.02		

Note: ***1% level of significance, **5% level of significance, *10% level of significance

Source: Based on primary data collected by authors

TABLE 6.13B: Who wants to be an entrepreneur?

	Whole sample	Male	Female
Household monthly family income (Rs)			
25,000–50,000	0.21	0.19	0.18
50,000–75,000	0.29	0.33	0.23
75,000–1 lakh	−0.58***	−0.64***	−0.48***
Above 1 lakh	0.59***	0.85 **	0.1 8*
Father's education			
12th standard	−0.28	−0.25	−0.27
Graduate	−0.04	−0.06	−0.07
Postgraduate	0.12*	0.27*	0.04
Professional	0.62*	0.46*	0.80**
Father's occupation			
Private job	0.18**	0.28**	0.38*
Business	0.16***	0.47***	0.37***
Retired and others	−0.62**	−0.39**	−0.64**
Age	0.12**	0.19**	0.21**
Age2	−0.004	−0.005	−0.003
Entrepreneurs in the family	0.18**	0.19**	0.29***
Pursuing postgraduation degree	0.16*	0.16**	0.09
Studying in private institutions	0.16*	0.13	0.18***
Pursuing non-technical courses	0.04*	0.04	0.07**
Institute has separate courses on entrepreneurship	0.15**	0.17**	0.24***
Risk-taker	0.16***	0.21**	0.19*
General self-efficacy	0.11**	0.13**	0.07
Internal vs. external locus of control	0.08*	0.11*	0.09
Proactiveness	0.09**	0.10*	0.13***
Autonomy	0.19**	0.14**	0.21
Innovativeness	0.25**	0.30**	0.20*
General optimism	0.32**	0.35**	0.27**
Competitiveness	0.21**	0.25**	0.29***
α_1	2.79		
α_2	4.09		

Note: ***1% level of significance, **5% level of significance, *10% level of significance

Source: Based on primary data collected by authors

DISCUSSION OF THE FINDINGS

In this chapter, we attempted to identify factors that were likely to motivate youth in higher education institutions to pursue entrepreneurship. While the existence of a gender gap in entrepreneurship was widely documented in the literature, the knowledge on determinants of this gender gap was limited. External factors like business environment, access to finance or work-family conflicts contributed to the gender gap (Klapper and Parker 2010). To develop a better understanding of why the gender gap exists and how appropriate entrepreneurship policy measures can be designed, it is pertinent to examine the contribution of individual level factors.

The previous chapter focused on external factors, like business environment, to explain the gender gap in entrepreneurship. In contrast, our survey research highlighted the role of individual behavioural traits using an IEA score among students. The results of our empirical analysis based on data obtained from a survey of 940 students enrolled across 28 higher education institutions in India's NCR provide relevant findings that enhance our understanding of the gender gap in entrepreneurship.

We found that most students expressed interest in entrepreneurship as a career option. However, only 5 per cent expressed their intention to pursue entrepreneurship immediately after completing their college education. This number increased to nearly 60 per cent when the students were given a larger time horizon and asked whether they desire to become an entrepreneur sometime later in life, for instance, in the next five to ten years. The percentage of male students inclined to pursue entrepreneurship was slightly higher compared to female students. Students in technical colleges were less inclined to pursue entrepreneurship compared to those in non-technical colleges (Kolvereid and Moen 1997; Wu S. and Wu L. 2008).

Our survey results extended the knowledge from prior literature on women entrepreneurship. Some of our results were aligned with findings from past studies from different contexts. Similar to findings by Anat BarNir, Warren E. Watson and Holly

M. Hutchins (BarNir, Watson and Hutchins 2011), we also found that having entrepreneurial parents positively influenced both male and female students to pursue entrepreneurship. Further, we found female respondents felt more encouraged if there were entrepreneurs within the family. Similar to the findings of Amentie and Negash (2014), our survey findings revealed that women felt the need for education, support, information and training for starting a business.

We explored whether the IEA score for respondents differed by institute type, course taken, type of degree, or gender. For all IEA components, except proactiveness, we found male respondents had higher mean scores than female respondents. Overall, the IEA score for public institutes was statistically significantly higher than for private institutions. Additionally, there were gender differences within public and private institutions in terms of personality traits. Male students in public institutions were more likely to be risk-takers, have more control on life decisions, and show greater optimism, competitiveness and innovativeness. On the contrary, there was very little significant gender difference in private colleges. A plausible explanation could be that students in private colleges come from upper-class households where girls were equally encouraged and motivated.

We did not find any differences in personality traits between technical courses and non-technical courses in the overall sample, but there were gender differences within technical and non-technical courses. In most cases, gender differences for personality traits within technical courses were insignificant. However, gender differences for non-technical courses exist for components like being a risk-taker, internal versus external control, and general optimism. A possible explanation for this could be that technical institutions have selective admission processes and usually enroll the brightest students in India, irrespective of gender. Therefore, the variation in personality traits was very low. In the case of non-technical courses, there is greater diversity in the student population in terms of ability, aptitude and interest. Possibly, this was reflected in the differences in personality traits by gender. The overall average IEA score for postgraduate respondents were higher than graduate respondents. However, there was no gender difference in terms of personality traits within graduation and postgraduation levels.

Using factor analysis, we identified motivation and obstacles factors for entrepreneurship. When we considered the total sample of respondents (including those who want and do not want to pursue entrepreneurship), we found male students perceived business development as the main motivational factor for entrepreneurship, while female students perceived independence as the main motivational factor. However, when the same analysis was done for only the sample of respondents who wanted to be an entrepreneur, there was little or no difference between male and female in terms of motivational factors. This is an important result and implies that female students who clearly want to become an entrepreneur do not perceive entrepreneurship differently than male students.

Similarly, for obstructing factors, we found no difference among male and female students who wanted to become entrepreneurs. In the total sample, male respondents considered lack of support as a critical obstacle, and females reported lack of adequate skills as the main obstacle factor. Similar results were found for obstacle factors for females by Olawale Olufunso Fatoki and Lynety Chindoga (Fatoki and Chindoga 2011).

We found low awareness on entrepreneurship-related programmes in educational institutions in the NCR. Most of the institutions surveyed invite resource persons as guest speakers to inspire students to pursue entrepreneurship. The participation of male students in such programmes is relatively higher compared to female students. Most of the respondents felt the need for more entrepreneurship-related training programmes and awareness-generating programmes in their educational institutions.

We explored the determinants of willingness to become an entrepreneur using an ordered probit model. Our results suggest that income had a significant impact on willingness. However, behaviour of willingness was different in middle, upper-middle and upper-income groups. We found that respondents from lower and particularly upper-middle income households did not show willingness to become an entrepreneur, while those from upper-income households showed greater willingness. A possible explanation for this could be that respondents from upper-income households were likely to garner income (financial) support from home for starting a business, and consequently, their risk-taking ability was likely to be higher as compared to respondents from middle-income households.

Further, presence of an entrepreneur within the family increased the willingness to become an entrepreneur more in the case of female respondents as compared to male respondents. Family occupation also had an impact on entrepreneurship. In general, the presence of an entrepreneur in the family was likely to increase willingness to become an entrepreneur for both male and female respondents.

We explored whether type of educational institute and courses had an impact on a student's willingness to become an entrepreneur. We found female students studying in private institutions more inclined to become entrepreneurs as compared to female students studying in public institutions. Further, studying non-technical courses tended to increase the willingness to become an entrepreneur for female respondents. Additionally, institutes offering separate courses on entrepreneurship positively influence the willingness to become an entrepreneur for both male and female respondents.

CASE STUDIES OF WOMEN ENTREPRENEURS

In addition to the survey of youth in India's NCR, we present two case studies of women entrepreneurs who studied in higher education institutions in India and later started their own businesses. The first case is of a genomics firm called MapMyGenome from the healthcare industry. The second case is of Ampere Vehicles that manufactures electronic vehicles in India. These cases emphasise the motivation and personality traits that allowed these women entrepreneurs to overcome obstacles, follow their desire to pursue entrepreneurship and succeed as serial entrepreneurs.

In both cases, the entrepreneurs grew up in a family where education was considered important. Parents greatly encouraged and motivated them to pursue higher education. Both women entrepreneurs emphasise that education played an important role in their entrepreneurial careers. The cases reveal challenges faced by women while launching enterprises in India and offer practical implications for women aspiring to start their own businesses.

CASE STUDY 9: **From IIT to Launching a Genomics Firm**

Entrepreneur: Anu Acharya
Company: Mapmygenome India Limited
Industry: Healthcare (Genomics)

Anu Acharya was born in Bikaner to a physicist father and a homemaker mother. She spent most of her childhood in Kharagpur, where her father was a professor at the Indian Institute of Technology (IIT). She grew up in an environment that valued education, hard work, critical thinking, reasoning and debate. As a child, Anu used to spend a lot of time in her father's laboratory at IIT, which inspired her to work in the field of science and technology. In 1995, Anu graduated from IIT Kharagpur with an engineering degree. She later went to USA to obtain a Master's degree in Physics and Management Information Systems from the University of Illinois, Chicago. This education motivated her to identify an opportunity in the field and set up a business in the industry of her expertise and choice.

Prior to launching her own firm, Anu had worked in the IT and telecommunications industry. For two years (1997–99) she had worked for a telecommunications start-up called Mantiss Information. In 2000, Anu worked with a consulting firm called SEI Information where she helped create a social networking site for entrepreneurs. In 2000, she co-founded a firm called Ocimum Biosolutions with her husband and worked as the CEO till April 2013. Ocimum Biosolutions was mainly led by her husband and was headquartered in Hyderabad. It was a genomics outsourcing company that served as a solution provider in the pharma and biotechnology sector.

Two things drove Anu to start MapMyGenome. First was the rich experience that she possessed in biotechnology and genomics. She had been working in genomics since 2000, and there were very few companies that had in-depth expertise in this niche and specialised area. Next was the vision to provide 'better health for Indians using technology'. 'One in six people in this world is an Indian and yet the [health-related] data available is limited...Why should all medical data and other things be normalised against a population that is not Indian? Can't we build something here?' Anu recalled thinking at the time.

As a result, MapMyGenome was launched in January 2013 as a molecular diagnostics company that offered preventive healthcare services. Anu co-founded MapMyGenome with her husband, Subhash Lingareddy, as a private limited company. The legal name of the company is Mapmygenome India Limited. The company offers genetic tests that help people understand their genetic health profile to lead a healthier life.

On the personal front, Anu considers her parents as her first mentors. Her father was the driving force behind her success and encouraged her to follow her dreams. She admired her mother's ability to manage the entire household efficiently even with low income levels. Anu shared that 'She [mother] never made us feel that we lacked for anything. I think that's a big thing that you don't even realise when you are growing up. That's what I tell a lot of people that today kids spend a lot more [money] but they are constantly complaining. I think something that my mom did was to never make us feel that way. It was also an age where we didn't have access to television or internet.'

On the professional front, board members of MapMyGenome and previous investors acted as her mentors. Anu believes that 'we learn a little from many people...mentors are not looking at you as a CEO but they know you as a person and when they say something, you know that they are saying it for your good'.

The initial startup capital for MapMyGenome came from Anu and her husband's personal wealth. Later, in March 2015, MapMyGenome raised funding from multiple investors. Anu and her husband had prior experience of incorporating and running a startup called Ocimum Biosolutions. Therefore, they were familiar with the legal process of how to incorporate a venture in India and whom to approach for facilitating it. But incorporating their first venture, Ocimum Biosolutions, was definitely a challenge. Anu shared that things have changed in India and people are able to carry out many legal formalities digitally. Therefore, the process is much easier now compared to the complicated process that she faced for her first venture. 'The Indian [legal] system is definitely more complicated. In the US one can incorporate a company in one day. Here it is not investor-friendly. We got our trademark after our company was registered,' she said.

Recommendations for women entrepreneurs

Learn from failure: 'Even though you don't want that [failure] to ever hit you, it's always a good thing for you to experience failure. When you're in the dark, you think about things more clearly. For me, I started thinking about everything more clearly. It made me ask myself what I really wanted to do, whether it was making money, whether it was creating an impact, whether it was doing something else...,' said Anu.

Know your customer: Anu emphasised that it is critical for any startup to understand the customer well. 'If you don't get a first-hand sense of what your customers want, you won't have a good grasp of how your customers [will] behave,' she said and suggests that an entrepreneur should get involved in every aspect of their business operation to build a deeper understanding of customer behaviour.

Use humour to overcome bias against women entrepreneurs: Anu shares that there are biases against women entrepreneurs in the industry, and part of it depends on how the woman entrepreneur wants other people to view her. She recommends using humour as a tool to break the bias barrier. 'I have a sense of humour, so many times...when someone had a bias against women...humour eased the tension. Now that I have been here [in the industry] for 13 years, people think about me differently than when I was completely fresh. There are many instances when people will have biases, and it is a question of whether you want to focus on that [bias] or not, as long as your work is getting done,' she said.

CASE STUDY 10: **The First Woman Entrepreneur from Her Community**

Entrepreneur: Hemalatha Anamalai
Company: Ampere Vehicles Private Limited
Industry: Manufacturing (Automobiles)

Hemalatha Anamalai was born in Salem and grew up in Chennai, the fifth daughter in a family of six children. Both her parents are academics. Hemalatha's father worked as a professor and her mother was a teacher. Hemalatha had a humble upbringing, with no exposure to television, media or fancy gadgets. Her father was a completely self-made man, and the first graduate in their family. He greatly stressed the importance of education and hard work. As a result, she and all her siblings are double degree holders.

Hemalatha holds an engineering degree in Computer Science from Government College of Technology (GCT), Coimbatore and an MBA from Royal Melbourne Institute of Technology (RMIT), Australia. She is the first engineer in her family and also the first to study at a foreign university. In addition, Hemalatha is the only entrepreneur in her family and the only woman entrepreneur in the manufacturing sector from her community.

Prior to launching Ampere, Hemalatha worked in embedded software development and design with Wipro in Bangalore for five years. She then started working with Cayenne Software where she got the opportunity to set up a complete business channel for regional distribution in Southeast Asia, covering Singapore, Malaysia, Thailand and Philippines. She next completed an MBA degree and worked in the area of business development for an American firm in ASEAN countries. She chose Singapore as her work base, and got married to an Indian in Singapore. At the age of 27 she decided to become an entrepreneur, and launched her own venture in professional services and technology training in Singapore. In 2007, she moved back to India and launched her next firm, Ampere Vehicles.

Ampere Vehicles is Hemalatha's fifth venture. Her earlier ventures were much smaller, and largely led by her husband. The idea of producing electric vehicles originated in May 2007 when Hemalatha's husband called her from a technology conference in Japan to seek her views on the forecast of Toyota's chief technology officer (CTO): 'The need for IC [internal combustion] engine is going to go away!' The statement became a trigger for Hemalatha, and she did a lot of research on the subject. Within three months, she decided she should do something in this area as the opportunity was huge and the concept very new in India. She deliberately selected the automobile-manufacturing sector. Hemalatha felt there were three fundamental unanswered questions in the electronic vehicle manufacturing space: '(a) If China can consume 31 million electric vehicles in one year, then why not India? (b) Many villagers in India are commuting 30–40 km per day; can electric cycles be brought to Indian villages at affordable costs? And (c) Can the auto industry be democratised by smaller players which have the potential to offer disruptive technological solutions?'

Within a span of just three months, Hemalatha moved to Chennai from Singapore to launch her firm. Initially, her parents were very disappointed and felt that she was leaving a well-settled life for an uncertain future. However, they later supported her, and Hemalatha believes it was the best decision of her life. In 2009, she launched Ampere Vehicles as a private limited company with her husband Bala. Hemalatha is the founder-CEO of Ampere and holds a majority stake in the company. She named her company 'Ampere', after the French scientist who discovered electro-magnetism, as the concept was foundational to her business idea of electronic automobiles.

Hemalatha states that her parents were her first mentors and role models. During the startup phase of her firm, she sought mentoring support from one of her senior colleagues at Singapore who had studied in detail the success of electronic bikes in China. She would often discuss her ideas with him and seek his advice on the electronic vehicles industry. She also considers her husband Bala a mentor who helped her launch her business. Hemalatha was also influenced by the writings and work of late president of India, Dr. A. P. J. Abdul Kalam, and believes in his ideology of making technology reach the common man because 'then only it will serve its purpose, otherwise it will remain a white paper somewhere'.

Initially, Hemalatha and her husband put in their own seed money of Rs 5 crore to launch Ampere Vehicles. They even sold their house to generate the seed money. Her daughter was very unhappy when they sold the house and cried a lot. Later, the company raised funds from various investors over the years. Ratan Tata (chairman emeritus of Tata Sons) also supported the idea and the Tata Group invested an undisclosed amount in Ampere in July 2015.

Since Ampere Vehicles was her fifth venture, Hemalatha was familiar with the legal process of incorporating a venture. The process of incorporating a venture in India was still manual in 2008. 'The legal process is much easier now as nearly 40 per cent of the process is electronic/online. Ampere is under the category of woman-led Micro Small Medium Enterprise (MSME) and is registered with the National Small Industries Corporation (NSIC),' Hemalatha shared.

Hemalatha highlights that a woman-led company has many advantages and a woman entrepreneur can avail of government schemes. Hemalatha and Bala had done most of the paperwork for meeting the legal formalities for Ampere. She visited the District Industry Centre to meet the officer in-charge for her application status, and even reported a delay in getting the license after registering her company. She believes there are many good people working in Indian government offices, and that 'if one genuinely tries, one will get support'. She advises that, 'Instead of saying that the government is bad, one should take up the issue, solve it and move on!'

Recommendations for women entrepreneurs

Building the right team: Hemalatha said, 'The team is any venture's strength. If the team is not there, any idea can fizzle out. Once the team is there, scaling is possible'. She regards a good team the foundational block required to make a strong company. Hiring and retaining good talent are crucial. She made mistakes initially, hiring the wrong people who did not fit with Ampere's work culture. But she said with experience, such mistakes have come down drastically. 'When the wrong people are hired, one cannot even remove them abruptly because often they are senior people. So one has to be very careful in choosing the right blood to join the company,' she advised.

Being a woman leader: Hemalatha launched her company with her husband Bala. She was the key person behind the venture. However, in the early days, the staff saw Bala as the boss, and would often come up to her and ask, 'Where is Sir?' And she would reply, '*I am Sir!*' It took time, but when her work became visible, the employees gradually started accepting her as the boss at Ampere.

People are the backbone of a company: A few years ago, Ampere was facing a dire shortage of funds and there were no profits. Staff salaries were delayed by two months and Hemalatha was not even able to deposit her employees' provident fund (EPF). One night, a few weeks before Diwali, she was sitting in the factory, wondering how to give her staff Diwali bonuses and clear all the pending PF payments. She saw around 30 to 40 of her staff coming to meet her; she assumed that they were coming to demand their PF and possibly inform her that they were going to the labour court. To her surprise, they said, 'Madam, what is stopping the growth of our company? You go to the market, bring business and we will execute. You want us to work 12 hours, 24 hours...we will work for you'. Hemalatha was very moved by the support and understanding shown by her staff, who helped her company sail through the crisis.

Determination to succeed: Hemalatha feels that the lives of many people and their families depended on how well her company was doing. Therefore, it was more important to work hard with greater determination and teamwork to make the company succeed. She said, 'Sometimes the power of cosmic vibrations from employees can push one to even greater heights. People know that in the end two things are vital for any company: sales and cash flow. If sales are happening, then you manage the cash flow intelligently to be able to manage every issue. If these two things are not taken care of, any company will fail, big or small, no matter what.'

Listen to your customers: Hemalatha admitted that in the first two years of business they did not listen to their customers as much as they do now. They now regularly talked to their dealers and customers to record their ideas, observations and suggestions. She felt that knowing your customers well and listening to them are critical for any firm.

CONCLUSION

The chapter offers key insights on gender differences in attitudes and perception of youth towards entrepreneurship in India. Traditionally, India is a male-dominated society where women are more likely to be considered the weaker sex, and be socio-economically dependent on men throughout their lives. Women mostly occupy subordinate positions and execute decisions generally made by male family members (Shah 2013). This was also reflected in the lower IEA scores for women in our survey. Many male and female students in the survey expressed their desire to become entrepreneurs in future. Female respondents felt the need for more entrepreneurship training programmes, which can help improve their entrepreneurship-related skills. Further, this is likely to help close the gender gap in entrepreneurship. Largely, the case studies and survey findings presented in this chapter reveal that women in India consider higher education important and were more likely to succeed in their entrepreneurial careers with support, information and training related to starting a business. The survey and case studies offer relevant policy implications for women entrepreneurs in developing countries like India.

APPENDIX

TABLE 6A.1: Items under personality traits

Autonomy:	The possibility of being rejected by others for standing up for your decisions does not stop you from taking the decision.
General self-efficacy:	When facing difficult tasks, you are certain that you will accomplish them.
Innovativeness:	You are an inventive person who has ideas.
Internal versus external locus of control:	Your life is determined by your own actions, not by others or by chance.
Optimism:	You are optimistic about your future.
Proactiveness:	If you see something you do not like, you will change it.
Competitiveness:	You like situations in which you compete with others.
Risk-taking:	The general willingness to take risks.

Source: Authors' proposed indicators

TABLE 6A.2: Basic demographics of the sample

Age	Percentage
18–23	65.0
24–30	25.0
30–35	10.0
Caste	
SC	10.4
ST	12.4
OBC	2.0
Others	76.2
Father's education	
10th standard	5.12
12th standard	11.8
Graduate	43.4
Postgraduate	26.7
Professional	11.1

(Contd)

Table 6A.2 (Contd)

Father's occupation	
Government job	34.5
Private job	18.4
Business	38.2
Retired	3.7
Farmer	1.1
Others	4.1

Source: Based on primary data collected by authors

TABLE 6A.3: Household monthly income of respondents

Monthly income	%
Less than Rs 25,000	11.58
Rs 25,000–50,000	19.13
Rs 50,000–75,000	17.92
Rs 75,000 to 1 lakh	15.73
Above Rs 1 lakh	35.62

Source: Based on primary data collected by authors

TABLE 6A.4: Entrepreneurship-related courses and activities in college

Activities in college	**Percentage**
Institute offers separate courses/training on entrepreneurship	29
College invites people from industry to interact with students	82
College encourages extracurricular activities	78
You have pursued any course/training on entrepreneurship, from your own institute or outside	9
You wish to pursue any course/training on entrepreneurship	69

Source: Based on primary data collected by authors

TABLE 6A.5: Gender-wise mean difference in IEA score by type of institution, public–private

	Public		Mean difference	Private		Mean difference
	Male	Female	Public	Male	Female	Private
Risk-taker	3.80	3.59	0.21***	3.76	3.74	0.02
General self-efficacy	3.87	3.72	0.14	3.73	3.67	0.05
Internal vs. external locus of control)	3.96	3.73	0.22***	3.76	3.67	0.09
Proactiveness	3.59	3.73	−0.13	3.39	3.55	−0.16*
Autonomy	3.81	3.71	0.10	3.65	3.59	0.06
Innovativeness	3.76	3.60	0.16*	3.70	3.61	0.09
General optimism	4.12	3.92	0.19***	3.76	3.85	−0.92
Competitiveness	4.03	3.76	0.26***	3.68	3.84	−0.15*
IEA	31.01	29.76	1.25**	29.51	29.58	−0.06
N	336	234	–	168	202	–

Note: Difference: mean (male)–mean (female), Test Ho: difference in means = 0

***1% level of significance, **5% level of significance, *10% level of significance

Source: Based on primary data collected by authors

TABLE 6A.6: Gender-wise mean difference in IEA score by type of course, technical and non-technical

	Technical		Mean difference	Non-technical		Mean difference
	Male	Female	Technical	Male	Female	Non-technical
Risk-taker	3.78	3.72	0.06	3.79	3.63	0.16***
General self-efficacy	3.79	3.68	0.11	3.84	3.71	0.13*
Internal vs. external locus of control	3.97	3.82	0.15*	3.87	3.67	0.21***
Proactiveness	3.61	3.54	0.07	3.50	3.70	−0.20
Autonomy	3.81	3.62	0.18	3.74	3.65	0.08*
Innovativeness	3.75	3.62	0.13*	3.74	3.58	0.15*

(Contd)

Table 6A.6 (Contd)

	Technical		Mean difference	Non-technical		Mean difference
	Male	Female	Technical	Male	Female	Non-technical
General optimism	4.10	4.02	0.07	3.97	3.82	0.15***
Competitiveness	3.87	3.93	−0.06	3.92	3.72	0.19***
IEA	30.81	29.93	0.88*	30.41	29.54	0.87***
N	114	154	–	390	282	–

Note: Difference: mean (male)–mean (female), Test Ho: difference in means = 0

***1% level of significance, **5% level of significance, *10% level of significance

Source: Based on primary data collected by authors

TABLE 6A.7: Gender-wise mean difference in IEA score by graduate and postgraduate level

	Graduate		Mean difference	Postgraduate		Mean difference
	Male	Female	Graduate	Male	Female	Postgraduate
Risk-taker	3.78	3.67	0.11	3.81	3.65	0.15
General self-efficacy	3.77	3.65	0.12	3.92	3.78	0.14
Internal vs. external locus of control)	3.86	3.65	−0.21**	3.93	3.81	0.12
Proactiveness	3.46	3.58	−0.12	3.62	3.76	−0.13
Autonomy	3.69	3.58	0.11	3.84	3.73	0.12
Innovativeness	3.71	3.59	0.11	3.79	3.61	0.18
General optimism	3.94	3.82	0.12	4.08	4.05	−0.02
Competitiveness	3.80	3.81	−0.00	4.09	3.77	0.31***
IEA	30.09	29.34	0.74	31.11	30.11	0.89
N	294	284	–	210	152	–

Source: Based on primary data collected by authors

TABLE 6A.8: Motivation factors for male respondents

Male	Business development	Independence	Own success	Family
Focus on a technology that interests you	0.65			
Satisfy a need in a market	0.69			
Create something innovative	0.74			
Create jobs	0.39			
Have more flexibility and independence		0.49		
Have more free time		0.41		
Head an organisation		0.62		
Manage people		0.67		
Make more money			0.45	
Gain high social status			0.39	
To realise own dream			0.44	
Entrepreneurial family				0.45
Eigen value	9.54	6.54	4.8	3.13
% of variance	20.66	20.39	15.02	13.85

Source: Based on primary data collected by authors

TABLE 6A.9: Motivation factors for female respondents

Female	Independence	Business development	Family	Own success
Have more flexibility and independence	0.68			
Have more free time	0.59			
Head an organisation	0.72			
Manage people	0.54			
Focus on a technology that interests you		0.57		
Satisfy a need in a market		0.71		
Create something innovative		0.72		
Create jobs		0.43		

(Contd)

Table 6A.9 (Contd)

Female	Independence	Business development	Family	Own success
Entrepreneurial family			0.48	
Make more money				0.62
Gain high social status				0.53
To realise own dream				0.45
Eigen value	6.54	5.54	4.3	3.45
% of variance	21.34	18.29	14.11	12.15

Source: Based on primary data collected by authors

TABLE 6A.10: Obstacle factors for male respondents

Male	Finance	Market and job opportunities	Risk	Skill	Support
Lack of savings	0.68				
Difficulty in obtaining bank finance	0.78				
Lack of assets for collateral	0.73				
Irregular income		0.57			
Target market and market size		0.48			
Unwillingness to leave a job		0.44			
Ability to take risk			0.61		
Future uncertainty			0.63		
Lack of business skills (financial, marketing)				0.61	
Do not have an idea				0.60	
Lack of business experience				0.51	
Lack of information on funding agencies					0.43
Lack of family support					0.31
% of variance	31.34	18.29	24.11	10.15	9.15

Source: Based on primary data collected by authors

TABLE 6A.11: Obstacle factors for female respondents

Female	Finance	Market and job opportunities	Skill	Risk	Support
Lack of savings	0.67				
Difficulty in obtaining bank finance	0.74				
Lack of assets for collateral	0.73				
Irregular income		0.55			
Target market and market size		0.51			
Unwillingness to leave a job		0.44			
Lack of business skills (financial, marketing)			0.57		
Do not have an idea			0.58		
Lack of business experience			0.52		
Lack of family support					0.52
Lack of information on funding agencies					0.58
Ability to take risk				0.41	
Future uncertainty				0.42	
% of variance	25.26	19.34	15.21	11.25	8.44

Source: Based on primary data collected by authors

VII

Women Entrepreneurship

Going Forward

India faces twin problems of a bulging middle class and a growing unemployed labour force which includes educated youth. While both a growing middle class and the demographic dividend of a youth population have their merits for economic growth, these classes also come with mounting aspirations. When economic growth slows down and youth aspirations of increasing incomes and high living standards are not met, it can spell political and social turmoil for the country.

Women's participation in the labour force is very low in India and even more so in urban areas. However, as education levels of women rise, their aspirations also rise. Among women in the labour force, a very large proportion is self-employed. In this book, we argued that self-employed women were entrepreneurs, but distinguished between those who were dynamic and driven by business opportunity and those driven by necessity. We also distinguished between entrepreneurs who operated in the informal and formal sectors of the economy and looked for the drivers of such entrepreneurship. We found that women owners not only in the formal sector but those in the informal sector as well could be opportunity-based entrepreneurs expanding their business.

Further, we studied the two ends of the spectrum—women students aspiring to be entrepreneurs in future and successful women entrepreneurs who had already established a business—using a unique survey in colleges in the National Capital Region and case study research, respectively. Among students, we looked for what kindles the entrepreneurial spirit. Among established women business owners who had spent more than five years in business, we studied the challenges of launching and sustaining their enterprise in India.

WHAT DID WE LEARN?

This section describes the context of entrepreneurship in India and how we locate our work in the framework derived from Shaker Zahra (2007). We proposed the need for a multidisciplinary framework and used established theory to understand entrepreneurship in India, within the context of a dualistic structure of industry and a growing middle class. We summarise the findings within this multidisciplinary framework and highlight the drivers of women entrepreneurship within each theoretical school and within the formal and informal sectors.

Multidisciplinary Framework Derived from the Literature

Early management literature on entrepreneurship was gender-neutral. It did not distinguish between male and female entrepreneurs on generic or business characteristics. It was only in the late 1970s that a separate literature on women entrepreneurship emerged. Research on women entrepreneurship as a distinct domain gathered momentum in the early 2000s. This development witnessed the emergence of professional communities, dedicated conferences and niche journals in this area. We documented and followed this journey of growth of women entrepreneurship research within the management domain. Given the large proportion of micro and small enterprises in India, we drew on the idea from the literature that entrepreneurship did not always arise in pursuit of a business opportunity. People may also opt to be an entrepreneur out of necessity.

The management view of entrepreneurship has been challenged by a more pluralist multidisciplinary perspective. We reviewed the wider literature to see whether strands of behavioural economics could help us understand how the attitude of the agent, i.e. the entrepreneur, influences the decision to undertake business. In developing countries, institutional voids were said to exist which could inhibit entrepreneurship. We reviewed the literature from the institutional economics perspective. Further, we viewed this literature and our study of entrepreneurship from a gender perspective.

Prior literature defined entrepreneurship narrowly as the creation of new economic activity, which often entails the study of a start-up, or enterprise creation in the early stage. In this book, we defined entrepreneurship more broadly to include all enterprises, mainly those that were running for over three to five years, to understand how the attitudes of the entrepreneur and the external environment impacts, helps or inhibits growth of firms.

Karl Marx and Max Weber were the early proponents of class. Marx saw class from an economic perspective as conflict between capital and labour, while Weber looked at it from a social perspective as social stratification of society based on status and power. The term 'middle class' was more recent and in general there was consensus that the middle classes were not homogenous. The global literature distinguished the middle classes as those having discretionary purchasing power, being educated and tending to be salaried. They formed a class with distinct social, cultural, political and behavioural characteristics. The middle classes were broadly defined from the economic perspective by income groups, while the sociological perspective preferred to study class from an occupational perspective.

Our Building Blocks

We agree with the idea that the middle class is a heterogeneous group. In our multidisciplinary perspective, we combined economic and social factors to analyse entrepreneurship in the middle classes. There were multiple definitions of the middle class based on income in India. We chose to use Abhijit Banerjee and Esther Duflo's definition of the 'middle class' as those earning a daily income of $2 to $10 (Banerjee and Duflo 2008). Assuming heterogeneity in the middle class, we divided this group into the lower middle ($2–$4) and upper middle ($4–$10) classes. The lower middle class constituted nearly 39 per cent, while the upper middle was about 26 per cent of India's population in 2011–12. From the social perspective, we used activity status or occupation categories of wage employment and the heterogeneity within self-employment to understand entrepreneurship.

In 2013, the Economic Census of India recorded 58.2 million enterprises, 45.5 per cent being non-agricultural enterprises. A majority of these non-agricultural enterprises were micro and small enterprise, nearly 66 per cent being self-employment or own account enterprises (OAEs) operated with only family labour. After nearly 27 years of economic reforms India has retained a dualistic structure of industry, which is considered in the analysis of entrepreneurship.

According to the NSSO, nearly half the adult women in the urban labour force were self-employed, rising by 3 percentage points between 2004–05 and 2011–12. A majority of self-employed units, irrespective of gender, were OAEs. Women independent own account workers (OAWs) rose in the upper middle and upper classes. However, in the poor and lower middle classes, the proportion of women OAWs fell and that of dependent contributing family workers rose during the period. A major class difference was noted, where upper middle-class women were perhaps taking up business opportunities, while the poor and lower middle-class women were losing their independent status in business.

More than half of the self-employed women were in the manufacturing sector, much of this being undertaken at home, perhaps as sub-contracted homeworkers. Trade was the next largest economic activity among self-employed women, with growth occurring among the upper middle class. In terms of class, a positive feature was growth of self-employed women in the real estate and business services, mainly in the upper middle and upper classes. Hence, we note a definite class difference among self-employed women, with the poor and lower middle classes engaged in home-based manufacturing and trade, while the upper middle and affluent women were venturing into real estate and business services.

Further, our case studies revealed women starting businesses across diverse industry sectors in India like manufacturing electronic vehicles, healthcare, e-commerce, social enterprises in travel and tourism, agribusiness, and sustainability-driven enterprises in solid waste management and bamboo-based construction. Clearly, the self-employed were an entrepreneurial class. While those in the poor and lower middle classes were more likely to be necessity-driven, self-employed women in the upper middle and upper classes were chasing a business opportunity.

Behavioural factors

A puzzle identified in the literature was why do a large proportion of entrepreneurs persist with low return enterprises for long periods of time? We explored the idea emanating from the management literature that entrepreneurs can be driven by necessity, and not just the pursuit of an opportunity. This puzzle was partly influenced by opportunity business from high-income households and necessity-driven entrepreneurship in the lower income classes. This puzzle of low return entrepreneurship was also explained by three behavioural traits of the agent: the entrepreneur's preference for risk-taking, overconfidence or optimism regarding the business environment, and non-pecuniary benefits like having a role model to help reduce uncertainty. The gender differential in behaviour we found was that male opportunity entrepreneurs in the top one-third income decile were most likely to prefer risk-taking. However, women entrepreneurs did fear failure and were risk averse, but undertook entrepreneurship due to necessity. The other two traits of self-confidence and non-pecuniary benefit arising from role models were observed among both male and female entrepreneurs. Thus, we use established theory from management and behavioural economics literature to arrive at a more nuanced understanding of a new phenomenon, the context of low return entrepreneurship.

Institutional factors

It is important to understand the institutional context in which entrepreneurship thrives, the dualistic structure of industry in India, which might provide differential responses to the existing institutional environment. The management literature talks of the impact of institutional voids on business creation and growth. We use the ideas from established theory in management and institutional economics to study growth and expansion of enterprises in the informal sector and innovation in firms in the formal sector within a given institutional environment.

We found that women proprietary enterprises in the informal sector were more likely to be home-based and smaller in scale of operation but being home-based did not inhibit expansion of the enterprise. The use of internet by the enterprise and registration with any statutory authority appeared to drive business opportunity. Our case studies also revealed that many women started small as sole proprietors and then later grew their businesses by adopting the private limited legal form. Further, the informal enterprises that received some form of government assistance had higher odds of expanding. This showed the importance of government support to help micro and small enterprises in the informal sector expand. Another interesting result was that among informal enterprises, there was no gender differential in all the three positive drivers of expansion of business. Thus, being relatively small in scale and largely home-based did not inhibit women-owned enterprises from expanding, particularly when provided with support.

We analysed what drives or inhibits innovative entrepreneurship by gender of ownership in the formal sector. We explored how the external economic environment influenced innovation in enterprises by gender of ownership. We found that firms with women owners were more likely to be older, larger and corporate entities. This might mean that firms with larger scale and scope were more likely to have a gender-balanced ownership in a competitive business environment. This was a distinct difference from the women-owned units in the informal sector, partly because the formal units in the sample had mixed ownership, both men and women. A major gender differential observed was that a poor regulatory environment inhibited innovation in formal firms with women-owners, but did not seem to impact firms owned by men. Perhaps men were better able to tackle the obstacles of dealing with the official regulatory systems. Lack of support from the local private ecosystem inhibited innovation in both men- and women-owned firms. Competition from informal enterprises inhibited innovation in all firms in medium-sized towns. Thus, we used ideas from established theory of institutional voids and institutional economics to study women entrepreneurship in the context of a dualistic structure of industry in India.

Aspirations of youth

For a country aspiring to be entrepreneurial, and with the government encouraging start-ups and innovation, we felt it important to explore if colleges were contributing to inculcating the entrepreneurial spirit among the youth. We surveyed male and female 940 students in 28 colleges in the NCR, covering graduate and postgraduate courses in technical and non-technical colleges, private and public institutions. We found that students from upper-class households were most likely to aspire to be entrepreneurs. Further, students from entrepreneurial families whose parents were in business were more inclined to become entrepreneurs, this being more significant among women students.

Students in public colleges were more likely to aspire to be entrepreneurs. However, the gender difference in personality traits in public colleges was larger, with male students more likely to be risk-takers, have more control on life decisions, and in general show more optimism, competitiveness and innovativeness as compared to female students. We found that gender did not matter in private colleges in terms of the aspiration to be an entrepreneur. It is likely that students in private elite colleges came from upper-class households where girls were equally motivated as boys.

Unlike public and private colleges, we found no significant gender difference in personality traits in technical courses compared to non-technical ones. Students in technical courses were generally the cream of the youth in India, and hence their motivations and aspirations were perhaps very similar. Additionally, colleges offering separate courses on entrepreneurship positively influenced willingness to become entrepreneurs, both male and female. Our youth survey also revealed that the effect of proactiveness and competitiveness was more significant for female students compared to male students. A majority of students articulated the need for some form of education and training in entrepreneurship. This was particularly so among women students.

In the sample, as a whole, we found that irrespective of whether they wanted to be entrepreneurs or not, business development stood out as the main factor motivating entrepreneurship for males, while independence figured as the main motivational factor for females. However, among those who wanted to be an entrepreneur, there was little or no gender difference in motivational factors or perceived obstacles, except that males considered support and females reported skills as more critical. Thus, women in private colleges, technical courses and with parents pursuing business, and those who were highly motivated to become an entrepreneur did not differ from men in their aspiration for entrepreneurship. Women did, however, articulate a need for training in entrepreneurship.

Established women entrepreneurs

To see the other side of the spectrum of entrepreneurship, in Chapters 2 to 6, we present case studies of established women entrepreneurs. Contrary to past literature, the 10 case studies revealed that middle-class women entrepreneurs in India were launching enterprises in sectors that have not been covered earlier in academic literature. We presented cases of women entrepreneurs who launched firms across eight different industry sectors, namely manufacturing, healthcare, e-commerce, agribusiness, construction, specialty niche products (pet industry), travel and tourism. In light of our research findings, the argument in the literature on women mainly launching small-scale, beauty parlour type of businesses did not hold true for upper and upper middle-class women entrepreneurs.

Some women entrepreneurs started by launching a proprietorship firm and later registered the business as a private limited company. This transition from a relatively informal system to a formal organisation helped to scale up the business and target new markets. Some women entrepreneurs were clear that they wanted to use the private limited legal form for their business at the onset itself. This further corroborates our observation in Chapter 5 that informal enterprises also expand.

The women entrepreneurs usually had some industry work experience before launching their own firms. Some were even serial entrepreneurs. We found that prior work experience was likely to help women entrepreneurs gain knowledge of business operations and help them build entrepreneurial careers.

Our case studies revealed that many women preferred to launch firms with their husbands as co-founders. However, we also reported three cases of women entrepreneurs who launched firms professionally with their friends or colleagues as co-founders. Financially, most of the women entrepreneurs used informal sources of finance, which was their own money or money borrowed from family or friends. This again corroborates the observation in Chapter 5 that credit was not a significant factor in expansion of informal enterprises.

Women entrepreneurs from the manufacturing or construction sectors, however, availed bank loans to buy machinery and set up their units. In two cases, women entrepreneurs sought funding from venture capitalists to scale their business. At the same time, two other women entrepreneurs shared that they preferred to stay away from the venture capitalist network due to the fear of losing control and the core essence of their business.

Our cases revealed that there was a gender bias against women entrepreneurs in industry, society and government departments. Our study noted that there was a need to design 'woman-friendly' entrepreneurial ecosystems in India. The importance of a 'social support network' was recommended as a key factor to entrepreneurial success in the case of women entrepreneurs. Overall, all cases recommended having faith in oneself and pursuing the business idea with passion as the key to launching a venture successfully. This corroborated the idea noted in Chapter 5 that self-confidence was a significant factor in expansion of enterprises. Hence, both behavioural traits of the agent and the institutional environment influenced the growth of these successful women entrepreneurs.

AND MILES TO GO IN THE FIELD OF WOMEN ENTREPRENEURSHIP

While the multidisciplinary framework adopted by us helped us understand the drivers and constraints faced by women entrepreneurs within a dualistic structure of industry better, there were many issues that we were unable to address or fully tackle in this book. In this section, we discuss some of these issues that require further probing by researchers.

Theory-building

One of the key contributions of literature on women entrepreneurship was the emphasis on the need to study both opportunity-driven and necessity-based entrepreneurship. The objective function of a woman-led enterprise may not be the conventional model of capturing a business opportunity and growing to scale. Women entrepreneurs may prefer working on a social cause on a limited scale, as noted in some of our case studies. There is a need to consider feminist theory on socialisation of girls and boys that might lead to differences in the way men and women think and grow businesses, as observed in our study of students aspiring to be entrepreneurs. A fruitful and difficult line of research to pursue is theory building on women entrepreneurship using the lenses of various disciplines.

A major contribution to the knowledge on entrepreneurship from our study is the understanding that women entrepreneurship requires the use of a multidisciplinary framework. A study purely from the angle of strategic management would not be able to bring out the various dimensions of the problem. An ideal study of women entrepreneurship should include insights from the disciplines of management, economics, psychology and gender at the very least.

A major limitation of studying women entrepreneurship is lack of a comprehensive data source on all the various aspects influencing it. The existing secondary national-level data sets do not give us a holistic picture. We have therefore used several data sources, such as the Economic Census, the Employment, Unemployment and Informal Enterprises Surveys from the NSSO, *Global Entrepreneurship Monitor* and the World Bank Enterprise Surveys to highlight the various dimensions of women entrepreneurship. We ideally require gender disaggregated data from the various disciplines of psychology, sociology and economics, on both subjective perceptions and objective factors. In this study we used, and highly recommend, mixed research (quantitative and qualitative) methods for a comprehensive and holistic understanding of women entrepreneurship.

This study does not build a theory of women entrepreneurship, but it points to the need for a multidisciplinary framework. Following Zahra, we build a broad framework for our study using established theory from the existing literature on management, behavioural economics and institutional economics (Zahra 2007) with a gender perspective, and apply this to the context of entrepreneurship in India. The context we described in detail was the existence of a large proportion of micro and small self-employment enterprises, along with large, technologically advanced enterprises. That is, the context of a dualistic structure of industry. However, due to a lack of comprehensive data, we were unable to build a unique model incorporating all disciplinary perspectives as well as both small and large enterprises. This is a major challenge for future research.

Entrepreneurship is very context-specific and women entrepreneurship even more so. While cross-country patterns of the problem provide many insights, there is a need to probe into the economic and social context which drives or inhibits women entrepreneurship in countries and regions. For example, there is probably very little literature on this issue from the Middle East and North Africa (MENA) regions where women's participation is low, as in India, and women face large social and mobility barriers. Such cross-country studies along with in-depth study of the regional barriers are potential topics for future research.

Environment and Competition

The management literature focuses on institutional voids that can inhibit entrepreneurship. Additionally, formal firms in low-income countries face challenges related to the external environment and competition from informal firms, while the latter face competition from multinational corporations with a global presence. How do women entrepreneurs deal with such competition to expand and grow their enterprise, reach new markets or find new product lines? Is innovation key to successful growth? These are questions for a larger study.

Resources and Capabilities

The strategic management literature focuses on resources and capabilities for the growth of firms. That is, besides institutional environmental challenges, small firms face constraints related to developing and acquiring resources and capabilities. Some firms overcome these challenges and grow large. However, some do not, and academic research is silent on why and how some firms grow large in low-income countries. How do women entrepreneurs garner human and physical resources to grow the enterprises? The issue of financial constraint or credit access was identified as a key issue for certain classes. How do women entrepreneurs deal with and overcome the challenge of human capital, skilled workers and access to training to improve capabilities of the existing and new workforce? While our case studies of middle-class women entrepreneurs address some of these issues, the context faced by lower middle-class women could be quite different and requires in-depth study.

Large-scale Data with Gender and Social Variables

A major part of the multidimensional nature of the problem is the social and family circumstances that influence women entrepreneurship. Women in all societies perform a social reproduction function. One of the major constraints to research on women entrepreneurship is therefore data sources on all these multidimensional aspects. In this context, research focusing on and emphasising the need for systematic large-scale national databases with basic data on gender, social, family and educational background of the entrepreneur should be a priority. Without such background information, research on women entrepreneurship is severely limited.

The NSSO provides a comprehensive database on entrepreneurship in India by gender through its Unorganised/Informal Non-Agricultural Enterprises Surveys. This source, however, only provides data on unregistered enterprises and is hence a truncated data set with respect to any meaningful analysis of entrepreneurship. The Annual Survey of Industries (ASI), India provides comprehensive data on enterprises in the organised/formal sector but does not probe the gender of the entrepreneur. Current national data sets do not allow distinction between necessity versus opportunity in line with existing literature, and we recommend that future research should study this dimension. Further, these secondary national data sets in

India do not have any variable to proxy for innovation. Further, these data sets also do not include any variable to proxy for social reproduction functions of women. Some prime aspects of entrepreneurship remain unexplored if we restrict our analysis to the existing standard national-level enterprise data sets.

STARTING TO BUILD POLICY

Women entrepreneurship today can address the current concerns of boosting job creation and economic growth. According to Darond Acemoglu and Fabrizo Zilibotti, entrepreneurs that can generate real growth and job creation can be found in the middle class (Acemoglu and Zilibotti 1997). Hence, the international literature suggests that public policy should focus on entrepreneurs who are opportunity-driven, who are innovative, who can seize an opportunity and can create jobs. Public policy needs to specifically focus on innovative approaches to skill training and building an ecosystem for women entrepreneurship development. In this book, we beg to differ and argue that necessity-based women entrepreneurs can also expand their business with necessary support from the government and the private entrepreneurial ecosystem.

Training in Entrepreneurship and Mentoring

A major issue identified by the youth in colleges was training in entrepreneurship. Students in colleges that were able to organise such courses or events were more likely to aspire to be an entrepreneur. This is a need of the hour in a country aspiring to encourage a start-up culture.

Women entrepreneurs in our case studies and the quantitative analysis studying behavioural traits of entrepreneurs noted the need for mentors and role models. There is a need to visualise how women can contact mentors and gain from mentoring. This could be part of fostering an eco-system that encourages entrepreneurship. Among the institutional factors, we noted that lack of a private eco-system in terms of local chambers of commerce or associations inhibited innovation of firms. This is an area of concern to be addressed in public policy.

Incentivised, Demand-driven Approach to Skill Training

Skill training is equally important, and we propose an incentivised, demand-driven policy approach to skill training. Some suggestions for implementing this approach are:

- Create an incentive system for skill training in technical education institutions that can find jobs in which to place their trainees and students.
- Create incentives for firms to invest in their workers' training. On-the-job training is a major method engaged by formal and informal enterprises to train their employees. The idea is to rejuvenate the old apprentice scheme of the Government of India, which was meant for the public sector, in a privatised form.
- Incentivise educational institutions and enterprises that maintain diversity of students and employees. Gender, social and economic diversity will benefit the enterprises, institutions and the country, and drive up participation rates of women.

We argue that if students and workers see the benefits of education and training, they would be willing to invest in it themselves. Further, if most enterprises see the benefits of conducting training for their employees, there will be no poaching across enterprises. The enterprises will be able to reap the benefits of their investment and be willing to undertake on-the-job training activities. Such a demand-driven incentive structure can replace the supply-driven approach to training and help to reduce the skill mismatch and improve employability of workers in small, medium and large enterprises. Of course, all this is based on the premise that there will be high economic growth which will create increasing demand for workers.

Align Policies to Promote an Ecosystem for Women Entrepreneurship Development

The key to women entrepreneurship development is to provide women with an enabling entrepreneurial ecosystem. Providing an environment and skills necessary to succeed as business leaders will help boost women entrepreneurs. To achieve this goal, the challenges faced by women entrepreneurs need to be addressed. Preeti Goyal and Vanita Yadav reported that women entrepreneurs in developing countries like India faced challenges of much greater magnitude than those faced by women in the context of developed countries (Goyal and Yadav 2014). Specifically, women in India face challenges with access to finance, socio-cultural biases, legal concerns, familial obligations, institutional voids and lack of business-related training and skills.

One may argue that some of the challenges like institutional voids and lack of skills are equally applicable to male entrepreneurs in India. We find that the complexity of all these challenges is much greater in the case of women entrepreneurs. The rich findings from our quantitative and qualitative studies presented in this book can guide policy-making on the challenges that need to be addressed to create an ecosystem of women entrepreneurship development in India. We propose a model in Figure 7.1 as a guiding tool to formulate policies for women entrepreneurship development in India. This model is based on the findings of our case studies and extends Goyal and Yadav's work on women entrepreneurship challenges (Goyal and Yadav 2014).

CONCLUSION

To conclude, there is a vast difference between women entrepreneurs in the informal sector and those in the formal sector. Female proprietors in the informal sector tend to be home-based and smaller in scale of operation than male

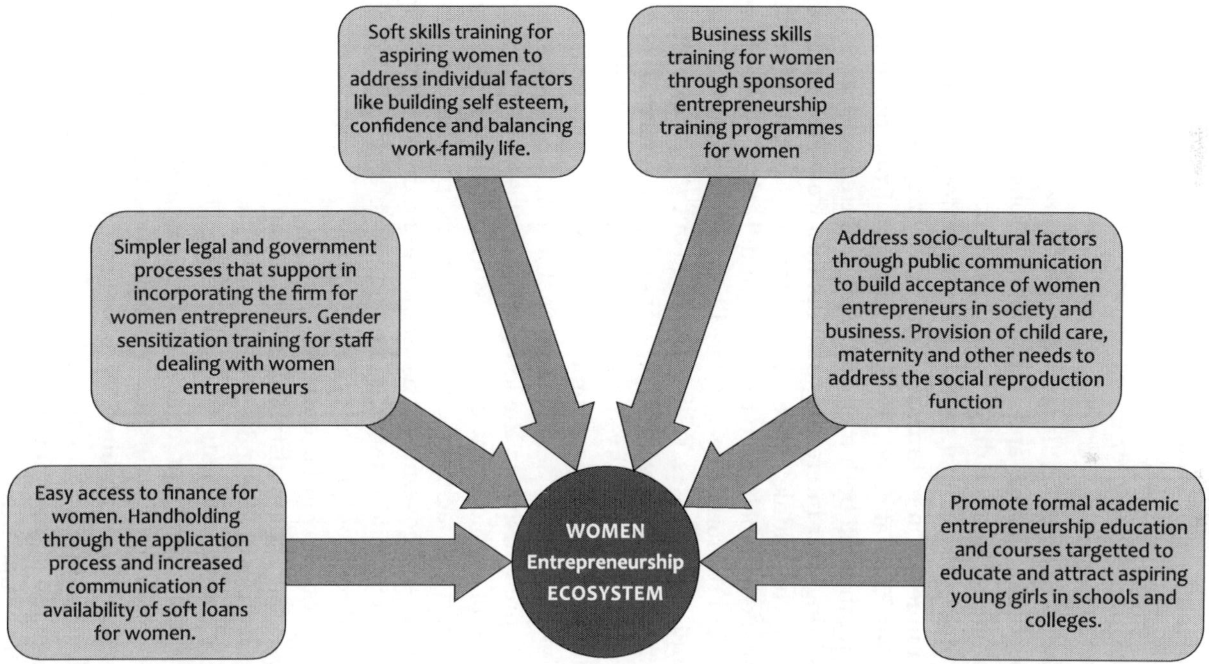

FIGURE 7.1: Policy framework for building a women entrepreneurship ecosystem in India

Source: Authors' proposed model

proprietors. However, there was no gender difference in the drivers of business expansion in the informal sector. Use of internet and registration with a statutory body and reported assistance from the government significantly helped to drive expansion of business.

In the formal sector, firms with women owners were more likely in older, larger and incorporated businesses. There were significant gender differences in the drivers of business opportunity in the formal sector. Poor regulatory environment inhibited innovation in firms with women owners, though male owners were not affected. Lack of support from the private ecosystem inhibited both men and women entrepreneurs.

This brings out interesting insights into women's entrepreneurship in the middle classes. The enterprises in the informal sector are likely to belong to the lower middle class, while those we studied in the formal sector were likely to be owned by upper middle and upper classes. While we started out with the idea that entrepreneurs in the lower middle classes in the informal sector were likely to be necessity-driven, we found that a significant proportion were also expanding their business. Given the larger proportion of enterprises in the informal sector, this is a positive sign. Entrepreneurship in the lower middle classes can be seen as a source of employment creation. With a little upgradation of infrastructure facilities, such as electricity and internet connectivity, and government assistance in credit or marketing channels, they could grow in scale and scope and help in job creation and to boost growth of the economy.

Our cases of women entrepreneurs in the upper middle and upper classes demonstrated that given an opportunity they could undertake diversified activities and grow their businesses to scale. Women students from the upper middle class and with support of entrepreneurial parents also showed higher aptitude for entrepreneurship. Women entrepreneurs in the formal sector were inhibited by poor regulatory environment and lack of support from the private ecosystem, such as the local chamber of commerce. If these impediments are taken care of and a supportive entrepreneurial ecosystem, as proposed in this chapter, is created, then women will further add to the growth of the Indian economy. Overall, our study found that women entrepreneurs in lower middle, upper middle and upper classes could become the future engines of growth of the Indian economy. The multidisciplinary framework used in this book, applying established theory to the context of the dualistic structure of Indian industry, helps to frame the debate afresh and provide the building blocks for a comprehensive theory of women entrepreneurship in future.

Bibliography

Aboobaker, Nimitha. 2015. 'Entrepreneurial Sociological Capital among Postgraduate Management and Non-Management Students in Kerala, India'. *International Journal of Advance Research in Computer Science and Management Studies* 3(7): 42–49.

Acemoglu, Darond and Zilibotti, Fabrizo. 1997. 'Was Prometheus Unbound by Chance? Risk, Diversification, and Growth'. *Journal of Political Economy* 105(4): 709–751.

Acs, Zoltan J. and Amorós, José Ernesto. 2008. 'Entrepreneurship and Competitiveness Dynamics in Latin America'. *Small Business Economics* 31(3): 305–322.

Adanali, Y. K. 2017. 'Rational Choice Theory: Its Merits and Limits in Explaining and Predicting Cultural Behavior'. *Erasmus Journal for Philosophy and Economics* 10(1): 137–141.

Agarwal, B. 2003. 'Gender and Land Rights Revisited: Exploring New Prospects via the State, Family and Market'. *Journal of Agrarian Change* 3(1–2): 184–224.

Agarwal, T. 2013. 'Vocational Education and Training Programs (VET): An Asian Perspective'. *Asia-Pacific Journal of Cooperative Education* 14(1): 15–26.

Ahl, Helene J. 2002. 'The Making of the Female Entrepreneur: A Discourse Analysis of Research Texts on Women's Entrepreneurship. *JIBS Dissertation Series* 15. Jönköping International Business School.

______. 2006. 'Why Research on Women Entrepreneurs Needs New Directions'. *Entrepreneurship Theory and Practice* 30: 595–621.

Ahl, Helene and Marlow, Susan. 2012. 'Exploring the Dynamics of Gender, Feminism and Entrepreneurship: Advancing Debate to Escape a Dead End?'. *Organization* 19(5): 543–562.

Ahl, Helene and Nelson, Teresa. 2010. 'Moving Forward: Institutional Perspectives on Gender and Entrepreneurship'. *International Journal of Gender and Entrepreneurship* 2(1): 5–9.

Ajzen, Icek. 1991. 'The Theory of Planned Behavior'. *Organizational Behavior and Human Decision Processes* 50(2): 179–211.

———. 2001. 'Nature and Operation of Attitudes'. *Annual Review of Psychology* 52(1): 27–58.

———. 2002. 'Residual Effects of Past on Later Behavior: Habituation and Reasoned Action Perspectives'. *Personality and Social Psychology Review* 6(2): 107–122.

———. 2011. 'The Theory of Planned Behaviour: Reactions and Reflections'. *Psychology & Health* 26(9): 1113–1127.

Ali, Akhtar, Topping, Keith, J. Tariq, Riaz H. 2010. 'Entrepreneurial Attributes among Postgraduate Students of a Pakistani University'. *US-China Education Review* 7(5): 66–77.

Allen E., Langowitz N. and Minniti, M. 2008. *Global Entrepreneurship Monitor* 2007, Report on Women and Entrepreneurship. The Center for Women's Leadership at Babson College, London Business School.

Allen, E., Elam, A., Langowitz, N., Dean, M. 2016. *Global Entrepreneurship Monitor* 2007, Report on Women and Entrepreneurship. Available at: https://www.gemconsortium.org/report/gem-2007-report-on-women-and-entrepreneurship-summary.

Allen, I. Elaine, Elam, Amanda, Langowitz, Nan, Dean, Monica and Global Entrepreneurship Research Association. 2008. *Global Entrepreneurship Monitor:* 2007 Report on Women and Entrepreneurship. Babson Park, Massachusetts: Babson College, London Business School.

Altinay, Levent, Madanoglu, Melih, Daniele, Roberto and Lashley, Conrad. 2012. 'The. Influence of Family Tradition and Psychological Traits on Entrepreneurial Intention'. *International Journal of Hospitality Management* 31(2): 489–499.

Amentie, Chalchissa and Negash, Emnet. 2014. 'The Study on Female Undergraduates' Attitudes and Perceptions of Entrepreneurship Development (Comparison Public and Private Universities in Ethiopia'. *International Journal of Scientific and Research Publications* 4(12): 123–139.

Anna, Alexandra L., Chandler, Gaylen N., Jansen, Erik and Mero, Neal P. 2000. 'Women Business Owners in Traditional and Non-Traditional Industries'. *Journal of Business Venturing* 15(3): 279–303.

Ardagna, S. and Lusardi, A. 2008. '*Explaining International Differences in Entrepreneurship: The Role of Individual Characteristics and Regulatory Constraints*'. Technical report, National Bureau of Economic Research.

Armstrong, Steven J. and Hird, Andrew. 2009. 'Cognitive Style and Entrepreneurial Drive of New and Mature Business Owner-Managers'. *Journal of Business and Psychology* 24(4): 419.

Arrington, Michael. 2010. 'Too Few Women in Tech? Stop Blaming the Men'. *TechCrunch* August 2010. Available at https://techcrunch.com/2010/08/28/women-in-tech-stop-blaming-me/.

Arum, Richard and Müller, Walter, eds. 2004. *The Reemergence of Self-employment: A Comparative Study of Self-employment Dynamics and Social Inequality*. Princeton: Princeton University Press.

Astebro, Thomas B., Herz, Holger, Nanda, Ramana, Weber, Roberto A. 2014. 'Seeking the Roots of Entrepreneurship: Insights from Behavioral Economics'. *The Journal of Economic Perspectives* 28(3): 49–70.

Aterido, Reyes, Hallward-Driemeier, Mary, Pagés, Carmen. 2007. 'Investment Climate and Employment Growth: The Impact of Access to Finance, Corruption and Regulations across Firms. *IZA Discussion Papers* 3138. Bonn: Institute for the Study of Labor.

Baker, Ted, Aldrich, Howard E., and Liou, Nina. 1997. 'Invisible Entrepreneurs: The Neglect of Women Business Owners by Mass Media and Scholarly Journals in the USA'. *Entrepreneurship and Regional Development* 9(3): 221–238.

Bandura, Albert. 1978. 'Reflections on Self-efficacy'. *Advances in Behaviour Research and Therapy* 1(4): 237–269.

Banerjee, Abhijit V. and Duflo, Esther. 2005. 'Growth Theory through the Lens of Development Economics'. *Handbook of Economic Growth* 1A: 473–552.

———. 2008. 'What is Middle Class About the Middle Classes Around the World?' *Journal of Economic Perspectives* 22(2): 3–28.

Bardhan, Pranab. 1999. *The Political Economy of Development in India: Expanded Edition with an Epilogue on the Political Economy of Reform in India*. Delhi: Oxford University Press India.

BarNir, Anat, Watson, Warren E. and Hutchins, Holly M. 2011. 'Mediation and Moderated Mediation in the Relationship Among Role Models, Self-Efficacy, Entrepreneurial Career Intention, and Gender'. *Journal of Applied Social Psychology* 41(2): 270–297.

Baron, R. A. and Henry, R. A. 2011. 'Entrepreneurship: The Genesis of Organizations'. In *Handbook of Industrial and Organizational Psychology 1*, pp. 241–273. Ed. S. Zedeck. Washington D.C.: American Psychological Association.

Bates T. 2002. 'Restricted Access to Markets Characterizes Women Owned Businesses'. *Journal of Business Venturing* 17: 313–324.

Bates, T., Jackson III, W. E. and Johnson Jr, J. H. 2007. 'Advancing Research on Minority Entrepreneurship'. *The Annals of the American Academy of Political and Social Science* 613(1): 10–17.

Baumol, William J. 1996. 'Entrepreneurship: Productive, Unproductive, and Destructive'. In *Journal of Business Venturing* 11(1): 3–22. Amsterdam: Elsevier.

Beinhocker, E. D., Farrell, D. and Zainulbhai, A. S. 2007. 'Tracking the growth of India's middle class'. In *McKinsey Quarterly 3*: 50.

Bhandari, Narendra C. 2006. 'Intention for Entrepreneurship Among Students in India'. *The Journal of Entrepreneurship* 15(2): 169–179.

Birdsall, Nancy. 2010. 'The (Indispensable) Middle Class in Developing Countries; or, The Rich and The Rest, Not The Poor and The Rest'. In *Equity and Growth in Globalizing World*. Eds. Ravi Kanbur and Michael Spence. Washington D.C.: The World Bank.

Birley, Sue. 1989. 'Female Entrepreneurs: Are They Really Different?'. *Journal of Small Business Management* 27: 32–37.

Blanchflower, David, Oswald, Andrew and Stutzer, Alois. 2001. 'Latent Entrepreneurship across Nations'. *European Economic Review* 45(4–6): 680–691.

Boeri, Natascia. 2018. Challenging the Gendered Entrepreneurial Subject: Gender, Development, and the Informal Economy in India. *Gender & Society* 32(2): 157–179.

Bönte, W. and M. Jarosch. 2011. 'Gender Differences in Competitiveness, Risk Tolerance, and Other Personality Traits: Do They Contribute to the Gender Gap in Entrepreneurship?' Schumpeter Discussion Papers, 2011–012, University of Wuppertal

Bönte, Werner and Piegeler, Monika. 2013. 'Gender Gap in Latent and Nascent Entrepreneurship: Driven by Competitiveness'. *Small Business Economics* 41(4): 961–987.

Bosma, N., Acs, Z., Autio, E. and Levie, J. 2009. *Global Entrepreneurship Monitor – 2008 Executive Report*, Babson College and Universidad de Desrrollo.

Boushey, Heather and Hersh, Adam. 2012. 'The American Middle Class, Income Inequality, and the Strength of Our Economy'.

Available at: https://www.americanprogress.org/issues/economy/reports/2012/05/17/11628/the-american-middle-class-income-inequality-and-the-strength-of-our-economy/ (accessed 7 September 2021).

Bowen, D. D. and Hisrich, R. D. 1986. 'The Female Entrepreneur: A Career Development Perspective'. *Academy of Management Review* 11: 393–407.

Boyd, R.L. 2005. 'Race, gender, and survival entrepreneurship in large Northern cities during the great depression'. *Journal of Socio-Economics* 34(3): 331–39.

Breman, Jan. 2013. *At Work in the Informal Economy of India: A Perspective from the Bottom Up*. New Delhi: Oxford University Press.

Bruni, Attila, Gherardi, Silvia, and Poggio, Barbara. 2004. *Gender and Entrepreneurship: An Ethnographic Approach*. New York: Routledge.

Brush Candida, G. 1992. 'Research on Women Business Owners: Past Trends, A New Perspective and Future Directions'. *Entrepreneurship Theory and Practice* 16(4): 5–30.

______. 1997. 'Women-owned Businesses: Obstacles and Opportunities'. *Journal of Developmental Entrepreneurship* 2(1): 1–24.

______. 1998. 'A Resource Perspective on Women's Entrepreneurship: Research, Relevance and Recognition'. Proceedings of the Organisation for Economic Co-operation and Development (OECD) Conference on Women Entrepreneurs in Small and Medium Sized Enterprises: A Major Force in Innovation and Job Creation (Chapter 7). Paris, France, 155–168.

Brush, Candida, G., de Bruin, Anne and Welter, Friederike. 2009. 'A Gender-aware Framework for Women's Entrepreneurship'. *International Journal of Gender and Entrepreneurship* 1(1): 8–24.

Caliendo, Marco, Fossen, Frank M. and Kritikos, Alexander S. 2009. 'Risk Attitudes of Nascent Entrepreneurs—New Evidence From an Experimentally Validated Survey'. *Small Business Economics* 32(2): 153–167.

______. 2014. 'Personality Characteristics and the Decision to Become and Stay Self-Employed'. *Small Business Economics* 42(4): 787–814.

Carter, Nancy M., Williams, Mary and Reynolds, Paul D. 1997. 'Discontinuance Among New Firms in Retail: The Influence of Initial Resources, Strategy and Gender'. *Journal of Business Venturing* 12(2): 125–145.

Carter, S. 2000. 'Gender and Enterprise'. In *Enterprise and Small Business: Principles, Practice and Policy*, pp. 168–181. Eds. Sara Carter and Dylan Jones-Evans. London: Prentice Hall.

Catley, Suzanne, Hamilton, R.T. 1998. 'Small business development and gender of owner'. *Journal of Management Development* 17(1): 75–82.

Chepurenko A. 2015. 'Entrepreneurship Theory: New Challenges and Future Prospects'. *Foresight-Russia* 9(2): 44–57.

Co, Mary Jesselyn and Mitchell, Bruce. 2006. 'Entrepreneurship education in South Africa: a nationwide survey'. *Education + Training* 48(5): 348–359, June.

Commander, Simon J. and Svejnar, Jan. 2007. 'Do Institutions, Ownership, Exporting and Competition Explain Firm Performance? Evidence from 26 Transition Countries'. *IZA Discussion Papers* 2637. Bonn: Institute for the Study of Labor.

Como, D. R. 2018. *The Rise of Religious Conflict in the Parliamentarian Coalition. Contemporary India: A Sociological View*, Chapter 6. Penguin Books.

Cooper, A. C. and K. W. Artz. 1995. 'Determinants of satisfaction for entrepreneurs'. *Journal of Business Venturing* 10(6): 439–457.

Credit Suisse. 2015. *Global Wealth Report 2015*. Available at https://www.credit-suisse.com/corporate/en/articles/news-and-expertise/global-wealth-in-2015-underlying-trends-remain-positive-201510.html. Credit Suisse.

Das, Pinaki and Das, Bhabasankar. 2017. 'Characteristics and Status of Growth of Micro Manufacturing Enterprises in West Bengal: An Analysis Based on NSSO Unit Level Data'. *Sarvekshana* 102 (1–24).

Davidsson, Per. 2006. 'Nascent Entrepreneurship: Empirical Studies and Developments'. *Foundations and Trends in Entrepreneurship* 2(1): 1–76. Available at https://papers.ssrn.com/sol3/papers.cfm?abstract_id=1629306.

Daymard, Arnaud. 2015. 'Determinants of Female Entrepreneurship in India'. OECD Economics Department Working Papers No. 1191. Organisation for Economic Co-operation and Development.

De Bruin Anne, Brush, Candida G. and Welter, Friedrike. 2006. 'Introduction to the Special Issue: Towards Building Cumulative Knowledge on Women's Entrepreneurship'. *Entrepreneurship Theory and Practice* 30(5): 585–594.

———. 2007. 'Advancing a Framework for Coherent Research on Women's Entrepreneurship'. *Entrepreneurship Theory and Practice* 31(3): 323–339.

De Clercq, Dirk, Honig, Benson and Martin, Bruce. 2013. 'The roles of learning orientation and passion for work in the formation of entrepreneurial intention'. *International Small Business Journal* 31(6): 652–676.

De Groot, Tezer Ulusay. 2001. 'Challenges Faced by Women in Industrial Development'. In *Women Entrepreneurs in Africa: Experience from Selected Countries*, Section III. Vienna: United Nations Industrial Development Organisation.

De Mel, Suresh, McKenzie, David and Woodruff, Christopher. 2008. 'Who Are the Microenterprise Owners? Evidence from Sri Lanka on Tokman v. de Soto'. IZA Discussion Paper Series No. 3511, May. Bonn: IZA Institute of Labor Economics.

Delmar, F., Holmquist, C. 2004. 'Women's entrepreneurship: issues and policies'. 2nd OECD Conference of Ministers Responsible for Small and Medium-Sized Enterprises (SMEs). Istanbul, Turkey 3–5 June 2004. Organisation for Economic Co-operation and Development.

Deshpande, Satish. 2003. 'The centrality of the middle class'. *In Contemporary India: A Sociological View*, ed. Satish Deshpande. New Delhi: Penguin Books.

Dethier, Jean-Jacques, Hirn, Maximilian and Straub, Stephane. 2011. 'Explaining Enterprise Performance in Developing Countries with Business Climate Survey Data'. *World Bank Research Observer* 26(2): 258–309.

Dhaliwal, Spinder. 2000. 'Entrepreneurship as a training process: The experiences of South Asian female entrepreneurs and women in business'. *Education + Training* 42(8): 445–452.

Döckel, J. A., and Ligthelm, A. A. 2005. 'Factors responsible for the growth of small businesses: Management'. *South African Journal of Economic and Management Sciences* 8(1): 54–62.

Dollar, David, Hallward-Driemeier, Mary and Mengistae, Taye. 2005. Investment Climate and Firm Performance in Developing Economies. *Economic Development and Cultural Change* 54(1): 1–31.

Douglas, Evan J. and Shepherd, Dean A. 2000. 'Entrepreneurship as a Utility-Maximizing Response'. *Journal of Business Venturing* 15(3): 231–251.

———. 2002. 'Self-Employment as a Career Choice: Attitudes, Entrepreneurial Intentions, and Utility Maximization'. *Entrepreneurship Theory and Practice* 26(3): 81–90.

Duflo, E. 2005. 'Gender Equality in Development'. *BREAD Policy Paper* 11(4).

Easterly, W. 1999. 'The middle class consensus and economic development'. *Journal of Economic Growth* 6(4): 317–335.

Edelman, Linda F., Brush, Candida G., Manolova, Tatiana S. and Greene, Patricia G. 2010. 'Start-up Motivations and Growth Intentions of Minority Nascent Entrepreneurs'. *Journal of Small Business Management* 48(2): 174–196.

Eisenhauer, Joseph G. 1995. 'The Entrepreneurial Decision: Economic Theory and Empirical Evidence'. *Entrepreneurship Theory and Practice* 19(4).

Engle, Robert L., Dimitriadi, Nikolay, Gavidia, Jose V., Schlaegel, Christopher, Delanoe, Servane, Alvarado, Irene, He, Xiaohong, Buame, Samuel and Wolff, Birgitta. 2010. 'Entrepreneurial intent: A twelve-country evaluation of Ajzen's model of planned behavior'. *International Journal of Entrepreneurial Behavior & Research* 16(1): 35–57.

Erikson, Robert, Goldthorpe, John H., and Portocarero, Lucienne. 1979. 'Intergenerational class mobility in three Western European societies: England, France and Sweden'. *The British Journal of Sociology* 30(4): 415–441.

Ewoh, Ethel Reuben. 2014. *Female Entrepreneurs' Performance: A Systematic Review of Forces Influencing the Performance of African Female Entrepreneurs*. Jyväskylä: University of Jyväskylä School of Business and Economics. Available at https://jyx.jyu.fi/handle/123456789/43564 (accessed 7 September 2021).

Fatoki, Olawale Olufunso and Chindoga, Lynety. 2011. 'An Investigation into the Obstacles to Youth Entrepreneurship in South Africa'. *International Business Research* 49(2): 161–169.

Fatoki, Olawale Olufunso. 2010. 'Graduate Entrepreneurial Intention in South Africa: Motivations and Obstacles'. *International Journal of Business and Management* 5(9): 87–98.

———. 2014. 'The Entrepreneurial Intention of Undergraduate Students in South Africa: The Influences of Entrepreneurship Education and Previous Work Experience'. *Mediterranean Journal of Social Sciences* 5(7): 294–297.

Field, Erica, Jayachandran, Seema and Pande, Rohini. 2010. 'Do Traditional Institutions Constrain Female Entrepreneurship? A Field Experiment on Business Training in India'. *American Economic Review* 100(2): 125–29.

Fischer, Eileen M., Reuber, A. Rebecca and Dyke, Lorraine S. 1993. 'A Theoretical Overview and Extension of Research on Sex, Gender, and Entrepreneurship'. *Journal of Business Venturing,* 8(2): 151–168.

Fitzsimmons, Jason R. and Douglas Evan J. 2011. 'Interaction between feasibility and desirability in the formation of entrepreneurial intentions'. *Journal of Business Venturing* 26(4): 431–440.

Fossen, Frank M. 2012. 'Gender Differences in Entrepreneurial Choice and Risk Aversion—A Decomposition Based on a Microeconometric Model'. *Applied Economics* 44(14): 1795–1812.

Förster, Michael. 2014. 'Income Inequality and Redistribution in the OECD Area: Trends and Driving Forces'. 2nd Queen's 2014 International Institute on Social Policy, Session I: Inequality and the middle class: The big picture, August 18–20. Organisation for Economic Co-operation and Development.

Fritsch, M. 2017. 'The theory of economic development—An inquiry into profits, capital, credit, interest, and the business cycle'. *Regional Studies* 51(4): 654–655.

Gatewood, E. J., N. M. Carter, C. G. Brush, P. G. Greene, and M. M. Hart. 2003. *Women entrepreneurs, their ventures, and the venture capital industry: An Annotated Bibliography*. Entrepreneurship and Small Business Research Institute (ESBRI).

Gelb, A., V. Ramachandran, M. K. Shah, and G. Turner. 2008. *What Matters to African Firms? The Relevance of Perceptions Data*. The World Bank.

Global Entrepreneurship Monitor (GEM). 2003. *GEM 2003 Global Report*. Babson and Kauffman Foundation. Available at: https://www.gemconsortium.org/file/open?fileId=47102 (accessed 7 September 2021).

———. 2004. *GEM 2004 Global Report.* Babson and Kauffman Foundation. Available at: https://www.gemconsortium.org/report/gem-2004-global-report (accessed 22 June 2021).

———. 2013. *Global Report*. Available at: https://www.gemconsortium.org/report/gem-2013-global-report (accessed 22 June 2021).

———. 2014. *India Report*. London: Global Entrepreneurship Research Association.

———. 2012–2013–2014. Adult Population Survey (APS), 2012, 2013 and 2014 (Pooled sample). Available at: https://www.gemconsortium.org/data/sets (accessed 22 June 2021).

Gentry, William M. and Hubbard, R. Glenn. 2004. 'Entrepreneurship and Household Saving'. *Advances in Economic Analysis & Policy* 4(1): 1053–1053.

Ghani, Ejaz, Kerr, William R. and O'Connell, Stephen D. 2012. 'What Explains Big Gender Disparities in India? Local Industrial Structures and Female Entrepreneurship'. *Policy Research Working Paper* 6228. Washington D.C.: The World Bank.

Gibb, Allan. A. 1993. 'Enterprise Culture and Education: Understanding Enterprise Education and Its Links with Small Business, Entrepreneurship and Wider Educational Goals'. *International Small Business Journal* 11(3): 11–34.

Gichuki, Castro N., Mulu-Mutuku, Milcah, and Kinuthia, Lydia N. 2014. 'Performance of women owned enterprises accessing credit from village credit and savings associations in Kenya'. *Journal of Global Entrepreneurship Research* 4(1): 1–13.

Gist, M. E. 1987. 'Self-efficacy: Implications for organizational behavior and human resource management'. *Academy of Management Review* 12(3): 472–485.

Goffee, Robert and Scase, Richard. 1985. *Women in Charge: The Experiences of Female Entrepreneurs*. London: George Allen and Unwin.

Gohmann, Stephen F. 2012. 'Institutions, Latent Entrepreneurship, and Self-Employment: An International Comparison'. *Entrepreneurship Theory and Practice* 36(2): 295–321.

Government of India (GOI) 2001. Census of India 20011: Registrar General and Census Commissioner of India, Ministry of Home Affairs, New Delhi, India.

Central Statistical Office. 2016. All India Report of Sixth Economic Census. New Delhi: Ministry of Statistics and Programme Implementation.

Goyal, Preeti and Yadav, Vanita. 2014. 'To Be or Not to Be a Woman Entrepreneur in a Developing Country?' *Psychosociological Issues in Human Resource Management* 2(2): 68–78.

Graevenitz, Georg von, Harhoff, Dietmar and Weber, Richard. 2010. 'The Effects of Entrepreneurship Education'. *Journal of Economic Behavior and Organization* 76(1): 90–112.

Grusky, D. B. and Sørensen, J. B. 1998. 'Can class analysis be salvaged?' *American Journal of Sociology* 103(5): 1187–1234.

Grusky, David B., Weeden, Kim A. and Sørensen, Jesper B. 2001. 'The case for realism in class analysis'. *Political Power and Social Theory Volume* 14: 291–305.

Guarín, Alejandro and Knorringa, Peter. 2014. 'New Middle-Class Consumers in Rising Powers: Responsible Consumption and Private Standards'. *Oxford Development Studies* 42(2): 151–171.

Gundry, Lisa K., Ben-Yoseph, Miriam and Posig, Margaret. 2002. 'Contemporary Perspectives on Women's Entrepreneurship: A Review and Strategic Recommendations'. *Journal of Enterprising Culture* 10(1): 67–86.

Gundry, Lisa K., and Welsch, Harold P. 2001. 'The ambitious entrepreneur: High growth strategies of women-owned enterprises. *Journal of Business Venturing* 16(5): 453–470.

Gurbuz, Gulruh and Aykol, Sinem. 2008. 'Entrepreneurial Intentions of Young Educated Public in Turkey'. *Journal of Global Strategic Management* 2(2): 47–55.

Hamilton, Barton H. 2000. 'Does Entrepreneurship Pay? An Empirical Analysis of the Returns to Self-Employment'. *Journal of Political Economy* 108(3): 604–631.

Haq, Mahbub ul. 2000. *Human Development in South Asia: The Gender Question*. Oxford: Oxford University Press. Available at: http://mhhdc.org/w content/themes/mhdc/reports/HDRSA%202000.pdf

Harriss-White, Barbara. 2003. *India Working: Essays on Society and Economy*. Cambridge: Cambridge University Press.

Harzing, Anne-Wil. 2016. Journal Quality List 57. Available at https://harzing.com/blog/2016/04/57th-edition-of-the-journal-quality-list-online.

Heintz, James. 2008. 'Revisiting Labour Markets: Implications for Macroeconomics and Social Protection'. *IDS Bulletin* 39(2): 11–17.

Henry, Colette, Foss, Lene and Ahl, Helene. 2016. 'Gender and Entrepreneurship Research: A Review of Methodological Approaches'. *International Small Business Journal* 34(3): 217–241.

Hill, Francis M., Leitch, Claire, and Harrison, Richard T. 2006. 'Desperately seeking finance?: The demand for finance by women-owned and -led businesses'. *Venture Capital* 8(2): 159–182.

Hisrich, R. D., and O'Brien, M. 1981. 'The woman entrepreneur as a reflection of the type of business'. In *Frontiers of Entrepreneurial Research*, pp. 54–67. Ed. K. H. Vesper. Boston, MA: Babson College.

Hisrich, R. D., and Brush, C. G. 1983. 'The woman entrepreneur: Implications of family, education, and occupation'. In J. A. Hornaday, J. A. Timmons, and K. H. Vesper (Eds.), *Frontiers of Entrepreneurship Research*—Proceedings of the Babson College Conference on Entrepreneurship, pp. 255–270. Wellesley: Babson College.

Holienka, M., Z. Jančovičová, and Z. Kovačičová. 2016. 'Drivers of women entrepreneurship in Visegrad Countries: Gem evidence'. *Procedia-Social and Behavioral Sciences* 220: 124–133.

Hotch, Janet. 2000. 'Classing the Self-Employed: New Possibilities of Power and Collectivity'. In *Class and its Others*, pp. 143–162, Eds. J. K. Gibson-Graham, Stephen A. Resnick and Richard D. Wolff. Minneapolis and Saint Paul: University of Minnesota Press.

Horn, Gideon. 2006. 'Educational Solutions to Improve the Employability of Senior High School Learners'. *South African Journal of Education* 26(1): 113–128.

Huynh, Phu and Kapsos, Steven. 2013. *Economic class and labour market inclusion: Poor and middle class workers in developing Asia and the Pacific*. Bangkok: Regional Office for Asia and the Pacific, International Labour Organisation.

Hughes, Helen and Woldekidan, Berhanu. 1994. 'The Emergence of the Middle Class in ASEAN Countries'. *ASEAN Economic Bulletin* 11(2): 150–157.

Hughes, Karen D. 2003. 'Pushed or Pulled? Women's Entry into Self-Employment and Small Business Ownership'. *Gender, Work & Organization* 10(4): 433–454.

Hughes, Karen D., Jennings, Jennifer E., Brush, Candida G., Carter, Sara, and Welter, Friederike. 2012. 'Extending Women's Entrepreneurship Research in New Directions'. *Entrepreneurship Theory and Practice* 36(3): 429–442.

Hurley A. 1991. 'Incorporating feminist theories into sociological theories of entrepreneurship'. Paper presented at the Annual Meetings of the Academy of Management, Miami, FL.

Hurst, Erik, and Pugsley, Benjamin Wild. 2011. 'What do small businesses do?' Brookings Papers on Economic Activity, 43(2), Fall. Economic Studies Program, The Brookings Institution. Cambridge: National Bureau of Economic Research.

Huynh, P., and Kapsos, S. 2013. 'Economic class and labour market inclusion: Poor and middle class workers in developing Asia and the Pacific'. Working paper. International Labour Organization.

International Labour Organization. 2006. *Vulnerability and young women entrepreneurs: A case study of Ethiopian informal economy*. Geneva: ILO.

———. 2008. *Women Entrepreneurs in Kenya (A Preliminary Report) and Factors Affecting Women Entrepreneurs in Micro and Small Enterprises in Kenya (A Primary Research Report)*. Geneva, ILO.

Indrawati, Nur Khusniyah, Salim, Ubud, Djumahir, A. Helmi Djawahir. 2015. 'Moderation Effects of Entrepreneurial Self-efficacy in Relation between Environmental Dimensions and Entrepreneurial Alertness and the Effect on Entrepreneurial Commitment'. *Procedia-Social and Behavioral Sciences* 169: 13–22.

Jennings, Jennifer. E. and Cash, Michelle Provorny. 2006. 'Women's Entrepreneurship in Canada: Progress, Puzzles and Priorities'. In *Growth-oriented Women Entrepreneurs and their Businesses: A Global Research Perspective*, pp. 53–87. Eds. Candida G. Brush, Nancy M. Carter, Elizabeth J. Gatewood, Patricia G. Greene, and Myra M. Hart. Cheltenham, UK: Edward Elgar.

Jennings, Jennifer. E. and Brush, Candida. G. 2013. 'Research on Women Entrepreneurs: Challenges to (and from) the Broader Entrepreneurship Literature?'. *The Academy of Management Annals* 7 (1): 663–715.

Jeppesen, S. 2005. 'Enhancing competitiveness and securing equitable development: Can small, micro, and medium-sized enterprises (SMEs) do the trick?'. *Development in Practice* 15(3–4): 463–474.

Kabeer, Naila. 2010. 'Women's Empowerment, Development Interventions and the Management of Information Flows'. IDS Bulletin, 17 November. Available at: https://doi.org/10.1111/j.1759-5436.2010.00188.x (accessed 7 September 2021).

Kadir, M. B. A., M. Salim, and H. Kamarudin. 2012. 'The relationship between educational support and entrepreneurial intentions in Malaysian higher learning'. *Procedia-Social and Behavioral Sciences* 69: 2164–2173.

Kalecki, Michael. 1972. 'Political Aspects of Full Employment'. In *A Critique of Economic Theory*, eds E. K. Hunt and J. G. Schwartz. Harmondsworth: Penguin.

Karides, Marina. 2010. 'Theorizing the Rise of Microenterprise Development in a Caribbean Context'. *Journal of World-Systems Research* 16(2): 192–216.

Kautonen, Teemu, Gelderen, Marco van and Tornikoski Erno T. 2013. 'Predicting Entrepreneurial Behaviour: A Test of the Theory of Planned Behaviour'. *Applied Economics* 45(6): 697–707.

Kessides, Ioannis N. 2004. *Reforming Infrastructure: Privatization, Regulation, and Competition*. Policy Research Report. Washington D.C.: The World Bank and Oxford University Press.

Khokhar, Amit Singh and Singh, Bharat. 2016. 'Status of Women Entrepreneurship in India'. In *Asian Journal of Multidisciplinary Studies* 4(5): 199–204.

Kim-Soon, Ng, Ahmad, Abd Rahman, Saberi, Abu Zar Md and Tat, Huam Hon. 2013. 'Discriminate analyses of motivators and obstacles on youth entrepreneurial intention'. *Asian Social Science* 9(17): 53.

Kirzner, Israel M. 1997. 'Entrepreneurial Discovery and the Competitive Market Process: An Austrian Approach'. *Journal of Economic Literature* 35(1): 60–85.

Klapper, Leora F.; Parker, Simon C. 2010. 'Gender and the Business Environment for New Firm Creation'. *The World Bank Research Observer* 26(2): 237–257.

Kobeissi, N. 2010. 'Gender factors and female entrepreneurship: International evidence and policy implications'. *Journal of International Entrepreneurship* 8(1): 1–35.

Koellinger, Phillipp, Minniti, Maria and C. Schade, Christine. 2013. 'Gender Differences in Entrepreneurial Propensity'. *Oxford Bulletin of Economics and Statistics* 75(2): 213–234.

Kolvereid, Lars and Moen, Øystein. 1997. 'Entrepreneurship among business graduates: does a major in entrepreneurship make a difference?' *Journal of European Industrial Training* 21(4): 154–160.

Kothari, Hem Chandra. 2013. 'Impact of Contextual Factors on Entrepreneurial Intention'. *International Journal of Engineering and Management Research* 3(6): 76–82.

Kremer, Michael, Rao, Gautam and Schilbach, Frank. 2019. 'Behavioural Development Economics', Chapter 5. In B. Douglas Bernheim, Stefano DellaVigna and David Laibson eds, *Handbook of Behavioural Economics*, Volume 2, pp. 415–417. North Holland.

Krueger Jr, Norris F., Reilly, Michael D. and Carsrud, Alan L. 2000. 'Competing Models of Entrepreneurial Intentions'. *Journal of Business Venturing* 15(5–6): 411–432.

Krishnan, Sandhya and Hatekar, Neeraj. 2017. 'Rise of the New Middle Class in India and its Changing Structure'. *Economic and Political Weekly* 52(22): 40–48.

Kumara, S. A. Vasantha and Sahasranam, C. 2008a. 'An Empirical Study on Students' Soft Skills Inventory Test: Reliability and Non-Parametric Analysis'. *IUP Journal of Soft Skills* 2(3): 35–45.

______. 2008b. 'Motivational Patterns for Entrepreneurship among Business Students: An Empirical Study'. *Review of Business and Technology Research* 1(1): 1–10.

______. 2009. 'Entrepreneurial Characteristics among Business Management Students: An Empirical Study'. *IUP Journal of Management Research* 8(6): 7.

Kumara, S. A. Vasantha and Kumar, Y. Vijaya. 2010. 'Examining Entrepreneurial Competencies and Their Relationship to Self-Employment Intentions among Engineering Students: A Case Study from India'. *Industry and Higher Education* 24(4): 269–278.

Lahiri, Ashok K. 2014. 'The Middle Class and Economic Reforms'. *Economic and Political Weekly* 49(11): 15.

Lee Siew Kim, J. and Seow Ling, Choo. 2001. 'Work-Family Conflict of Women Entrepreneurs in Singapore'. *Women in Management Review* 16(5): 204–221.

Levent, Tüzin Baycan, Masurel, Enno and Nijkamp, Peter. 2003. 'Diversity in Entrepreneurship: Ethnic and Female Roles in Urban Economic Life'. *International Journal of Social Economics* 30 (11–12): 1131–1161.

Lituchy, Terry and Reavley, Martha. 2004. 'Women Entrepreneurs: A Comparison of International Small Business Owners in Poland and the Czech Republic'. *Journal of International Entrepreneurship* 2(1/2): 61–87.

Maes, Johan, Leroy, Hannes and Sels, L. 2014. 'Gender differences in entrepreneurial intentions: A TPB multi-group analysis at factor and indicator level'. *European Management Journal* 32(5): 784–794.

Makena, Phylis, Kubaison, Simon Thiaine, Ibuathu, Charles and Njati, Ibuathu. 2014. 'Challenges facing women entrepreneurs in accessing business finance in Kenya: Case of Ruiru Township, Kiambu County'. *IOSR Journal of Business and Management* 16: 83–91.

Malebana, Justice. 2014. 'Entrepreneurial intentions of South African rural university students: A test of the theory of planned behaviour'. *Journal of Economics and Behavioral Studies* 6(2): 130–143.

Mann, Michael. 2012. *The Sources of Social Power: The Rise of Classes and Nation-States, 1760–1914*, Volume 2. Cambridge: Cambridge University Press.

Marglin, Stephen A. 1974. 'What do bosses do? The origins and functions of hierarchy in capitalist production'. *Review of Radical Political Economics* 6(2): 60–112.

Marlow, Susan and Patton, Dean. 2005. 'All Credit To Men? Entrepreneurship, Finance, and Gender'. *Entrepreneurship Theory and Practice* 29(6): 717–735.

Marques, Carla S., Ferreira, Joao J., Gomes, Daniela N. and Rodrigues, Ricardo Gouveia. 2012. 'Entrepreneurship Education: How Psychological, Demographic and Behavioural Factors Predict the Entrepreneurial Intention'. *Education + Training* 54(8/9): 657–672.

Marx, Karl. 1956[1964]. *Karl Marx Selected Writings in Sociology and Social Philosophy*, eds. T. B. Bottomore and Maximilien Rubel and Erich Fromm. McGraw-Hill Book Company.

Masters, R., and Meier, Robert D. 1988. 'Sex Differences and Risk-taking Propensity of Entrepreneurs'. *Journal of Small Business Management* 26(1): 31–35.

McClelland, D. C. 1967. *Achieving Society*, Volume 92051. Simon and Schuster.

McDonald, Seonaidh, Gan, Bee Ching, Fraser, Simon S., Oke, Adekunle and Anderson, Alastair R. 2015. 'A review of research methods in entrepreneurship 1985–2013'. *International Journal of Entrepreneurial Behavior & Research* 21(3): 291–315.

McKinsey & Company. 2007. 'Tracking the growth of India's middle class'. In *The 'Bird of Gold': The Rise of India's Consumer Market*. McKinsey Global Institute.

Mehrotra, Santosh. 2009. 'The Impact of the Economic Crisis on the Informal Sector and Poverty in East Asia'. *Global Social Policy* 9: 101–118.

Minniti, M. 2010. 'Female entrepreneurship and economic activity'. *The European Journal of Development Research* 22(3): 294–312.

Mirchandani, Kiran. 1999. 'Feminist Insight on Gendered Work: New Directions in Research on Women and Entrepreneurship'. *Gender, Work & Organization* 6(4): 224–235.

Moore, Don and Healy, Paul J. 2008. 'The Trouble With Overconfidence'. *Psychological Review* 115(2): 502–517.

Moore, Dorothy P. 1990. 'An examination of present research on the female entrepreneur-suggested research strategies for the 1990's'. *Journal of Business Ethics* 9: 275–281.

Mroczkowski, Tomasz. 1997. 'Women as Employees and Entrepreneurs in the Polish Transformation'. *Industrial Relations Journal* 28(2): 83–91.

Mulholland, K. 1996. 'Entrepreneurialism, Masculinity and the Self-Made Man'. In Collinson, D. L. and Hearn, J. eds, *Men As Managers, Managers As Men: Critical Perspectives On Men, Masculinity And Management*, pp. 123–149. London: Sage.

Mumtaz, B. A. K, Munirah, S. and Halimahton, K. 2012. 'The relationship between educational support and entrepreneurial intentions in Malaysian higher learning institutions'. *Procedia–Social and Behavioral Sciences* 69(24): 2164–2173.

National Crime Records Bureau, Ministry of Home Affairs, Government of India. http://ncrb.nic.in/ (accessed 2 May 2013).

Naudé, W. A., and Krugell, W. F. 2003. 'An inquiry into cities and their role in subnational economic growth in South Africa'. *Journal of African Economies* 12(4): 476–499.

Ndao, M., A. Hima, A. Rabiou, and J. Lama. 2004. *World Development Report 2005: A Better Investment Climate for Everyone*. The World Bank.

Niethammer, Carmen. 2013. 'Women Entrepreneurship and the Opportunity to Promote Development and Business'. In *The 2013 Brookings Blum Roundtable Policy Briefs*. Washington D.C.: The Brookings Institution.

North, D. C. 1990. *Institutions, Institutional Change and Economic Performance*. Cambridge: Cambridge University Press.

Nunnally, Jum C. 1978. *Psychometric Theory*. Hillsdale: Mcgraw Hill.

Organisation for Economic Co-operation and Development. 2002. *The Keys for Successful Women Entrepreneurs*. The OECD Bologna Process, December 2002. OECD.

Oliver, Adam. 2015. 'Nudging, Shoving, and Budging: Behavioural Economic-Informed policy'. *Public Administration* 93(3): 700–714.

Oosterbeek, Hessel, Praag, Mirjam van and Ijsselstein, Auke. 2010. 'The Impact of Entrepreneurship Education on Entrepreneurship Skills and Motivation'. *European Economic Review* 54(3): 442–454.

Ordenana, X. and E. Arteaga. 2012. 'Middle-Class Entrepreneurship and the Effect of Social Capital', IDB Working Paper Series No IDB-WP-318.

Orhan, Muriel and Scott, Don. 2001. 'Why Women Enter Into Entrepreneurship: An Explanatory Model'. *Women in Management Review* 16: 232–243.

Otuya, R., Kibas, P., Gichira, R. and Martin, W. 2013. 'Entrepreneurship education: Influencing students' entrepreneurial intentions'. *International Journal of Innovative Research & Studies* 2(4): 132–148.

Pande, Rohini and Udry, Christopher R. 2005. 'Institutions and Development: A View from Below'. *Yale University Economic Growth Center Discussion Paper* 928. New Haven: Yale University.

Parvin L., Rahman M W., Jia J. 2012. 'Determinates of Women Micro-entrepreneurship Development: An Empirical Investigation in Rural Bangladesh'. *International Journal of Economics and Finance* 4(5): 254–260.

Pavcnik, N. 2006. *World Development Report (2005): A Better Investment Climate for Everyone.*

Pines, A. M. 2002. 'The Female Entrepreneur: Burnout Treated Using a Psychodynamic Existential Approach'. *Clinical Case Studies* 1(2): 171–81.

Pines, A. M. and Schwartz, D. 2008. 'Now You See Them, Now You Don't: Gender Differences In Entrepreneurship'. *Journal of Managerial Psychology* 23: 811–32.

Porter, Michael E. 1979. 'The Structure within Industries and Companies' Performance'. *Review of Economics and Statistics* 61(2): 214–227.

———. 1979a. 'How Competitive Forces Shape Strategy'. *Harvard Business Review*, March/April.

———. 2008. 'The Five Competitive Forces That Shape Strategy'. *Harvard Business Review*, January.

Powell, Melanie, Ansic, David. 1997. 'Gender differences in risk behaviour in financial decision-making: An experimental analysis'. *Journal of Economic Psychology* 18(6): 605–628.

Puffer, Sheila M., McCarthy, Daniel J. and Boisot, Max. 2010. 'Entrepreneurship in Russia and China: The Impact of Formal Institutional Voids'. *Entrepreneurship Theory and Practice* 34(3): 441–467.

Raj, K. N. 1973. 'The Politics and Economics of "Intermediate regimes"'. *Economic and Political Weekly* 7: 1189–1198, July.

Ravallion, Martin. 2008. 'A Global Perspective on Poverty in India'. *Economic and Political Weekly* 43: 31–37.

———. 2009. 'The Developing World's Bulging (But Vulnerable) "Middle Class"'. Policy Research Working Papers 4816. Washington, D.C.: The World Bank.

Ravallion, Martin, Shaochua Chen and Prem Sangraula. 2009. 'Dollar a Day Revisited'. *World Bank Economic Review* 23(2): 163–184.

Rutton, M. 2003. 'The study of entrepreneurship in India: In need of a comparative perspective'. In *The Oxford Indian Companion to the Sociology and Social Anthropology*, Veena Das ed. London: Oxford University Press.

Ryan, Richard M. and Deci, Edward L. 2000. 'Self-Determination Theory and the Facilitation of Intrinsic Motivation, Social Development, and Well-Being'. *American Psychologist* 55(1):68–78.

Samuel, Yeboah Asuamah, Ernest, Kumi, Awuah, Jacob Baffour. 2013. 'An Assessment of Entrepreneurship Intention among Sunyani Polytechnic Marketing Students'. *International Review of Management and Marketing* 3(1): 37–49.

Sarfaraz, Leyla, Faghih, Nezameddin and Majd, Armaghan Asadi. 2014. 'The relationship between women entrepreneurship and gender equality'. *Journal of Global Entrepreneurship Research* 4(6): 1–11.

Schoar, Antoinette. 2010. 'The Divide between Subsistence and Transformational Entrepreneurship'. *Innovation Policy and the Economy* 10(1): 57–81.

Schumpeter, Joseph A. 1934a. *The Theory of Economic Development: An Inquiry into Profits, Capital, Credit, Interest, and the Business Cycle*. Cambridge: Harvard University Press.

———. 1934b. 'The Theory of Economic Development: An Inquiry into Profits, Capital, Credit, Interest, and the Business Cycle'. University of Illinois at Urbana-Champaign's Academy for Entrepreneurial Leadership Historical Research Reference in Entrepreneurship. Available at SSRN: https://ssrn.com/abstract=1496199 (accessed 7 September 2021).

Schwartz, Eleanor Brantley. 1976. 'Entrepreneurship: A new female frontier'. *Journal of Contemporary Business* 5(1): 47–76.

Seker, Murat. 2011. *Trade Policies, Investment Climate and Exports*. Washington D.C.: The World Bank.

Sexton, Donald L., and Bowman-Upton, Nancy. 1990. 'Female and Male Entrepreneurs: Psychological Characteristics and Their Role in Gender-Related Discrimination'. *Journal of Business Venturing* 5(1): 29–36.

Shah, Hina. 2013. 'Creating an Enabling Environment for Women's Entrepreneurship in India'. *Development Papers* 1304. Bangkok: United Nations Economic and Social Commission for Asia and the Pacific (ESCAP) South and South-West Asia Office.

Shane, Scott and Venkataraman S. 2000. 'The Promise of Entrepreneurship as a Field of Research'. *Academy of Management Review* 25(1): 217–226.

Shapero, Albert and Sokol, Lisa. 1982. 'The social dimensions of entrepreneurship'. In *Encyclopedia of Entrepreneurship*, pp. 72–90. Eds. Calvin A. Kent, Donald L. Sexton and Karl H. Vesper. Englewood Cliffs: Prentice-Hall.

Shepherd, Dean A. and DeTienne, Dawn R. 2005. 'Prior Knowledge, Potential Financial Reward, and Opportunity Identification'. *Entrepreneurship Theory and Practice* 29(1): 91–112.

Shivani, S., S. Mukherjee, and R. Sharan. 2006. 'Socio-cultural influences on Indian entrepreneurs: The need for appropriate structural interventions'. *Journal of Asian Economics* 17 (1): 5–13.

Sobel, Russell. 2008. 'Testing Baumol: Institutional quality and the productivity of entrepreneurship'. *Journal of Business Venturing* 23(6): 641–655.

Sridharan, E. 2004. 'The Growth and Sectoral Composition of India's Middle Class: Its Impact on the Politics of Economic Liberalization'. *India Review* 3(4): 405–428.

Stearns, P. N. and M. Mann. 1993. *The Sources of Social Power: Volume 2, The Rise of Classes and Nation States 1760–1914*.

Straub, Stéphane and Terada-Hagiwara, Akiko. 2010. 'Infrastructure and growth in developing Asia'. *Asian Development Bank Economics Working Paper Series* 231. Asian Development Bank.

Streiner, David L. 2003. 'Starting at the Beginning: An Introduction to Coefficient Alpha and Internal Consistency'. *Journal of Personality Assessment* 80(1): 99–103.

Sullivan, Diane M., and Meek, W.R. 2012. 'Gender and entrepreneurship: A review and process model'. *Journal of Managerial Psychology* 27(5): 428–458.

Sundaram, K and Tendulkar, S. 2006. 'Changing Structure of India Workforce, Quality of Employment and Real Earnings, 1983–2000'. Paper presented at conference on meeting the employment challenge, Institute for Human Development, New Delhi, 27–29 July.

Svejnar, J. and S. J. Commander. 2007. 'Do institutions, ownership, exporting and competition explain firm performance? Evidence from 26 transition countries'. Working paper No. 1067. Michigan Ross School of Business.

Terjesen, Siri and Lloyd, Ainsley. 2015. *The 2015 Female Entrepreneurship Index*. Washington D.C.: Global Entrepreneurship and Development Institute. Available at https://thegedi.org/research/womens-entrepreneurship-index/.

Thompson, Edmund R. 2009. 'Individual Entrepreneurial Intent: Construct Clarification and Development of an Internationally Reliable Metric'. *Entrepreneurship Theory and Practice* 33(3): 669–694.

Thurow, Lester C. 1987. 'A surge in inequality'. *Scientific American* 256(5): 30–37.

Timmons, J. A. and Spinelli, S. 2004. *New Venture Creation: Entrepreneurship for the 21st Century*, Volume 4. Burr Ridge: Irwin Burr Ridge.

Tkachev, Alexei and Kolvereid, Lars. 1999. 'Self-Employment Intentions among Russian Students'. *Entrepreneurship & Regional Development* 11(3): 269–280.

Torche, Florencia and Lopez-Calva Luis F. 2013. 'Stability and Vulnerability of the Latin American Middle Class.' *Oxford Development Studies* 41(4): 409–435.

Ummah, Salfiyah. 2009. 'Entrepreneurial Motivation and Self-Employment Intention: An Empirical Study on Management Undergraduates in Sri Lanka'. *Journal of Management* 5(1): 87–96.

United Nations. 2006. *Entrepreneurship and e-Business Development for Women*, pp. 1–14. United Nations Publications.

Unni, Jeemol. 2006. 'Contours of Conflict and Coalition: Rise of the Intermediate Classes and Castes'. In *Contested Transformations: Changing Economies and Identities in Contemporary India*, pp. 237–260. Eds. Mary E. John, Praveen Kumar Jha and Surinder S. Jodhka. New Delhi: Tulika Books.

Unni, Jeemol and Raveendran, G. 2006. 'Are the results of the economic census robust?' *Economic and Political Weekly* 41(33): 3558–3560.

Unni, Jeemol and Naik, Ravikiran. 2018. 'Gender Differentials in Expansion of Informal Enterprises'. CSE Working Paper 2018–12. Bengaluru: Centre for Sustainable Employment, Azim Premji University. Available at: https://cse.azimpremjiuniversity.edu.in/wp-content/uploads/2018/05/Unni_Naik_Informal_Enterprises.pdf (accessed 7 September 2021).

Üstüner, Tuba, and Holt, D. B. 2009. 'Toward a Theory of Status Consumption in Less Industrialized Countries'. *Journal of Consumer Research* 37(1): 37–56.

Kumara Vasantha, S. and C. Sahasranam. 2008. 'An empirical study on students' soft skills inventory test: Reliability and non-parametric analysis'. *IC-FAI Journal of Soft Skills* 2(3).

Verheul, Ingrid, van Stel, André, Thurik, Roy. 2004. 'Explaining Female and Male Entrepreneurship across 29 Countries'. *Entrepreneurship and Regional Development* 18(2).

———. 2006. 'Explaining Female and Male Entrepreneurship at the Country Level'. *Entrepreneurship and Regional Development* 18(2): 151–183.

Verheul, Ingrid, Uhlaner, Lorraine, Thurik, Roy. 2003. 'Business Accomplishments, Gender and Entrepreneurial Self-Image'. *Scales Research Reports N200312, EIM Business and Policy Research*. Rotterdam: Erasmus University.

Verheul, Ingrid and Thurik, Roy. 2001. 'Start-Up Capital: "Does Gender Matter?"'. *Small Business Economics* 16(4): 329–345.

Von Graevenitz, G., D. Harhoff, and R. Weber. 2010. 'The effects of entrepreneurship education'. *Journal of Economic Behavior & Organization* 76(1): 90–112.

Von Hippel, Eric. 1988. *The Sources of Innovation*. New York, Oxford: Oxford University Press.

Vossenberg, Saskia. 2013. 'Women Entrepreneurship Promotion in Developing Countries: What explains the gender gap in entrepreneurship and how to close it?' *Maastricht School of Management Working Paper* 2013/08. Maastricht School of Management.

Wagner, Joachim. 2007. 'What a Difference a Y Makes-Female and Male Nascent Entrepreneurs in Germany'. *Small Business Economics* 28(1): 1–21.

Watson, John. 2014. 'Examining the Impact on Performance of Demographic Differences between Male and Female Controlled SMES'. *Small Enterprise Research* 9(2): 55–70. Available at: https://doi.org/10.5172/ser.9.2.55 (accessed 22 June 2021).

Watson, John, and Robinson, Sherry. 2003. 'Adjusting for Risk in Comparing the Performances of Male- and Female-Controlled SMEs'. *Journal of Business Venturing* 18(6): 773–788.

Weber, Max. 1978[1909]. *Economy and Society: An Outline of Interpretive Sociology*, Volume 1. Oakland: University of California Press.

Webb, Justin. W., Khoury, Theodore A. and Hitt, Michael A. 2019. 'The Influence of Formal and Informal Institutional Voids on Entrepreneurship'. *Entrepreneurship Theory and Practice* 44(3).

Weeden, Kim A. and Grusky, David B. 2005. 'The Case for a New Class Map'. *American Journal of Sociology* 111(1): 141–212.

Weeks, Julie R., Seiler, Danielle. 2001. 'Women's Entrepreneurship in Latin America: An Exploration of Current Knowledge'. IDB Sustainable Development Department Technical Papers Series. Ref. No. MSM-111.

Weinstein, N. D. 1980. 'Unrealistic Optimism about Future Life Events'. *Journal of Personality and Social Psychology* 39(5): 806–820.

Wooldridge, Jeffrey M. 2003. 'Pooling Cross-sections Across Time: Simple Panel Data Methods'. In *Introductory Econometrics: A Modern Approach*. Mason, OH: Thomson/South-Western College Publishing.

World Bank. 2001. *Engendering Development through Gender Equality in Rights, Resources and Voice*. Washington D.C.: The World Bank.

______. 2004. *World Development Report 2005: A Better Business Climate for Everyone*. Washington D.C.: The World Bank.

______. 2009. *Enterprise Surveys*. Washington D.C.: The World Bank. Available at: http://www.enterprisesurveys.org (accessed 7 September 2021).

______. 2012. 'Gender Equality and Development'. *World Development Report 2012*. Washington D.C.: The World Bank.

______. 2013. *Enterprise Surveys*. Washington D.C.: The World Bank. Available at: http://www.enterprisesurveys.org (accessed 7 September 2021).

Wright, Erik Olin. 1985. *Classes*. London: Verso.

______. 2015. *Understanding Class*. London: Verso.

Wu, Sizong and Wu, Lingfei. 2008. 'The Impact of Higher Education on Entrepreneurial Intentions of University Students in China'. *Journal of Small Business and Enterprise Development* 15(4): 752–774.

Xavier, Siri Roland, Ahmad, S. Z., Perumal, S., Nor, L. M. and Mohan J. C. 2011. 'The Transition from Corporate Careers to Business Ownership: The Case for Women Entrepreneurs in Malaysia'. *International Journal of Business Administration* 2(3): 148–159.

Xavier, Siri Roland, Kelley, Donna, Kew, Jacqui, Herrington, Mike, Vorderwülbecke, Arne and Global Entrepreneurship Research Association. 2013. *Global Entrepreneurship Monitor: 2012 Global Report*. Global Entrepreneurship Monitor Consortia.

Yadav, Vanita and Unni, Jeemol. 2016. 'Women Entrepreneurship: Research Review and Future Directions'. *Journal of Global Entrepreneurship Research* 6(12): 1–18. Available at: https://doi.org/10.1186/s40497-016-0055-x (accessed 5 September 2021).

Yurdagul, Emircan. 2017. 'Production Complementarities and Flexibility in a Model of Entrepreneurship. *Journal of Monetary Economics* 86, Issue C: 36–51.

Zahra, Shaker A. 2007. 'Contextualizing Theory Building in Entrepreneurship Research'. *Journal of Business Venturing* 22(3): 443–452.

Zain, Zahariah Mohd., Akram, Amalina Mohd., and Ghani, Erlane K. 2010. 'Entrepreneurship Intention among Malaysian Business Students'. *Canadian Social Science* 6(3): 34–44.

Zhang, Ying, Duysters, Geert and Cloodt, Myriam. 2014. 'The Role of Entrepreneurship Education as a Predictor of University Students' Entrepreneurial Intention'. *International Entrepreneurship and Management Journal* 10(3): 623–641.

Zhao, Hao, Seibert, Scott E. and Hills, Gerald E. 2005. 'The Mediating Role of Self-Efficacy in the Development of Entrepreneurial Intentions'. *Journal of Applied Psychology* 90(6): 1265–1272.

Index